INTERVIEWS BY A CLUELESS
White Woman

AMY THORNTON SHANKLAND

ISBN: 978-1-957723-61-7 (Hard Cover)
       978-1-957723-62-4 (Soft Cover)

Shankland. Amy Thornton.

Edited by: Amy Ashby

Published by Warren Publishing
Charlotte, NC
www.warrenpublishing.net
Printed in the United States

This book is dedicated to
Bryan Fonseca.

COVID-19 may have taken you from us too soon,
but through this and countless other efforts,
you are still changing the world.
Gracias, mi amigo.

INTRODUCTION

I am eager and excited to share this book with you. I'm also completely, totally, and utterly terrified. The title may give you some indication as to why I feel this way. The book may bring you heartache, readers, and then, of course, there is my cluelessness regarding the experiences of those who have shared their stories.

When I began writing this book, the year 2020 was drawing to a close. It not only brought the devastation of COVID-19, but it also widened the gaps between numerous groups of people.

More than ever, the struggles of millions of marginalized individuals have been brought to light, revealing truths that many Americans cannot even begin to comprehend. I'm talking about people who struggle because they have, as Parker Palmer says, "otherness."[1] Perhaps they are people of color or members of the LGBTQ+ community. Or both. Maybe they have a physical, mental, or emotional disability. Perhaps they practice a religion other than Christianity.

My objective was to speak with and learn from those who have experienced discrimination and share their stories and impart their truths, knowing I would probably screw up along the way. Why? Because, as I told my dear friend and client Bryan Fonseca when I first began toying with the idea of collecting these stories, I'm just a clueless white woman. Okay, I was not 100 percent clueless. But when it came to issues of inequity between different races, gender identities, sexual preferences, abilities, religions, and other aspects that divide our country, I felt, deep inside, like I was *way* behind the times, that I had so much to learn. I still do have a lot to learn, and I'm sure many people are in the same boat.

I grew up in a place that some called the "Oreo Cookie." I was raised in Mishawaka, a city in northern Indiana between South Bend (home of the University of Notre Dame) and Elkhart (RV Capital of the World). We maybe had a half-dozen Black or Asian kids in my entire high school, which at the time had about 1,200 students. Mishawaka had mostly White people, whereas South Bend and Elkhart had more Black people. Thus, the sad and unamusing Oreo Cookie nickname.

Despite the odds, one of my closest friends as a child was a Korean girl named Yumi. We were friends until she and her family moved to Elkhart before our junior year in high school. Yumi and I still kept in touch, however, and she even came to my first wedding when I was twenty-two years old.

We drifted apart as the years went on, but thanks to the magic of social media, we reunited in 2018. She and I met for lunch and, as we reminisced, I felt this tug in my heart. Yumi shared some of the trials she had gone through as an Asian girl. (You will have the honor of reading her story on page 260.) It killed me to realize I'd never known the pain she experienced during our younger years. I suppose it's typical for children and teenagers to focus on their own problems growing up, but I still felt racked with guilt.

Then along came 2020 with its ferocious worldwide pandemic—and with it more headlines revealing our unequal and unjust society. The headlines shared horrible stories about the fate of Black men like Ahmaud Arbery—an unarmed twenty-five-year-old man shot and killed while jogging in his own neighborhood—and George Floyd, who was arrested and died after an officer knelt upon his neck for approximately eight minutes. These incidents and others catapulted the Black Lives Matter movement into the spotlight. Protests, unrest, and riots sprang up around the country.

The year also highlighted the ongoing troubles the LGBTQ community continues to endure. According to the Human Rights Campaign (HRC), at least forty-four transgender and gender-nonconforming people were violently killed in 2020. That is more than any year since the organization began tracking statistics in 2013.[2] HRC has now tracked over 202 deaths in those eight years.[3]

According to a 2020 survey from the Center for American Progress, more than one in three LGBTQ Americans faced discrimination of some kind, with one out of two reporting moderate or significant negative psychological impacts.[4]

Many of these Americans also experienced mental health issues related to the pandemic. In 2020, COVID-19 caused rates of anxiety and depression to rise almost 20 percent.[5] My research has found that for those in marginalized communities—people who were already facing emotional, mental, physical, and other disabilities—the pandemic dealt an even greater blow.

Thankfully, hundreds of organizations were there to help. I'm blessed to work for one of them—Fonseca Theatre Company (FTC)—through my consulting business. I began working with its founder, Bryan Fonseca, in 2018. FTC exists to amplify and celebrate the minority communities of Indianapolis through the prism of purposeful theater and civic engagement. The goal is to bring about social justice through programs that educate, illuminate, and ignite conversations on equity, diversity, and inclusion. The organization is primarily run by people of color, LGBTQ individuals, and those with disabilities. After consulting for the organization for two months, I quickly realized what little I knew about these individuals' worlds. I went to nearly every play held at the theater over the past couple of years, and walked away deep in thought after each performance. Silly me, I thought the sixties had settled so many issues of inequality. Yep, clueless White woman.

I realized there was one important thing I could do to transform not only *this* White woman, but hopefully millions of people like me. I could write. I could talk to people, listen to their stories, and share those narratives with the goal of increasing understanding between groups of individuals.

I wanted to interview Bryan first, as he was a member of the LGBTQ community and a Mexican American. He helped formulate the idea for this book and was the first person to agree to an interview. However, before I could interview him, Bryan passed away in September of 2020 due to complications with COVID-19.

I may not have been able to interview Bryan, but I know his spirit will be felt throughout this book. This pandemic has caused so many of us to want to learn how to be better. It's my greatest hope that these stories make us all more empathetic, that they open our eyes, turn our hearts upside down, and, most of all, motivate us to help bring important change to our communities.

You will not find victims in this book. Everyone I interviewed has fought and struggled against their particular stigmas and stereotypes, and some do not acknowledge any marginalization. Others were not as fortunate.

I was surprised to find that people with mental illness are among the most marginalized in the world. Lack of understanding, fear, and inaccurate media representations of mental illness contribute to this problem. Additionally, those suffering from diseases, such as cancer, even if there are not outward signs of their suffering, are often marginalized as people distance themselves from potential heartache.

Each interviewee has shared not only their past and present story but also their advice to others on how to support people like themselves. I encourage you to consider what speaks to your heart. We all have different socioeconomic statuses, talents, available time, and interests. I believe if we all do a little something, it will create major transformation and a stronger, less divided country.

Please keep in mind, these stories are just glimpses into what it's like to not be your typical White Anglo-Saxon Protestant American. They do not reflect the definitive experience of any group as a whole. And I also realize that most of these people are from the Midwest. Their stories may not be like those of someone from another region.

Although I am eager and excited to share these sixteen stories, part of my terror comes from knowing I've made mistakes along the way. I know I didn't always say or ask the right things, but I requested that each of the storytellers gently guide me to the correct path and way of thinking. I can't thank them enough for their courage, time, and strength of heart.

Author, educator, and Center for Courage & Renewal founder Parker Palmer, a White man, stated things beautifully in a 2015 commencement address:

"The old majority in this society, people who look like me, is on its way out. By 2045 the majority of Americans will be people of color. Many in the old majority fear that fact and their fear, shamelessly manipulated by too many politicians, is bringing us down. The renewal this nation needs will not come from people who are afraid of otherness in race, ethnicity, religion, or sexual orientation."[6]

Let's stop being afraid and, instead, start opening our minds and hearts.

Author's Note: Some names in this book have been changed at the request of the interviewees or their friends or family.

Trigger Warning

This book includes material that may be upsetting to some individuals. Subjects include the following:

- Sexual assault
- Homophobia
- Transphobia
- Racism
- Ableism
- Violence toward marginalized ethnicities

Empathy is seeing with
the eyes of another,
listening with the ears of another,
and feeling with the heart of another.

–WADE WALKER

SONYA

I admit, I almost didn't interview Sonya. She is a former hoop–dance friend of mine and also gave my son music lessons when he was little. Sonya is a brilliant, beautiful soul, but when she battled depression, we drifted apart. Or so I thought. Before I even spoke with her, she let me know that I could have done some things differently to help her years ago. I decided to face the music—pun intended—and hear what she had to say so I could do better for others.

NAME: Sonya
AGE: Prefers not to say
IDENTIFIES AS: Female
ETHNICITY: Southeast Asian
OCCUPATION: Music Teacher

SONYA: I can't speak for everybody because some people do want to stand out, but maybe [some want the] chance to blend in and be seen as a normal human being. If you look at the nature [of the questions you sent me prior to the interview], it kind of made me think, *Oh, so now I'm being spotlighted, but the thing you want to spotlight me for is,* "Oh yeah, *there goes the sad woman.*" Who wants that kind of label, right?

[I decided to do the interview because] I wanted to be honest instead of just saying, "Oh, I'm offended, I'm not going to do this." This is what happens to our country when it's all torn apart. Everybody's like, "I'm all offended. I don't want to deal with this. I don't want to talk to you, so I'm going to camp out in my camp and you're just going to camp out in your camp."

[If we stay in our own camps], we're going to build fences instead of bridges. In order to build bridges, there has to be understanding. So when we talk, hopefully there's more understanding. I may not agree with everything or where you're coming from, but at least we leave less ignorant of each other, you know what I mean?

ME: *Yeah, exactly! Nicely said. Let's start with my initial questions. Tell me about you and your family growing up.*

SONYA: I grew up in Southeast Asia. I came to America a few months before my twenty-fifth birthday. I lived half a life in Asia. I was pretty immature, but I was my own grounded person already, when I came here … When you're a high schooler, and you come here [to the United States], you absorb different values, and you don't know your person. I did have my values. I did grow up Asian.

Every one of my family is in Southeast Asia. Well, and Australia. So nobody was in America. I came here on a scholarship—full ride—with two suitcases. That's it. My scholarship [was for] music and music ed. As a grad student, I was asked to teach classes and immediately take on private students as part of my internship. So I was pretty much thrown into being a full-time student and full-time teaching.

ME: *Holy mackerel!*

SONYA: Yep, straightaway, and having to adjust to being an international with an accent, mind you. I did have an accent. I did not sound like this. I wasn't Americanized yet. So this accent that I have [now] is Survival 101. It wasn't because I'd lived here so long [that] I blended in, or because I was trying to be pretentious and wanted to sound American. It wasn't that. [When I came here], I spoke too fast and I was on a whole different wavelength from my students. It was a miracle my first-semester kids passed ….

I observed a lot of my mentors teaching and I kind of learned how they phrased sentences, how they verbalized themselves, and I absorbed myself into the culture. Slowly but surely that transformed down to my speech. Plus, also for me, speech is kind of like music. I can pick up things by ear.

ME: Oh, that's really hard. I'm assuming you studied English before you came here?

SONYA: Yes, I've been studying English since kindergarten. I grew up trilingual, so writing was not a problem for me. It was just a matter of learning to verbalize, learning to clearly state what I need to say.

ME: That's awesome. I had no idea, Sonya. I just kind of assumed you and your family came here when you were young and then they moved back. How often do you get to see them?

SONYA: When I was a student, when I was single/premarried or [even] postmarried, I would go home once a year or every two years. You know, COVID has put a damper on everything. When I was married it was difficult, too, because my money was not my own.

ME: Did you meet your husband at college?

SONYA: Yeah. We were set up by friends. When we met, I [had been] in the country for maybe two–three years. I was still pretty naive and pretty green to the people here and the dating scene. With me being a full-time student and a full-time teacher at the same time, I didn't have much time to socialize.

ME: Probably hard to cut loose!

SONYA: It kind of was. I was still awkward and not very comfortable with American norms and culture, society, and just social events. I hung out mostly with the international crowd and we didn't always party. There was not a lot of dating or socializing going on. At my peak while I was at college, I was practicing [piano] six hours a day. I practiced like an athlete. So I didn't really have much time. My former husband was like the first serious relationship I had in a long time.

ME: [As an Asian woman, did] you encounter any issues when you first got here? Were you treated well?

SONYA: When I first came, I hung out mostly with internationals. I was very naive in the sense that I just believed everybody at point value. I did not get subliminal messages yet …. If there was any kind of discrimination, I did not perceive it. Definitely not at college … The discrimination that I felt I received was probably ten to fifteen years later. I was married to a White guy, and no less from a small town in Wisconsin. I thought I blended in, but maybe I didn't.

ME: *Did his family treat you okay or were there issues?*

SONYA: Let's just say that I was gracious, and because we were married, I overlooked a lot of sins, and that was also part of my personality. Part of my failure in the marriage [was] not sticking up for myself, not saying, "No, I will not take that." I just let it go. I didn't know anything and then I just let it go. I thought I was the dumb one, you know?

It's taken awhile for me to learn to grow a backbone. I think the more backbone I grew, the more I saw the discrimination and the subliminal lines between certain things people say …. I did not stand up or ask for [my husband] to stand up for me. He did not stand up for me. Your partner should be there for you and when you marry somebody, that's what you expect. It's not like I had experience being married. I was married to a foreigner and trying to adapt to a country not my own. And having identity issues. Am I White? Am I Yellow? Am I Asian? Am I Southeast Asian? Am I American? So I wasn't sure of myself.

ME: *Well, I think you raise a good point. As women, sometimes we're taught to be nice, you know, we can't say anything. And then all of a sudden in our forties and fifties we're like, "Wait a minute, that's not right. Why did that happen?" Suddenly we mature and we realize we need to speak up …. Sonya, we've emailed back and forth about the other issue that you face: When did you start battling depression?*

SONYA: I did the Myers-Briggs three times throughout my life, maybe ten years apart each time. I scored the same personality type. This was a paper test, and they gave you the chart and everything back in the early 2000s. My introversion topped the chart—like it hit the roof! I had nearly zero extroversion, so I didn't really understand people. My personality type is the type that feels not understood, misunderstood. We walk around the world thinking nobody understands us.

I'm a musician. As an artist, [this feeling of being nisunderstood] is already probably elevated. I tend to be more, you know, they call it the "emo" musician—very emotional. That's kind of how we process music so well—because we feel emotions through our music. We channel it and also I think my personality tends to go more melancholy, not so much sanguine. That was already my leaning.

Being in a foreign country, being young, and not really understanding who I [was] as a person, and then thrown into an interracial marriage ... was causing a lot of problems. So my depression clinically was diagnosed two years into my marriage. I was clinically severely depressed for eight years out of the ten that I was with him. I was on a bunch of medication. A lot of therapy, a lot of medication, you barely hang on to work and all that. Miraculously, after the divorce, within two years, I cleaned everything out—no more medication. I was officially discharged by therapists and psychiatrists—everything.

I chose to stay in therapy, but not like all the time. I check in because I think depression is kind of like cancer. You talk to any cancer survivor, they have doctors, every few years they go back. They check to make sure the cancer doesn't come back. They watch their lifestyle, they watch their food, maybe they exercise. They change their lifestyle, right? But they always go back for that checkup just in case the cancer comes back.

Same thing with depressed people. I opted to stay in therapy sort of to keep myself in check, to make sure I am managing my emotions. I had to change my lifestyle, my mental outlook, retrain my brain, you know, different things. You take proactive steps. You learn if you start feeling like this, it could be a sign of something that needs to get checked [out]. I know my markers. If I'm feeling a certain way or if I know I'm headed toward that depression route, then it's, "Okay, time to rein it back in." It's a discipline.

ME: What is life like when you have depression and you're trying to live and make money? It's different for everybody, but what was your experience?

SONYA: I felt alone, isolated, and maybe that's a very common thing with depression. I felt misunderstood by my church, misunderstood by people, students, my students' parents. I felt like they didn't understand what was going on.

My husband kind of took on the role as primary caretaker for me so a lot of people saw him as the saintly husband that had to take care of this poor woman. They felt bad for him. They felt compassion for him because this wife of his was completely deranged, off her rocker. So I felt even more isolated because now I'm not just depressed—I'm deranged. I'm crazy, you know, and they don't know how to reach me. I have burnt a lot of bridges.

I had not, at that point, built any relationships with church people because the church that I was a part of when I got married, that church broke apart. It was a pioneering church. The pastor died, [then] my dad died. Throughout that whole eight-year depression period, a lot of people left so it was very difficult for me.

ME: I am very sorry about that, Sonya. I was one of the people that heard you were battling depression. I heard you were having troubles and didn't know when you'd return to teaching. I remember that phone call when I said, "Hey, you know my son's starting to lose interest. I have to find a new [music] teacher."

SONYA: There were parents that stuck with me and I appreciated them for it. Ironically, it's kind of funny, the parents that did stick with me through those periods also stuck with me when the studio failed and we had to dissolve the business. They said, "You know what, we're still continuing with you," and some of them are still with me today.

ME: That's great.

SONYA: [Others], instead of understanding, it made people walk away from my life when people should not have done so. Every person that walks away at that point when you need them ... it's like fifty steps backward. It's like, "There goes another betrayal, there goes another one that let you down. There goes another bridge burnt." So, in that case, being different is not a blessing, it's a curse.

Do you understand why I do not like that label? [Different.] Because all I wanted to do was to belong. It didn't help that sometimes when I had to cancel lessons, I did not take charge of my own life. I depended too much on [my husband] to the point he was making calls [on] my behalf. It caused me to sound even more deranged than I already was.

ME: *I'm sorry I'm one of the people that left. I could have reached out to you ....*

SONYA: You can judge me based on Sonya back in 2010 or you can look at me now and decide for yourself.

ME: *It sounds to me like what you wish people had done differently was just talk to you, reach out to you.*

SONYA: And really be a safe place—create a safe place, because safety was huge. You know there was a friend that lived right next door but I still clammed up. And there were plenty of people at my church ... and I clammed up. It was because I didn't feel safe anywhere.

ME: *If you'd had people that made you feel safe, that would have helped you?*

SONYA: Maybe. I felt like I was screaming but nobody was listening. And so I resorted to bad ways of trying to get attention, canceling work and stopping work altogether. And just trying to get my act together, trying to heal, and, you know, tantrums. I was screaming for attention. You know I was suicidal all those years, but I never died. Why did I not die? I'm smart enough to kill myself, so at one point you have to understand—did that person really want to die? Or is that person crying for help?

But people just think, *Oh man, she just wants to die. So man, let's stay away. She's not safe.* So instead of you creating a safe place, you just tell that person, "Stay away from my family." You know, that's it. It's crazy.

ME: *You mentioned something about cancer earlier, right? Well people don't [typically] avoid somebody with cancer. They support them and they say, "How can I help?" But you didn't have that.*

SONYA: No.

ME: *That's really sad. I so wish I could go back and change it ... I can't.*

SONYA: You have to understand throughout this bad—all this bad because I had nothing, literally nothing—I will say the one thing that I clung to is my faith. That did not fail me. I tell this to a lot of people, including non-Christians: when you're suicidal, you think there's no other higher being than you and you are the highest being in existence …. Then there's no point to life. [You think], *I might as well just die because I am pathetic right now. I feel like I'm the worst. If I died, I would probably do everybody a favor.* That was truth in my life at one point, and so if you're going to come to me like most atheists and say, "We are our supreme being," then I just want to die. I've lost hope.

The one thing that has kept me hopeful and thus given me some shred of will to fight has been my faith that there is a higher power. That maybe my suffering is gonna matter someday and that maybe I will have a story to tell. If I can get out of this tunnel and get out into the light … that is probably why I am as strong as I am.

As unapologetic as I am in my faith—because rather than write all these bad things and about these bad people—I would rather you write a story about a survivor. About a fighter. It's not easy for me to share these things because, like I told you before, I would rather you just judge me by my actions and my work. You can always judge me based on what people knew about me ten years ago. You make the decision, so I don't really feel the need to scream injustice. I was mislabeled and people didn't understand me back then. I could whine and scream all day about that, but what's the point? It happened, it was then. I pulled through. This is now.

ME: *What would you tell the world to do differently for people with depression?*
SONYA: I would say, be a safe person. I think there's a book out there called *Safe People* by Henry Cloud and John Townsend …. Be a safe person, even if you cannot do business with them, be a safe friend. Create safe environments because you don't know who you're talking to. People have the happiest and the most positive social media accounts. But you have to think, *Do they have inner peace or is this surface happy? Are they laughing a little too hard? That's something. Are they trying a little too hard to get this attention or that?* Those are little signs sometimes that people will put out that they are struggling with something. I'm very sensitive now to these things because I have been that person.

Maybe not call it out in them that, "Hey, I think you're depressed." There goes [their] safety. But just be a friend and not treat people differently. That's where I, in some degree, disagree with your book. Because I disagree with the premise that people are different. You might be different in the language you speak, or in the geographical region that you grew up, or in the food and groceries that you buy, or even with your upbringing and values. But if you look at the core things, everybody wants to be loved. Everybody wants to feel safe. Everyone wants to feel seen and heard and understood. So when you look on those values, then we're not really that different, are we?

If someone says, "I want to be different," why do you want to be different? Maybe what [they're] trying to say is, "I want to be understood. That's why I'm sticking out, because I need you to hear me. Because otherwise you would not hear me, you would not see me." So if they say they want to be different, why? Why is the question to ask.

ME: *I think you're going to help me phrase things a little better as I go along. The big purpose of the book is just to let everybody know kind of what you're saying. Hey, we all want the same things, and just because this person is bisexual or they have muscular dystrophy ... that doesn't mean we have to stay away from them.*

SONYA: But that also is not the thing that defines them as a person. I mean, how would you want to be defined? Think of yourself. Would you want to be defined based on your worst? Or would you want to be defined by, "Okay, there goes Amy Shankland. She's the hoop lady." That's it. That's all you have—hoop lady. You're not a writer, you're not a mom, you're not a wife, you're just a hoop lady. No, that's not who you are. But that's one part of you. My depression is one part of me, but it's not my entire being.

At one point, when I lost myself and was in the deep pits of despair and my darkest days, possibly it was all of me, but that wasn't the truth. That was just the lie that I created for myself—the facade and the self-pity. That wasn't me. That wasn't all of me. I just refused to acknowledge all the other parts. I just saw that one part—tunnel vision, you know?

ME: *Sonya, do you know of any organizations that help people with depression? Are there any nonprofits?*

SONYA: I'm sure there're a ton. I'm not a part of any social organization out there. I was a part of NAMI (National Alliance on Mental Illness) at one point. I was a part of Prevail for a while. They helped me. I'm still with Aspire. Those are good. I did a fundraiser for the Julian Center.

I would say for people that are going through depression … fight the isolation. I had to fight to create an atmosphere for myself, a community of people for myself. I had to fight to build myself a home. So essentially in my twenty years here in America, I seriously rebuilt my life twice. The first time when I came with two suitcases and nothing else, and the second time when I had to rebuild my life after divorce.

I think the best thing for people with isolation is to find a community. It could be church, it could be friends, it could be even online support groups. There's a lot of those [support groups] now through [videoconferencing], because depressed people may not want to be out that door. It might be hard for them and also for others that are trying to learn or be more receptive.

Learn and be more receptive. Learn to be a safe person. Educate yourself so that you can pick up signs and understand.

ME: *I'd like to go into the homestretch by asking, What have you learned through your struggles with depression?*

SONYA: I've learned that God is faithful and God is good, that God is very real in my life. I've learned to understand myself better, that I do have a backbone. I've learned that I might be an immigrant and I might have suffered through a lot of depression and a lot of dark years, but I'd like to be known not as the sad person that keeps walking around but actually as the survivor and the fighter. A reputation takes years to build and seconds to destroy … I'm in a business where I am teaching children. Never have I ever jeopardized or felt the desire to jeopardize any of my students. Not even in my worst days.

ME: *Well, for your final words, Sonya, what would you say to the world right now?*
SONYA: It's a journey. Life's a journey. Appreciate it.

Organizations mentioned during this interview:
- NAMI (National Alliance on Mental Illness): www.nami.org
- Prevail: www.prevailinc.com
- Aspire: www.aspireindiana.org
- The Julian Center: www.juliancenter.org

When we look at things from a broader perspective, we may notice that human beings are social animals. Even as individuals, we survive in dependence on the community in which we live. Therefore, showing compassion and concern for other members of our community is ultimately good for us too. If we're selfish instead, we tend not to be happy.

–THE DALAI LAMA

PATRICIA

*M*y heart is so happy to share my dear friend Patricia with the world. We've known each other for almost twenty-seven years now. I thank God we worked together so we could meet and I could walk up to her and say, "You're someone I'd like to get to know better." She is one of my soul mates, and I was eager to learn more about her experiences. As you'll see, Patricia is a passionate, powerful woman. I want to be like her when I grow up.

NAME: Patricia
AGE: 52
IDENTIFIES AS: Female
ETHNICITY: Latina
OCCUPATION: Banker (Program Manager) and Actress

PATRICIA: I identify as Latina; that's my preference—pronouns are she/her/ella. I know there are all sorts of terms out there for people that come from Latin America or who are of Latino descent in the United States. There's Chicano, there's Hispanic, and the most recent one, Latinx. But I like the term *Latina* because it says several things about me. It says that I identify as female and it also says that my background or my ethnicity is of Latino descent. So I like it because it is specific, it's intersectional.

ME: *Thank you. I'm glad you explained because there is some confusion out there.*

PATRICIA: I think that with any kind of identity question, you ask, "What is your preference?"

ME: *Excellent explanation. Well, I start everybody off with the same thing—you and your family growing up. Where were you born?*

PATRICIA: My brothers, my sister, and I were all born in Lima, Peru. When I was five, we moved because of my father's job. We moved to Mexico and that's really where I grew up. That's [where] everything that I remember about being a child up to high school [took place]. I lived in a city of three million people—very industrial—three blocks away from the main plaza where they had all the festivals, all the dancers, singers, and storytellers. Every Sunday there was something to look forward to.

I'm the youngest of four. My brothers are eighteen and fourteen years older than I am, and my sister is thirteen years older. I'm the baby. When they were of age, they went to college in the United States. So I didn't actually grow up with my brothers or my sister. I always grew up knowing that eventually I was going to move here [to the United States], though, because everybody was here, building their lives. When my brothers moved to the US, they went to college, they fell in love, got married, had a family, had kids, got divorced, you know ... the American dream. They've been here since I came to the United States, right out of high school.

Actually, in Mexico, you go to school eleven years instead of twelve, so I had to complete an extra semester here to get a high school diploma. I went to high school in Indianapolis for one semester. Even while I was living in Mexico, I was adapting to US culture. I lived close enough—like two and a half/three hours away from the border—always knowing that I was going to be of this culture. So you kind of start preparing yourself subconsciously. The whole world receives American culture, right?

My mother said that when I was in Lima as a little girl, I would walk around the house going, "Blah blah blah blah" and she would say, "What are you doing? What are you saying?" and I would say, "I'm speaking English."

ME: That's so cute!

PATRICIA: English was an expectation in my household. Everybody knows English outside of the United States to a certain degree. I'm very fortunate that I was educated in both English and Spanish as far as traditional education. I not only know how to speak it, but I also know how to write it, to be truly fluent …. Not everybody who speaks Spanish in the United States has that ability. They know Spanish because they hear it. You learn just spoken Spanish but not writing and grammar.

ME: Yeah. So you all just came on your own at that young age? You all went to college and your parents were still in Mexico?

PATRICIA: At this point, one of my brothers was a teacher in high school in Ohio and my other brother worked for Allison Transmission. Both of them are retired now. But one had the bigger house and I came to stay with him. When my dad retired from his job in Mexico, that's when my mother, he, and I moved here. At that time it was really easy. My brothers are both US citizens. They petitioned for my parents to become US [citizens]. It took a couple of years of processing. Now it takes as long as twenty-four years for something like that. Very different.

Before you get citizenship, you have to wait five years to be able to apply. Since I was a minor, it took six months for me to get my documentation in order, but even then, it was an interesting experience. I was sixteen–seventeen, something like that, when I went through that experience. I remember going through the process of giving my fingerprints for the FBI, so yes, they have a file on me and anyone else who has requested residency. Then you go through an interview, and since I'm a minor, my mother was there but she wasn't allowed to speak. It was very surreal, especially for someone who has known no other reality than one which always had me ending up in the US. Every other country where I lived, including mine, I was just passing by.

Then you go through a physical. And the physical was kind of traumatizing because you are in a row of people, and you're just kind of like cattle going from one test to another, and going from one room to the next to the next.

And this is in the eighties, at a time when we started hearing about AIDS, and I remember that one of the people that was in our little group, he was told—in front of us, mind you—that he didn't pass because he had tested positive for AIDS. He had tested positive for HIV. He was told that in front of us!

ME: *Wow! Where's the privacy and the HIPAA and all that?*

PATRICIA: Oh, that didn't come until years later. But it was really devastating to him. I remember that. I still think about him. Anyway, I passed all that and that's how you get your green card, your passport gets a stamp. I ended up in Indianapolis.

ME: *So, I have to ask, what were your struggles initially coming to the United States? How were you treated overall?*

PATRICIA: Again, a very different time. When I came to Indianapolis, I was "the cute girl with the funny accent," trying to figure things out, and people wanted to help me. I struggled with the language sometimes, but people were very kind in helping me out. I was fearless in terms of always trying to add a new word or a new saying into my vocabulary.

At that time, I was always working in some kind of service job, whether it was at a restaurant or a hotel, always in front of people. So I had to use my English for work, and at school as well. In math I was an ace because I know that language. It doesn't matter what you speak; math is math in every language! Trying to obtain language quickly was always a goal of mine. Like I said, people were very kind. I had the privilege of being not only young but also pretty bright in terms of figuring things out—that's the logical part of me.

I also never had a fear to sit at a table where I wasn't invited. I'm light skinned. My skin is white. It's whiter than a lot of people that I know that are from the US. I don't want to say that I "passed," because my accent always gave it away, but I was viewed in a different way than people who have darker skin that have the same accent.

I'm very aware of the fact that my skin color opened a lot of doors for me ... very aware. In many cases, actually, the fact that I was bilingual opened even more doors for me that normally would not have been open. When I first got here, I would do things like just get in the car and drive until I got lost, just to find my way back home. When I think about that now—you know, an eighteen-year-old immigrant girl with a funny accent in some of the places that I ended up—I'm thinking, *How did I survive?* But at that time, I didn't think about it at all.

ME: *Ladies and Gentlemen, she's always been fearless! I've known her since 1994.*

PATRICIA: I think that age gets us to be more afraid of things. But that's okay, you have more to lose .... It changed when—I would put it right around 2000—when the census came out and we highlighted this "new" community. There was a lot of emphasis on the Latino population in central Indiana. There were people that were welcoming with open arms and there were people that were saying, "Wait a minute, what are you getting that I'm not getting?" So I was really shocked to see, after so many years of really building a life and a community, how people that didn't know me changed their approach toward me.

I've always considered one of my superpowers is [the ability] to find commonality with someone I disagree with in order to have a civil conversation. No matter how far apart we are, in our ideology or in our beliefs or anything else, finding that point of connection is a powerful place around which to build dialogue. It got a little harder right around that time. Definitely a lot harder now than then. If anything, I think we've regressed. I attribute it to the polarized political state of our country, how we talk about each other, and how we view each other— starting from the very top. I can't help but connect some dots here.

ME: *I think readers might like to hear about your husband and your family now.*

PATRICIA: Well, I met my husband [Carlos] in the nineties doing a play together at a semiprofessional theater here in Indianapolis—he played my father. We're only five years apart, but the play used magical realism. So the character had a magic watch that actually made him age backwards; it was a Latino-themed play.

Bryan Fonseca was always good to produce a [Latino-themed] play every season, answering to his own Latino roots. He did this beginning in 1991. I can still see him. I came in through the doors of the old Phoenix Theatre building, and Bryan is sitting there at the end of the hallway with his little desk, making notes, just watching everybody auditioning to see how they entered the room. He cast me and Carlos. I still maintain friendships from that particular play, and I married one of them.

Carlos and I were friends for a number of years, and he was the kind of friend that I could always count on to be there to help me out. Like if I ran out of gas or if I needed to go somewhere with someone; he was like a big brother. I actually tried to set him up with several people, including my niece who's seven years younger than I am! As it turns out, ten years after we met, we did another play together and in that one we played husband and wife. So that stuck! And we have two beautiful children that are now fifteen and seventeen.

ME: And Carlos is Puerto Rican, right?

PATRICIA: He is "Newyorican"—he is Puerto Rican from New York. Many Puerto Ricans from the island will tell you they're not the same kind of Puerto Rican ... Newyoricans and Puerto Ricans—they don't claim each other. The term *island culture*, one island is a tropical island and the other island is Manhattan ... very different environments, right?

ME: Okay, wow! All right, so here you are, a Latino family ... I don't know how to phrase it.

PATRICIA: Yeah, a Latino family. We call ourselves "Incaricans" because of my heritage from Peru—Incas and Puerto Ricans. So our children are Incaricans; that is a label that Carlos actually coined. It's not something that you're going to find somewhere else. *Incaricans, Newyoricans,* I love these terms! You're learning a lot this evening.

ME: We're in this climate [that often disrespects immigrants]. How are you navigating this climate raising your sons?

PATRICIA: Being very open with them. I think that has been a main theme for us as parents from the time they were little. Age appropriate, but always being very real with them and keeping them safe, but not sheltered. I think it's probably the best way to describe it. Thankfully, they have not experienced much in terms of repercussions for having their dark curly hair.

I think the most troubling issue that has happened to my son was when he went to high school. People think he's Jewish, which actually going back—way back—both Carlos's family and my family, back in Spain, we have Jewish last names. Sephardic Jews. During the great conversion, a lot of our families converted to Catholicism, particularly when they came to the New World. So we're part of that wave of Jews that were forced to convert to Catholicism. So anyway, because he has dark curly hair and fair skin and certain features, people think that he's Jewish. In AP biology class, one of his classmates showed him his wrist. He said, "Look at this. Does this offend you?" And it was a swastika.

ME: *Wow!*

PATRICIA: So not repercussions about being Puerto Rican or Latino or anything like that, but anti-Semitism ... imagine that.

ME: *How did your son handle that?*

PATRICIA: He said, "No, it doesn't offend me, but you do," or something like that.

ME: *Was it a tattoo on his wrist or a drawing?*

PATRICIA: No, he just drew it with a pen. They were both freshmen.

ME: *That's crazy.*

PATRICIA: It's a real problem in Indianapolis and in many places. You see it at schools. I serve on a board with the executive director of the Jewish Community Relations Council, and she explained to me that they do a lot of intervening at high schools across the city—public and private. This is seen everywhere.

ME: *Wow, I did not expect that at all tonight.*

PATRICIA: It's a different experience.

ME: *So your family, fortunately, hasn't run into a lot of issues due to being Latino, but I'm sure you're seeing others that are running into issues.*

PATRICIA: It's something that when I talk to my kids about it, they're very well aware of it when they see it happening. I'll give you another example that happened to my son—again, freshman. While he was in honors English class, someone from administration came and pulled him out of class and said, "You're not supposed to be in this class. You're supposed to be in the ELL [English Language Learner] class."

And he said, "Uh, no, what do you mean?"

"Because you don't speak English."

He's like, "Yes I do." And this is right after he had won a school-wide award in English class. So he says, "Let's go talk to my teacher."

And the teacher confirmed, "Yeah, he's supposed to be here."

But it was because of his last name. It was an assumption that was made that because his last name ends in a vowel that he must not speak English, you know, fluently. It was also a label that was placed by his original school that stayed with him throughout his whole educational career. Yes, he only spoke Spanish when he entered school, and that was by design.

That same assumption happened when he was born, actually at a hospital here in Indianapolis. The hospital sent a social services person and an interpreter to talk to me and Carlos, and we were like, "We're okay, but thank you." It was because of the last name—that's how sometimes assumptions happen. It may be well meaning, but it can be detrimental at a point. We are fortunate enough that Carlos and I are both professionals. We are okay financially and we're connected enough to be able to receive information and even distribute information to those who usually can't receive it in their own language. But that kind of bothers me sometimes when assumptions are made just because of your last name.

Recently, there's been a lot of conversation about the "majority" population is equated to White population and the minority population is equated to everybody else. In the last few years, we've been talking about "majority minority." What is that about? If you're the majority, you're the majority, but calling a group of people the "majority minority," to me it's a form of oppressing that group of people by continually using the "lesser" label, even though they're the majority.

It's oppressive language. So I've been really taking stock of how we use language, and how we label people, and how we need to kind of undo some of the things that have been done by us or by others. Just to make sure that we don't continue to create those microaggressions that happen when you label somebody one way or you use this language with another person. I think it's our responsibility to continue to do that.

ME: *I hope my book helps with that. I should say "our" book—the interviewees and me—I hope this helps in that area.*

PATRICIA: I think so, Amy. Until we come together, and we talk together, and we break bread together, and we go to each other's homes, and we see what's on their shelves—what kind of books they read or what kind of decor they have, that sort of thing … We may have different music playing or different food that we eat, but we still eat food and listen to music and read; that's where we can come together. Then we expand on our experiences and how we feel about things and what our experience is like.

I live in a city, and so I hear gunshots pretty much, you know, as a matter of fact, because it happens around here. I remember [a] moment [when] my kids were coming back from school, which is three blocks away. They had stayed over for some after-school activity. They were probably ten and twelve and it was dark at seven o'clock that night because of winter. So they were walking home together and it's pretty safe. And I saw … they decided to run down the sidewalk, and my heart just jumped.

I remember when they got home, I sat them down and I said, "You can't do that!" Because [my son] was running down the street—it was winter—he had his hood up …. And in the shadows you can't tell if he's a kid or if he's a grown-up, and my heart jumped. And I'm yelling at them saying, "Don't do that! You can't do that! You don't know what anybody's gonna think of!" I'm explaining to them. You know I'm shaking inside. And they're looking up at me like, *What did I do wrong?* And it just broke my heart that I had to have that conversation with them. That, no, you can't be a kid and run down the street with your hood up because you may get shot.

In the end when I had to explain that to them … it was a little like their innocence was broken at that point.

ME: *Yes, that's where my mind went to when you said that.*

PATRICIA: Carlos and I made a conscious choice to live where we live so that they could experience city life. We both come from cities, and that's our experience. We prefer to live in the city but there are some things that … I guess I'm thinking, *How did my parents do it?* Especially because I was a girl and I was walking around the city by myself from ten to twelve years old … using public transportation by myself, protecting myself. I did have one occasion where I had to use the straight pin my mother gave me. That's another experience—growing up as a woman, right?

ME: *Right.*

PATRICIA: I explained to my kids it's a very different experience: "You guys can walk down an alley without any worries or issue at any time of the day or night. I'm walking around anywhere and I'm worrying about who's looking at me, who's down the street, am I on the right side or the left side of the street?" You know, all those things.

ME: *So what do you think you've learned through the years as a Latina woman?*

PATRICIA: The label of "Latina" was something that was imposed on me when I stepped into this country. I was not Latina when I was in Mexico. I was not Latina when I was in Peru. Maybe Latino, as an identity, has extended to those countries now. But when I was growing up, I was Peruvian—from Peru, right? Peruvian living in Mexico. But I never identified as Latina because that's specifically a United States label. It's something that was created here; that's something interesting. I grew up as a Peruvian girl in Mexico, so from somewhere else—always from somewhere else. That's been a theme in my life.

What was interesting is that—again—skin tone. I was White until I came to the United States. I talk to my kids about that, too, because they wonder, what do we put on the census? What do we say that we are? There is such a thing as White Latina or White Latino.

ME: *I've seen that.*

PATRICIA: Going back to that majority-minority thing. It's really weird how we are forced to be placed into like a little cubby, when we are a lot of things. That's always been interesting to me. If there's a theme in my life, it's been about flexibility and adaptability. Being able to be in any room, at any table, and present myself as I am, not as a label and not as playing a part or ... representing anything or anyone. And being free from those things—I think that is the reason why I've been successful at [presenting myself as I am].

But at the same time, I know that it's because of my ethnicity, my last name, all of those things, that I'm allowed at some tables sometimes. Because there was a time where there weren't that many of us [Latinos] around. So I was asked to be on this board and to be on that board so that there could be representation. Now ... when somebody asks me to be on a board, [I say] I'm not joining any boards right now. I've reached that time in my life where I can say, "Thank you but no thank you. But let me pull somebody else for you to consider." There are so many qualified Latinas in Indianapolis that I ask, "What are the qualities that you're looking for? The gifts that people can bring to the board?" And if they tell me [they] need somebody to represent the Latino community, it's like okay, so you're checking the box. So I press further. I say, "Fine, but what kind of talents are you looking for? Are you looking for somebody who's in the legal profession? Somebody who is in education? Somebody who is in the arts? Do you need somebody with a financial background? If I have a choice, let us check the full three-dimensional box, not just ... the representation here."

So that's what I've learned. That I have to be fearless in making sure that people see me as a whole person, not just a check mark.

ME: *Well, that leads me to my next question. What sorts of things would you like to tell the world to do a little differently as far as Latino families or the population in general?*

PATRICIA: [I'd tell people] to have the full experience with someone that you want to have in your life. What I mean by that is the full experience of the conversation of their history ... of having this tough conversation. Create the space for the opportunity. It's not okay to do it necessarily at a cocktail party or if you're with a bunch of people. Then it's like, "Tell me about your experience?" Read the room, right? Say to somebody, "Hey, you know, I really want to know more about you and your life." Being brave enough to ask that question is a good thing.

I've had to ask that question of others that I don't understand completely. Sure it's easy for me to say, "Well, I'm not from here so I need to know this." But it's okay. You can say, "I'm not of your culture but I want to know this. I want to know about what makes you a full person." Most people are not going to be interviewing people for a book, so you're different in that. But most people are going to … look for the opportunity to interact with people not like themselves. If you extend yourself, you're going to have a relationship with somebody not like you. What I mean by that is a friendship, whether it's a co-worker or anybody in your immediate circle. Make the effort to extend yourself and put yourself out there. I think that if anybody were to ask me, "Can we have a conversation about you?" I'd be happy to—I love talking about myself! Who doesn't, right?

ME: *Who doesn't? Exactly! One of the things I had started to ask Bryan [Fonseca] is, "What would you recommend?" He told me about a great show that John Leguizamo did about Latin American history: [*John Leguizamo's Latin History for Morons*] … I'm so glad I asked him. I watched it a couple weeks later and I absolutely loved it. I was looking forward to learning more from him.*

PATRICIA: I think PBS did a wonderful three- or four-part series on Latinos in America: [*Latino Americans*]. That's a very good one too.

ME: *Okay, I will look that up too.*

PATRICIA: Bryan's experience was different from mine because he was born here of immigrant parents. He had that dual experience of the Mexican American experience and the Irish mom.

ME: *I didn't know that.*

PATRICIA: Yes, the Irish side was very much a part of his culture as well.

ME: *Well, you are going to be the perfect person to ask this next question. Do you belong to any organizations that help spread the message? Can you tell me about local or national organizations if people want to learn more or help?*

PATRICIA: Fiesta Indianapolis, which became La Plaza, the Indiana Latino Institute, Latino Expo—these are some local organizations. At the national level, you have LULAC (League of United Latin American Citizens), which is the largest and oldest Hispanic organization in the US dating back to 1929, NALEO (National Association of Latino Elected & Appointed Officials), and the [United States] National Hispanic Chamber of Commerce. ... We do have ... an intention to represent not only racially and ethnically, but also socioeconomically and location-wise.

The other organization that I'm involved with [and] specifically wanted to address ... is Enlace Academy. The intention was to address the educational needs of kids K–8 ... that spoke a language other than English at home—primarily Latinos because of our location, but many from Asia and Africa as well—and to make sure that they had an environment where they could excel. So in essence this is a 100 percent ELL (English language learner) school.

One of the things that we're finding out actually is that there are kids ... that typically would not be receiving ELL education ... [who are] benefiting from the model, because all of them are being taught as English Language Learners. But the kids that speak English from birth—whether they're White or Black—are actually excelling their peers at other schools because they're being taught in an ELL environment.

Another organization that I've been very involved with since 2000 actually is the Race and Cultural Relations Leadership Network. The RCRLN is a subcommittee of GIPC (Greater Indianapolis Progress Committee). The RCRLN gathers individuals from around greater Indianapolis that represent a variety of constituencies. We meet the first Friday of every month and we talk about the issues that are affecting the city that deal with race and culture. If there's anything that is a stress that is happening between communities or within a community, we discuss it. We find out more about it and then we go back to our own communities so that we can dispel any bad information or maybe even misinformation or assumptions. So the idea is that we come and represent different groups, and the fact that we've been meeting every first Friday of every month for over twenty years now—for me, but even before—you create relationships with others that are not like you .... When something happens that affects both your groups, you're able to come to the table and have a civil conversation about it because trust has been established. [The RCRLN] is something that the city of Indianapolis's mayor's office supports. Actually, I was chair of that organization for two years and continued to be involved in an advisory capacity. The prosecutor's office and the police department all are involved in it. Everything that we've been hearing with the police department, for instance, all of that is discussed in the open. Very much so.

And the Fonseca Theatre Company, which is specifically addressing societal issues through theater. Plays that are about or written by people of color particularly addressing Latinos, African Americans, Asian Americans, LGBTQ+, and others. That is something that I have found, because of the intersection of the arts and social issues playing out on stage, just how the arts are so important to be able to—impactfully and quickly—change people's attitudes about a specific topic through the theater.

If you're working with a social services agency or doing just education through talks and through community events and things like that, it takes so long for people to really get it. But you go to see one play and you see the experience of others being portrayed right there in front of you ... I mean, it can change your mind like *that*! The power of the arts and the power of the theater to be able to communicate and to express what people are feeling—the joys, the pains, the sorrows, and the wins—it is amazing. So I will always be involved in the arts for that reason.

ME: *It's exciting! And you mentioned Women4Change earlier, which I can certainly add more information in here, but what's great about Women4Change is that there are organizations like them popping up all over the country.*

PATRICIA: We're not affiliated with anybody outside of Indiana. We are unique to us. But the organizations that are popping up around the country are typically women organizations that are like-minded and talking about the issues that affect them. I don't know how coordinated they are though. It's usually like a book club of some sort or a Facebook page here and there.

One of the last events that we did before COVID was on March 5 [2020]. Women4Change brought over 1,500 postcards from women, and some men, who wrote about their experience of being sexually accosted in some way, and they represented each and every county in the state of Indiana. We put them up all over the state house and then we also sent copies of the words that were written by constituents to each representative to be delivered to their desks. Because sexual assault affects all, not only women, because you know it affects the men that love them too … And the fathers and the husbands and the brothers and everybody else. It's not glamorous work but it's great work.

ME: *Definitely! Oh, you've hooked me up to some good organizations! I appreciate it. Well, is there anything I forgot this evening that you might want to share?*

PATRICIA: Oh probably, but for now I think that's good. I thank you for the opportunity and for you having the guts to ask the questions and to go into this very difficult journey for yourself as well. Thank you for opening the space to do it.

Organizations mentioned during this interview:
- La Plaza: www.laplazaindy.org
- The Indiana Latino Institute: www.indianalatinoinstitute.org
- Indiana Latino Expo: www.indianalatinoexpo.org
- The Race and Cultural Relations Leadership Network: www.indygipc.org/initiatives/rcrln/
- Enlace: www.enlaceacademy.org
- Fonseca Theatre Company: www.fonsecatheatre.org
- The League of United Latin American Citizens: www.lulac.org
- The National Association of Latino Elected & Appointed Officials: www.naleo.org
- The United States Hispanic Chamber of Commerce: www.ushcc.com
- Women4Change: www.women4changeindiana.org

There is growing evidence that reading a story engages many of the same neural networks involved in empathy.

-RESEARCH LED BY PSYCHOLOGIST DAN JOHNSON, WRITTEN IN THE JOURNAL *BASIC AND APPLIED SOCIAL PSYCHOLOGY*

JORDAN

J ordan is currently the head of Fonseca Theatre Company and has done an incredible job leading the transition since Bryan's death. I met her two and a half years ago and instantly recognized her as an old soul. She is intelligent, driven, compassionate, and an all-around pleasure to be with. I love working with her but had never before heard her "Mexi-Jew" story!

NAME: Jordan
AGE: 27
IDENTIFIES AS: Female
ETHNICITY: "Mexi-Jew" (half Mexican and half Jewish)
OCCUPATION: Theater Producer

ME: *I'm so honored to work with you. You actually shared some of your story with me a couple years ago when we visited [our friend] Bryan [Fonseca], but I'm not going to remember everything. I would love to hear about you and your family growing up. Where did you live?*
JORDAN: I grew up in the suburbs of Atlanta. I'm an only child. It was just me, my mom, and my dad. I've actually got a cousin that's my same age and it was her and her parents. I grew up with my dad's side of the family, which was the Jewish side of the family. We would go to Texas fairly often to visit my mom's family, the Mexican side

of the family. It was one of those things where in my own home life, my parents were both very passionate about their cultures. They both did what they could to teach me about their history and their culture. *ME: I love hearing that both of your parents encouraged you to learn their cultures. Since your mother was Mexican, did you learn Spanish in your home growing up?*

JORDAN: I did, yes. That was part of my mom wanting to make sure that I knew my culture, that I knew my history. It was very important to her that I spoke the language. She worked with me herself when I was a little kid and I would go to some language camps during the summer. Once I got to the level in school where language classes were offered, I took Spanish all the way through to make sure that I had a place to practice and that I could obtain proper fluency. My mom wanted to make sure that I had some exposure to literature and writers from Spanish cultures and in the Spanish language.

ME: I like your mom! She is very smart. My sister-in-law grew up similar to your mom in Texas and she tried to help her daughter when she was learning Spanish in school. Her daughter was learning things that were different from what [my sister-in-law] knew. Did your mother encounter that?

JORDAN: Yep, absolutely. Like every language, there are different dialects of Spanish. There are colloquialisms, localisms, slang terms, all that sort of stuff. It was funny going back and forth between the two worlds. All my Spanish teachers in school at every level along the way—I don't know how it worked out—but they were all Venezuelan. From them, I was taught a different—very different—dialect. Different vocabulary, different structure.

I would definitely be talking in Spanish from school and my mom would be like, "Wait, I don't think that's a word ... is that a word?" Or conversely, the Spanish that my mom spoke and that her family spoke, if I would use them in an assignment, I would get it back with a circle and a question mark. So it's interesting trying to find that balance. Based on where I've been, how I've been using my Spanish, it's definitely evolved over the years.

Think about someone from the UK, or someone from Australia, or someone from Canada ... they've just got different words that they use. One of my Spanish teachers actually had a big sign at the front of her classroom that was a reminder that language is not based in science or logic, it's based in tradition and heritage, just to remind folks that things might not make sense.

ME: Exactly! So here you are growing up with two different cultures. Tell me about holidays and religious celebrations—how were those handled in your household?

JORDAN: Well, my mom being Mexican American, she was raised Catholic and my dad, of course, was raised Jewish. That meant we did both actually. So we would have a little menorah next to the Christmas tree. I did a mix of it. I've had varying affiliations and involvements throughout my life. I went to the temple for preschool so I had a little bit of religious education from the Jewish side of things. I learned my prayers, attended services, all that sort of stuff.

I also have been to a variety of Christian services over the years with my mom and with other folks in my life. I actually did a service trip as part of a youth group once—a Methodist church. I'm a member of the synagogue here in Indy. I've been connecting more with the Jewish side of my faith. It's very much been an ebb and flow. Going through that process, it's been, I think, really great to have exposure to multiple faiths like that. It's really given me room—at least the way my parents handled it—to kind of find my own sense of spirituality and my own belief system. It gave me an appreciation for a multitude of practices and beliefs.

What drew me to this particular synagogue is their reconstructionist congregation. The Jewish faith is strongly passionate about service and community in general. Reconstructionists take it to that next level. The big belief system at my synagogue is that it's not about praying to make the world better; it's about praying for the *strength* to make it better and really acknowledging we have to do the work ourselves. That's just something that spoke to me. Actually, the rabbi at the synagogue is also Latino. He's from Panama, so that's another connection that I just felt going into that space, going into that community.

ME: I love how you grew up. It sounds pretty wonderful. But were there some struggles because of your family being the mix that they were?

JORDAN: Well, it's interesting because being half Jewish, I'm very pale. I am White-passing. And on the flip side, my mother's actually Brown. My mother has a much-darker complexion than I do. That means that a lot of the inherent biases, a lot of those snap judgments, a lot of those assumptions ... I didn't necessarily deal with them myself, especially once I was more independent from my family. But I grew up watching my mom deal with those. I grew up watching my mom get comments from people at the grocery store. I grew up with people at school assuming that she was a nanny or a housekeeper or a babysitter there to pick me up.

Being White-passing, it's been like a coming-out process, sometimes having to explain to people, "I am not White; I am half Mexican. So what you're saying is affecting me. What you're saying is something I actually have a connection to." Especially over the past few years, dealing with the political climate and how extreme everything [has] gotten under the past administration, I really had to do a lot of work on myself to come to terms with what it meant to be White-passing. How could I be more vocal and be more of an advocate for my community, for my family? Especially in this day and age, especially in the United States where there are so many different cultures and nationalities coming together. There are so many people that are like myself—that are mixed—and it's just one of those things; you can't assume someone's cultural background. I really would like to see the day where we get to a place as a society that we acknowledge [those assumptions] and that people get those preconceived notions out of their head of what someone from a certain background, or that uses a certain label, is supposed to look like.

ME: Excellent points, my friend. I have to go back a little bit. So your mom heard these comments—or you heard them—how did that affect her?

JORDAN: It's one of those things that she's been dealing with all her life as a Brown person. It's something that she started recognizing from an early age. She actually went to an HBCU [historically Black college or university] law school specifically because she did not want to be at a predominantly White institution. She knew as a Brown woman from a border town that she would not fit in.

What's interesting … my mother and her side of the family are actually more American than my dad's side of the family because they are specifically *Tejano*—as in, from the Mexican state of *Tejas* that became Texas after the revolution there … Davy Crockett and all that. Her family can be traced to Texas from the very first census that was taken there in the 1800s. She's done the genealogy. So her side of the family is actually more American than my dad's side of the family by a couple of generations.

That's something that she's always felt a bit frustrated about, because you know, she's educated, she's born and raised in the United States. Several generations. It's frustrating for her to know that that won't necessarily protect her. She is Brown and if she's ever in a situation where she's at the Mexican market picking up something for dinner—and she was doing some work around the house or something—and just goes in yoga pants and a T-shirt with nothing but her credit card, she could end up detained, purely because some cop won't believe [she's a citizen]. Even if they see her ID, what White racist cop from Georgia is gonna believe that this Brown woman has a Jewish last name?

I thought a lot about what this could mean, especially back when I was growing up in the early 2000s and there was a lot going on policy-wise in Georgia. There were raids that were really heightened and everything. We actually had a plan. I had a list of people that I knew I was supposed to contact in the event that Mom did not show up to get me from school or in the event that she went to the store and did not come back. I think part of how it affected her too, though, was the anxiety. Knowing that purely because of the fact that she was a Brown woman from a border town, she had a target on her back. I think that growing up with that and seeing that, it gave me an appreciation for all the work that needs to be done.

One of the things that I remind myself and remind other folks of all the time ... my mom is roughly the same age as Ruby Bridges [late sixties]. That's what people forget. It's not ancient history; the water hoses and the dogs and the protests [are] not ancient history. Especially being here in the Midwest and thinking about engaging with folks of my parents' generation, of my parents age—and especially thinking about engaging with the White folks ... it's something that I just remind myself.

They might not have been the people that were hissing and throwing things at Ruby Bridges, but they probably were friends with them and didn't give it a second thought. They were probably perfectly comfortable sitting right there next to them in class, and playing on sports teams with them, and going to dances with them, and all that cliché high school stuff. That really is very recent history, and there is still so much that we have to undo and that we have to unlearn. It's not just one particular people or one particular group of people—it's everyone.

ME: *Exactly. And I won't pretend to think that this book is going to tell every single story possible. One person's Mexican/Jewish story is going to be very different from another one's. I'm kind of hoping to create a spark with this book so people can try to do more to help make [those assumptions/stereotypes go away] someday. Because you're right, we have a lot of work to do.*

It's funny you mentioned Ruby Bridges. I had no idea about all the different things she did until somebody posted on Facebook about her and said there's more to her. I've read about all she did, [and how she is an activist to this very day], and I thought, Wow, I never had heard about this! It's fascinating. She's amazing.

JORDAN: Yeah, and she is still out there ... she is still being very vocal and she's still ... part of the movement.

ME: *I love that, but like you said, I was thinking that was so long ago. It's just like I say in my introduction to this book. Growing up I thought, "Oh, everything's better." Not really.*

Well, another part of your story, something that you might have told me and I had forgotten about when I was telling you about who I was trying to interview for this book … you reminded me, "Hey, Amy, I am a lesbian." So I have to ask about that part of you as well. When did you realize that you might be or that you were [gay]?

JORDAN: I realized that when I was a teenager, when I was in high school. I had gone on a couple of "Let's go to the Starbucks and sit and talk" sort of dates with boys and stuff. It was just one of those things where you didn't really click, didn't really have that interest, never really felt that connection with someone. I had just kind of been dismissing it and thinking, *I'm focused on school and on trying to figure out my future because that's more who I am. I go to a girls' school anyway, so I don't know that many boys.*

I just hadn't really been giving a lot of thought to it. But as I was growing, I had the epiphany: "I am gay." Just realizing that I can feel that [romantic] connection with someone. I can feel that is an interest of mine. I just hadn't been doing that with the right people.

I grew up in a major city, [Atlanta], with progressive, supportive parents, and I went to a more progressive school. I was very fortunate. I even had some friends that came out around the same time. I know many, many people that had a much more difficult time of it … that did have those experiences where they were thrown out of their house, where it did affect their relationship with their families, where they did have to stop going to their religious group, where it did change key relationships in their life. I also grew up and came into this part of my identity in a time where we had much more language for [being queer], where we're having a much more open dialogue about it and thinking about [it]. It's something that I do feel very lucky that I had a relatively peaceful, nondramatic experience with it, and there were support systems for me there.

ME: *I am glad to hear that, Jordan. That's absolutely wonderful. You're right, even today with the more open-minded population, you still hear stories of families, friends that just turned their backs on people.*

JORDAN: Absolutely, and actually, Indiana is one of the highest states for suicide for queer folks and especially queer youth, statistically. [Support] really is important for folks and it can make all the difference. Even something as simple as just reading a queer romance novel can make all the difference for young folks that are going through that process and that are learning more about themselves.

A lot of it really is [having] open conversation, because especially in the States, we're so hesitant to talk about sexuality and it's such a taboo. It's something that makes so many people uncomfortable, especially in mixed company. That means that there are a lot of folks who grow up not even knowing that queerness is a thing. Not even knowing what the words are. Not even knowing that there are happy, successful people who have other types of relationships besides monogamous heterosexual relationships. Just having that awareness that there are other folks out there is a big, big, big thing for mental health and in finding a support system.

ME: Yeah. I like that you mentioned literature. I've been really excited. I joined the Book of the Month Club about five or six months ago. I like [it] because I'm reading more current releases. I'm noticing the authors are having more of, "Here's Tess and Mary, they're this couple, they've been together for years," or "Here's somebody [who was assigned female at birth] and now they identify as a man." It's neat to see these more modern books talking about these characters that aren't just heterosexual, that aren't just, you know, WASP. It's great to see the variety of characters. It makes me happy.

JORDAN: I'm taking a class through my master's program this semester called Anti-racism, Feminism, and Theater. A lot of the theory we've been reading talks about just how narrow this dominant norm is of White middle-class heterosexuality and how few people actually fit into those boxes and fit into that identity. Really, the overwhelming majority of folks do not. There is at least one thing different, if not multiple things—whether it's someone's cultural background, their sexual orientation, their gender identity, their socioeconomic status, where they grew up, what their family structure is. Some folks come from single-parent homes, some folks come from a traditional two-parent home, some come from a home with two moms or two dads. Some folks grew up without parents for any multitude of reasons and were raised by older siblings, or by aunts and uncles, or by grandparents. Some folks got separated from their families when they were very little. There are just so many different stories out there when it comes to family and heritage and identity. And that's beautiful and that's something that should be celebrated. I think that having these stories available, that more folks can see themselves in, and [because] more folks feel comfortable sharing their stories [and] because there was that brave author somewhere that wrote something that spoke [to them] ... they could connect.

Another thing I think about in this regard, too, is social justice as a trend and inclusion as a trend because, regardless, it's a good thing. Sometimes it comes from a really genuine place and sometimes it comes from, "We're trying to be hip," or "We're trying to do something that'll sell," or "We're trying to do something that speaks to this particular younger demographic or to this particular cultural community." That's just something that you really have to think about. Who's in the room? Who's making the decisions about the project? Who's creating the content? Who's being hired to support it? How is it being distributed? What's the price point? Who's the real target audience?

Actually this week in my anti-racism class, we talked a lot about erasure and about how a lot of these stories [about marginalized individuals] are being made more comfortable and more accessible for "mainstream" audiences—meaning White audiences. In particular, what we were talking about was this whole idea around color-blind casting and what it means to put a person of color in a traditionally White role, especially if you're doing it in a way that forces them to assimilate. That they have to straighten their hair, that they have to unlearn an accent, that they have to move in a different way.

Just thinking about what that means for the theater industry specifically and then also thinking bigger picture, what that means in popular culture and in the content we're consuming from these different streaming platforms ... from these popular books that are coming out.

There was one book that came out, *American Dirt,* and it is basically the Latino version of *The Help.* So it's very much a book about the Latino culture from the White perspective and it reinforces a lot of stereotypes. It's very problematic and it's just something that thinking about those books—how the White gaze, the straight gaze, how the male gaze can affect how a story gets told. I think it's becoming increasingly important to me, especially in my job, especially in my work, to really be thinking about where stories are coming from, and who they aim for, and if they actually are doing good things, or if it really might be doing more harm than good.

ME: *Wow, I want to take your class. That sounds really great. That's one that I would look forward to. I wish that had been there when I went to IU [Indiana University] thirty years ago.*

JORDAN: That was one thing I've definitely had a big appreciation for, the fact that I am at a traditional, predominantly White, flagship institution and I have courses like this in my curriculum. I have content like this in my curriculum, and I've got professors in my department that are fighting to get this perspective as part of our learning. I think that's incredibly valuable and that's definitely one of the things that gives me a lot of hope for the world.

ME: *Yeah, me too. I agree with you, Jordan. I hope it's not just a trend, especially in what we do. We work together, obviously, and so often I'll see a foundation talk about, "We want to be more equitable." And I'm thinking,* Are you doing this because it's the right thing, or are you doing this because it's just the thing now? *I hope they're doing it for the right reasons but I kind of wonder,* Are you just hopping on this because everybody else is? *It's an interesting question.*

JORDAN: Here's the thing ... I don't know if you saw this or not, but a [nonprofit] recently put out a job description for a new director position and they actually specifically said as part of the job description, "maintaining their White traditional audience."

ME: *Whoa! I missed that!*

JORDAN: Yes, definitely take a look at that ... but the fact that that's still happening in the nonprofit world is just ridiculous to me. There are a lot of institutions and foundations out there that they might have some lingo around diversity or they might have a really cool side program that's not part of their mission. You have to really evaluate how they're doing that work, especially within larger institutions.

What percentage of their resources are they dedicating to that community engagement or to that diversity training that they put all over social media that their staff is going through? In the terms of foundations, what percentage of their funding is actually going to organizations of color and organizations that have leadership of color on their boards and in their executive staff? Because the numbers on that are still pretty dismal when it comes to the development side of things—the percentage of funds that go to organizations of color or leaders of color. Especially in the arts.

ME: *Yeah, it doesn't surprise me. So, Jordan, what have you learned by being who you are, a lesbian woman of Mexican/Jewish heritage?*

JORDAN: I've learned to have a strong sense of self and to be proud of who I am and where I come from. I've learned to have a more global perspective on where folks can come from and how folks can identify. I think it's given me an appreciation for my heritage, my family, and my background. It's taught me a lot about how to identify who are really my friends, the folks that are really in my corner and really do support me in all parts of me—not just the young professional that presents herself—that really understand where I come from, who I am, what's important to me.

I think [my background has] definitely helped shape my value system when it comes to the sort of work I do and how I want to spend my time and the organizations I want to be a part of. I think it's also a big part of why I do the work that I do at the theater. I engage with a lot of volunteerism as well. I think it's really where my passion comes from, where I find that drive to have these conversations and to be part of this big, ever-constantly growing group of people that want to make the world a better, more inclusive place. I want to help open folks' eyes to these different experiences. I'm proud of who I am and I'm proud of the communities that I'm a part of. I am proud that I have found people in my life who support that and embrace that, who encourage me to share that part of myself and be proud of that part of myself.

ME: I love it, Jordan. I am so glad you have that community, and I see now why you're so passionate and why you are where you are today. The position that you're in and the work that you do—it all makes even more sense to me today. One thing, though, I have to ask … is there something you don't like about who you are?

JORDAN: I think especially as a kid and especially just being younger, we all have that interest when we're a teenager, when we're in middle school, that we want to fit in. We want to just feel normal. I think that there were definitely some times where I would have to do odd things like skip swim practice because we had to go to a Jewish holiday thing, or when I had to sit down and have tough conversations with my mom about what's going on in the world and what that meant.

There were definitely times where I felt myself pushing back on that and where I've had myself feeling, *Why does it have to be this hard? Why can't I just be normal?* And I think that's something, in retrospect, I really didn't understand where I was coming from at the time. But I'm glad that I had adults in my life who pushed me through that and who encouraged me to really see that it's okay to be different. Folks are unique and that's a good thing.

I remember specifically there was a time during my first master's program. We were all out at a brewery after class and one of my cohorts made a joke about, "Oh, I guess the future of arts administration is all White women because we're all White women here." Ha ha ha. And I was [thinking], *But we're not.*

Or another example: I was having lunch with a newer friend. Someone that I was just getting to know. We were just hanging out and she asked, "Oh, are you seeing anyone? Do you have a boyfriend?" And she specifically said *boyfriend*. So then I went into the explanation of, "By the way, I'm gay …." And she stopped me at a certain point and she asked, "Why do gay people always have to say they're gay?" I had to explain, "You used the word *boyfriend* so I had to clarify. And if I didn't clarify then that meant you would have gone on assuming." I've just been in that position so many times where I've had to decide between identifying myself and potentially causing that conflict, or just letting that part of myself be erased in that context and just letting that part of myself be ignored. I think that's something that I still struggle with sometimes. I still have to pick those battles. Sometimes I wonder if that's ever gonna stop.

ME: *Good point. I think I probably have done that a couple times myself. Just not even thinking! "Why doesn't somebody like you have a girlfriend?" (Teasing a guy or something). I've just never thought about that. So maybe changing our language a little bit could help.*

JORDAN: That's part of why there is so much conversation around language, and around what words to use, and how to speak about these issues. Because those subtle things really can make a difference. Because my friend specifically using the word *boyfriend* put me in that uncomfortable situation where I had to decide to either let her keep assuming I was straight, or to out myself and potentially jeopardize that relationship, not knowing where she stood …. Or when my cohort made the comment about us all being White. I had to choose between just letting it roll off my back and not drawing attention to it, or actually being vocal and causing that conflict and being the one that ruined the "fun cohort outing after class." That time I actually did just let it roll off my back. She wasn't really directly speaking to me and it was still like my first or second semester. I was trying to get to know these folks and stuff, and I just didn't really know what to do.

That's why I really want us to get to a place eventually where we just realize we need to not make assumptions about anything. That it needs to just become a cultural norm to either use neutral language or to just ask …. Everyone should be given the opportunity to identify themselves how they want to be identified, to recognize that so many of these aspects of our identity—culture, gender, sexual orientation, physical ability—all those sorts of things are not something that you can necessarily see, that is necessarily readily visible. People just might not check your box for what you think that particular label looks like.

ME: *Yep, I'm learning that with every interview, I think. Jordan, it's been tremendous. I knew this experience would start to bring some change within me. I didn't realize it'd be happening so quickly. I've been losing some sleep here and there—but I embrace it because it's given me so much to think about as I go through this …. I have the joy of working with you and Fonseca Theatre Company. But I'm curious, have you faced people who don't like what your work is or what the theater's work is?*

JORDAN: So this past summer, in response to both the pandemic and to the Black Lives Matter movement, we threw out the last couple of shows in our season, and we produced two scripts that spoke specifically to the Black experience in America and to police brutality. We staged them outdoors—socially distant, masks, chairs spaced out, hand sanitizer, the whole nine yards. During that whole process we actually got an email from some random person—we had no recognition of them in our ticket system, I'm not sure how they ended up on our mailing list, no donor records, no nothing. They sent us a very incensed message asking us to please take them off our mailing list and condemning us for putting on this "divisivy" work— using the word *divisivy*. Clearly, they meant divisive, but that's what the email said.

ME: *Oh my gosh!*

JORDAN: It took me aback because it doesn't happen very often. We do have pushback every now and then and it comes in different ways. Sometimes it comes in the form of people leaving a performance early, sometimes it comes in the form of an email like that, sometimes it comes in the form of an awkward conversation. But, fortunately, especially with the community that we've built around the theater, there hasn't been a whole lot of that. But that email just sticks with me. I remember joking about it with some folks and just talking about renaming us the "divisivy theater." I will never forget the word *divisivy* as long as I live!

ME: *Yeah, me either now!*

JORDAN: It's just one of those things where it's an example of how even today, there's still so much learning to do that people think raising your voice in support of a community is divisive … is problematic … and knowing and thinking about the fact that politics have become so much about humanity, and about who has rights and who doesn't, and who is effectively a person and who isn't. How it is okay and not okay to treat certain groups of people based on certain arbitrary things.

Sure, you can argue that politics has always been about that—has always been about allocating rights and resources—but the fact that it is that those conversations around the allocation of rights and resources have gotten to such an inhumane point … I want to say that it's shocking but … I think it's something that was just such a long time brewing.

It's just gotten easier and easier to see how we got to the point when the previous administration got elected, and it's just highlighted for me the importance of those insidious things. Of what it means to take a certain lesson out of a history book in class, what it means to use the wrong word here and there, what it means to not engage with folks that are different from yourself just because you might not be comfortable.

What it means to really think about these issues and what it really means to acknowledge difference, to understand difference, and not only acknowledge and understand it, but to do so in a way that helps build that bridge.

ME: *Yes!*

JORDAN: And help find connection.

ME: *I think a lot of readers are going to agree with me that you have incredible wisdom for being twenty-seven. It just blows my mind, Jordan, just how thoughtful you are. A lot of people would say you have an old soul … I don't know what the word is I'm trying to come up with. I'm trying to compliment you—you're wise beyond your years—that doesn't quite cut it. I certainly don't think I knew all you did at age twenty-seven or had the understanding that you do. I think it's tremendous. What would you tell the world to do differently for people like you—either people who are gay or people who have mixed heritage?*

JORDAN: First off, to just reiterate, don't make assumptions and to make space for the people in your life to identify themselves how they want to be identified on all fronts. It's also about doing the internal work, like you're doing by going through these interview processes and working on this book. Just finding ways in your own life to do this learning for yourself. To read about these issues, about these ideas.

To learn about new language and why certain terms are coming into use more prominently. To do a little bit of work, a little bit of research when you're going to engage with an organization or with a project—with a piece of media or a piece of art—and think about the perspective it's coming from.

If you're reading a news story, [look up] the journalist real quick. Look at what their background is—look at other stuff that they've written—get a sense of what perspective they're writing from so that you know to just not necessarily take everything with a grain of salt, but to question things and to dig a little bit deeper. It's very hard [in] this day and age with the information overload, but go beyond that headline, go beyond the clickbait, and really try and figure out what's going on for yourself. Think about the source of whatever it is you're looking at.

ME: *Yeah, good point. It's pretty easy for us to do that nowadays, which is nice.*

JORDAN: Yeah, exactly, and just doing a quick search. Ruby Bridges has been mentioned a lot because there was an anniversary recently. Looking into her story and thinking about what it would be like to be a little six-year-old Black girl integrating a school in Louisiana and to have to have a federal marshal escort you to class in your little Mary Janes with your little ruffly socks … just trying to get to school. Think about what it meant.

… Also, just recognizing that, especially in the States, we have such a bad habit of altering our history, of teaching more propaganda than what actually happened. Really question those quaint stories you know in your head.

I had a great professor in my undergrad—I majored in history, and that's one of my big lenses for thinking about these issues. She taught a social movements class and this [recognition] was her whole approach. That's part of why I ended up a history major, because of just how much that perspective opened my eyes. Just thinking about that untold history. It's problematic to me that I had to get to a junior/senior-level undergraduate class at an elite liberal arts college to gain access to this information. Realizing what that [information] means for the majority of folks who don't take that history class when they're in college or who don't even get to go to college ... it's a very small percentage of people that even go that far educationally.

Just trying to find ways to take the resources we have at our disposal—you know [the internet] is an amazing thing—and just thinking about that ... those are my two big things. Don't make assumptions, and do your homework.

ME: Yep, great advice, Jordan. So, obviously you belong to an organization making a huge difference—you're leading it currently—but are there any other organizations that you might recommend? What if somebody is reading this in, I don't know, Nevada, and they're like, "Hey, I wanna make a difference. I wanna help make a difference for people." Are there any organizations you know of that people could join or support?

JORDAN: Locally, Indiana Youth Group is an incredible organization. I volunteer with them. They are a queer youth center—full service. They've got a clothing closet, they've got a food pantry, they've got all sorts of incredible programming just to build community and create that space for youth. They're a fantastic organization doing fantastic work.

I also highly recommend, locally, Indy Reads. A lot of people know them as a great independent bookstore, but they are actually a nonprofit, and all proceeds from that bookstore fund adult literacy classes, ESL (English as a second language) classes, and high school equivalency programs.

There's also RAICES [The Refugee and Immigrant Center for Education and Legal Services] in Texas, which actually does great work with the immigrant community. And I definitely recommend just taking a look at your local nonprofit scene and seeing what's around there because I'm sure that, regardless of what community you're in, there's probably an organization not too far away from you that's doing some pretty cool stuff.

ME: Is there anything that I forgot to ask you that you think would be good to share?

JORDAN: I would be happy to talk a little bit more about my background with Bryan and how the theater came to be, if that history would be useful for you.

ME: Yes, sure!

JORDAN: I started working for Bryan as an intern during my arts administration program and we hit it off. We had a great mentor-mentee relationship. I came back after I finished that degree right away. I started working for him full time and we got a fellowship from the local arts council, as you know. We started doing programming on the Near Westside of Indianapolis through that fellowship program. However, like many fellowships and grants, it had a time limit. Once the two years were coming to an end, we were looking for a solution on how to sustain these programs that we built and these relationships that we had started nurturing. We were really trying to avoid doing that thing where we "art and run" the second the grant was over.

We decided that the best way to continue the programming was to file for a 501c3. We did, and we went back and forth about what approach to take with the theater and what the mission should be. We knew community building should be part of it, and as you know, the Near Westside is a heavily Latino group. Bryan being Latino and myself being Latina, he was very tempted to do a purely Latino theater. But we went back and forth and we looked at other models that I showed him—really, the multicultural approach and the full-scope approach to diversity just made the most sense. We started just doing some research on what that meant. We decided to move forward with it and that's how we got to the conclusion we came to. Also, just looking specifically within the theater industry at the conversations that were going on, and knowing that the American theater right now really is having a reckoning when it comes to diversity and engagement and what institutions look like, and having had all these resources, we were very intentional about how we set up our board, how we set up our staff, about the artists that we invited to be part of our collective, the shows we picked, and all those sort of things ... to make sure that we were honoring our mission all the way from the top.

[We wanted to ensure] we were reflecting our community and reflecting a diverse group of folks, starting with the board, the executive leadership, and making sure it wasn't just supporting the community, but we were making room for folks at our table ... we were giving the decision-making power to folks that were part of our mission.

ME: Awesome, and fortunately when you worked with him, you discussed succession planning because Bryan was in his early sixties at the time. From what I've read, the plan was for you to take over when he would retire.

JORDAN: As his mentee and as a cofounder of the theater, that was definitely something we started talking about. Prior to his passing, he was already getting to that point in his career and just personally where he was hitting that three-to-five-year mark where he would be ready to retire. We talked about what that meant for the theater, and how to sustain it, and how to move forward. That's when we had discussed me stepping into this role. It was just not supposed to be this soon. I will always be sad for what I did not get a chance to learn from Bryan, but I am confident he taught me plenty. I do feel he prepared me well, and other experiences I've had professionally and personally have prepared me to tackle this and to really embrace this mission ... to continue doing this work.

ME: I'm just so thrilled that here we are, months later, with an incredible lineup for this summer. The vision and all that's happening ... I'm so happy that it's going to continue for many years to come. I know you have a lot on your plate, so making this time for me—for this book—it really means a lot, Jordan. Thank you!

JORDAN: Happy to be a part of it. Thank you, Amy.

Organizations mentioned during this interview:
- Indiana Youth Group: www.indianayouthgroup.org
- Indy Reads: www.indyreads.org
- RAICES (The Refugee and Immigrant Center for Education and Legal Services): www.raicestexas.org

If we can let ourselves, all of us, be united by the simple fact of having a difference, we will be bigger and stronger and more powerful than anyone who might otherwise make us feel small. And you know what? We'll have more fun too. We'll be the world's most colorful block party.

—PAIGE RAWL

CHIP

I met Chip in college through our coed service fraternity. Even though I was at Indiana University and he was at Ball State, we still connected quickly and easily. He's just that kind of a person—you're drawn to him! Chip and I lost touch for a while but thanks to the magic of Facebook, we reconnected. I got to visit him when I went to Washington, DC, in 2012 and 2019. We picked up like it was yesterday. I had never asked him about his coming-out journey and life as a gay man. We could have talked for a whole day!

> **NAME:** Chip (Charles)
> **AGE:** 52
> **IDENTIFIES AS:** Male
> **ETHNICITY:** White
> **OCCUPATION:** Director of Communications for the National Minority AIDS Council (NMAC)

CHIP: When I was born, we were living in a town called Markleville, Indiana. It's [a] little, tiny town. We moved from there when I was about four and moved to Pendleton.

ME: *Two sisters?*

CHIP: They're ten and eleven years older, so I was a bit of a surprise. It was difficult at times. Mom used to tell stories of Christmas mornings and family vacations. And everybody knows it and I'm like, "Nope, I don't know that one, you know." You feel a little disconnected.

ME: So how long were you in Pendleton then?

CHIP: We moved there in '72 [when I was four], we left in early '79 to move to Muncie [when I was eleven]. My mom was not happy with the school in Pendleton at the time and she wanted me to get into Burris in Muncie. I was much happier when I got into Burris. We were there until I moved out after grad school—with the exception of one year we lived in Florida, my freshman year in high school. That was an awful decision. That was one of the worst decisions my parents ever made. Awful, awful year. It's one of those years we don't even talk about anymore, it was so bad. It was a combination of Mom was really sick—that was going into the last year of her life. She was really sick and deteriorating noticeably while we were there.

ME: Remind me, what was she battling?

CHIP: Breast cancer. She was diagnosed with breast cancer in 1978 when I was ten years old. She died in October of '83 [when I was fifteen]. Then, after she passed, they moved everything back from Florida and we unpacked.

ME: So it was just your dad and you, then?

CHIP: Yeah, in this great big house. I mean, it's a beautiful house but it was just two of us. Then we moved to the house we lived in when I went to college, and I was there until December of '93 when I moved out to Indianapolis [for] my first job.

ME: I was going to ask what your struggles were growing up, and it sounds like that was definitely a big one.

CHIP: Yeah, of course it's gonna weigh on your mind a lot. You know, you try to do the normal life—going to school and doing all that—but boy, that weighs on you. I told my therapist ... I did a lot [of therapy] around my mom's dying, let me tell you. One of the hardest things [my therapist] ever had me do—this was like the second session with him—he had me write a letter to her and read it to him. I still have the letter. I saved it and I've not read it since then, but once I got through that, it was just like, "Wow, I feel much better, much lighter, freer."

ME: *At what point was this therapy session, Chip?*

CHIP: [It was] 2007–2008. [My therapist] was crying at the end, too, as I was reading it. It weighs on you in ways you don't realize until after you get through it. [My friend] Leslie told me one time—she and I first met in 1988, we were both [coed fraternity] pledges so that would have been about five years after Mom died—she said to me several years after that, "I think you were still in mourning when we met." I said, "Oh yeah, I think so too."

It'd be hard on anyone, but I think it's hard on a kid. Because I look back now and I have no solid memories of her that don't involve her being sick.

That was probably the struggle as far as childhood—that's the biggest one I was dealing with. A good friend of mine who I've been friends with since sixth grade, he would come over. He knew Mom, he knew my parents, he would come over a lot. When he came over after she passed away, he told his mom, "It's not the same. It's just so different." That and the double whammy of knowing I was a gay kid in the eighties. The two back to back.

ME: *When did you realize that?*

CHIP: At thirteen.

ME: *Was there some incident that brought [the realization] on or were you just like, "Wait a minute ..."?*

CHIP: I don't recall like a light-switch moment, but basically it was just like ... I put two and two together at some point and thought, *Guys turn me on and girls don't.* It was exactly like that—straightforward.

I know a lot of people who go back and forth. I understand that the journey's different for everyone, but that was not my journey. It was very cut and dry .... Looking back, there were certain things that would go in my head when I was younger, but I didn't put two and two together until I was a teenager. My sister, when I was six, went to Butler and we would go down to visit. We'd go to their basketball games at the time. In the seventies, they were not that great, but we would sit there and I'd just be mesmerized by the guys' legs. I'm still a leg man to this day! But I kept looking and looking. I didn't understand at the time why. At my sister's first wedding when I was nine years old, I kept looking at one of the groomsmen and couldn't understand why. It wasn't like I would stare, but that's my attention—Why am I looking at this man? Looking back, there were clues. My sister still says she knew when I was five years old.

ME: Really? How did she know?

CHIP: I don't know. She just said there was something, and she actually talked to Mom about it. Mom said, "Probably not." She was very sort of nonchalant about it. But [my sister] suspected when I was about five years old. I'm like, "Okay, I don't know what I could have done at five years old to elicit that response!"

ME: Interesting. But at thirteen you really knew?

CHIP: Yeah, no question about it.

ME: But like you said, it was the eighties.

CHIP: It was 1981, and you know the message you got at the time was, "That's bad, that's a bad thing." The sort of casual use of derogatory language or insults, especially among boys, ["gay" is] like the biggest insult you could throw out …. Of course, I never called anybody [those names] when I was a kid. Maybe something like "stupid" or something like that, but nothing around race or gender, nothing like that.

ME: What did you do when you realized it? I'm guessing you probably didn't tell people.

CHIP: Oh God no! I was doing everything I could to hide … it's trying to cover up, trying to feign being straight in a way … [and] I wasn't very good at it …. It became more of, "Just don't show any interest at all, don't show any inclination, don't approach it, don't talk about it." In some ways—you know this is a terrible thing to say—but in some ways, Mom's dying gave me cover. I literally had someone in college tell me that they thought that I didn't date because my mom died and I was still dealing with that. So, in some ways, it gave me cover; people didn't question it or didn't really think about it. And of course, on top of that, you know what's going on … starting in 1981, you start seeing these news stories of gay men dying.

ME: Exactly.

CHIP: Dying horribly from this horrible disease. So in addition to all this stuff that's being dumped on you—"You're evil," "You're sick," "You're perceived so low"—it's like, "Okay, well now I'm at risk of dying a horrible death."

My therapist—I keep going back to him—but there was a lot of insight that came out of my session[s] with him. He and I [have] had sessions for seven years. He said, "Your mom dying about that same time; you now have in your head her dying and HIV bound up together." She didn't die of [AIDS], but she died in a similar way that people died from it. So now because those two things happened around the same time, they're tied up together. I'm not sure how to pull them apart … and I don't know if I ever will be able to. But he said, "Those two things are bound up together and you have to deal with that."

It's funny … I went to my twenty-year high school reunion, which is now fifteen years ago, and I went to my reunion "out." I went by myself but I was out. This is pre–[social media], so I haven't seen or talked to most of these people literally since graduation day. We were a small group—the classes were small, my class had sixty-seven people in it.

ME: *That is small!*

CHIP: We knew everybody! Burris is part of the Teachers College of Ball State. So [Burris] was built and it functions as sort of a training center for student teachers. The mindset of the kids there was very different than what you'd see in a typical public school. So I go to this reunion, and everybody knows each other, [and] I'm telling everybody I'm out. It's not like I'm running in with the rainbow flag or anything, but I'm being very upfront. Everybody takes it and runs with it.

One of the guys and I were talking and he said, "You felt you couldn't tell us this in high school?" And I said, "No. I did not know what the reaction would be." He was very supportive. Somebody came over and said, "You guys are having a really serious conversation— what's going on here?" He said, "I'm just telling Chip that he's my friend and he's got my support."

ME: *Right. So, Chip, when did you come out? Was it college?*

CHIP: Yeah, I was twenty-three. It was toward the end of my first year of grad school. So I went through all of undergrad and the first year of grad school without coming out. It got to a point where I just could not keep it under wraps any longer. I don't know what was going on in my life, but I just got so tired ....

In 1988 was the very first National Coming Out Day, and I remember it because I was watching Oprah Winfrey that day. Her whole audience was people who were coming out that day. They had someone who talked about how it's so much energy that you have to put into staying in the closet. You have to keep the shields up all the time and you have to change the pronouns. You have to feign interest in things. It takes so much energy to hide who you are that eventually you just get tired of it. It's draining, exhausting.

At the time, I was still scared to death. That was 1988 [when I watched the show]. It was another four years before I came out. But that stuck with me. I thought, *Oh, I'll never get to that point*. But I did.

There were probably two things that happened that I think probably were just the final two straws. One was in the fall of '91. My service-fraternity chapter was doing volunteer security work at a display of the AIDS quilt at Ball State. That was put on by the gay student union at Ball State—the first time I'd been around the gay student union ever.

The first night we were walking through the display and I just started crying. And I cried and I cried and I cried ... all the way through that. We walked that whole display. In every panel I walked past, I just cried harder and harder and harder. We went back to the APO [fraternity] office because we were working on a panel that we were going to add for the quilt, and we started watching this documentary called *Common Threads*, which is a great [1989] documentary. It won the Oscar that year for best documentary.

It's about stories from people from the quilt. We were watching that ... and I lost it again. Not just crying, like heavy sobbing ... like putting my head on [my friend] Jeannie's shoulder and just sobbing uncontrollably. That whole weekend experience was one of the big things that really said, "It's time. It's time."

The next one ... I was sharing an apartment with two guys, Mark and Scott. We had a great time in that apartment, I really enjoyed that. They were out one night and I was watching this TV movie. I had it on VHS for a long time because I really loved it. It was called *Doing Time on Maple Drive*. It was one of those sort of TV movies about the apparently perfect suburban family. It has all these hidden secrets, and one of them was the youngest kid was gay and was hiding it. He was engaged to Lori Loughlin; she played his fiancée who finds this letter he wrote to his ex-boyfriend and dumps him. He doesn't want to tell his family at all, but it all comes out.

There's a scene where he's coming out to his best friend toward the end and his best friend makes a joke, and then gives him a big hug, and then makes a joke again. And I thought, *I wonder if anyone would do that? I wonder if that's actually the reaction I would get?*

So I got up all my courage and I went to the first person that I absolutely knew would have no problem with it. You remember Allison from our [coed service fraternity] chapter?

ME: *Vaguely.*

CHIP: She and I had known each other at that point, probably for three and a half years. She actually pledged APO because of me. So I pulled her aside one night, and we're at a party, and I said to her, "Come over to the apartment some night." I knew I was gonna be there alone. I said, "I have something to tell you, and don't let me off the hook." She had a very, very positive response. And then the positive responses just kept coming and coming and coming. The only bad reaction I had that stayed bad was [my roommate] Scott.

ME: *Really? What happened?*

CHIP: He confronted me. I didn't tell him. He and I were sort of drifting apart at that point anyway. We were not as good of friends. I'm sure he'd heard it because it was spreading around like wildfire.

ME: *Oh yeah, I found out really quickly.*

CHIP: Yeah, I'm sure you did. I'm sure everybody did. Not too long after that, I got a very nice letter from Bubbles [a chapter advisor]. It said, "You know, I heard this. I hope you know you've got all my support." Just awesome. A very nice, supportive note from her. It said, "What you're doing is very brave, very courageous, and I support you completely." I was kind of waiting to see what the fallout from that would be in a lot of circumstances, but I figured it would spread pretty quickly and it would get back to [Scott]. I didn't want to tell him because we were getting close to his graduation—he'd be gone soon anyway—and I just really didn't want to get into it.

Scott had very definitive ideas about what masculinity meant and what he thought being a man should be. [Being gay] clearly was not one of them and he was threatened. He confronted me and I said, "Yeah, it's true."

And he said, "Well, how long have you known this?"

I said, "Quite a while, but I've only been telling people for maybe three or four months."

He said to me, "Well, I don't agree with it, and I don't condone it." He asked if I told my family, and I said, "Not yet," because that was the next big bridge to cross. At that point, I was not ready. He said, "Don't tell my parents about it. If you tell your family, please tell them I was not involved with it in any way."

And that was it. We still had a month or two left on that apartment, but he and I really didn't speak after that. We didn't really interact.

ME: *That must have been a long month.*

CHIP: He threw out these conditions at me and I basically blew him off. It's just like, "You are not going to affect me. One, I'm never going to see your parents again so that's not an issue. Two, it's not like you're going to be a big part of my life going forward. It's not like you're going to be central in my story of my telling my family about this."

ME: *So how did things go with your family, Chip?*

CHIP: Really well.

ME: *Did you tell them all at once?*

CHIP: No, it was one at a time. I told Dad the night before I moved out, before I got my job in Indianapolis. I didn't know what the reaction [would be] actually, because Dad's politically and socially very liberal.

He and Mom were good friends with a gay couple when I was a kid—
Mom's hairdresser and his partner.

ME: Now there's a stereotype!

CHIP: Exactly. He was very flamboyant; he was very effeminate. His
partner was like this blue-collar warehouse worker, Vietnam vet …
really, really nice guys. They were very good to Mom when she was
sick. Bill actually did her hair for her funeral. So [Mom and Dad] were
always going to their house; they lived in Anderson.

Dad and Mom had [also] been friendly with a gay couple in Muncie,
who owned the local video store. But, you know, it's different between
someone who's your friend and someone who's your kid. I didn't know
what [Dad's] reaction was going to be, so I waited until he would have
no more power over me to tell him, just to be safe. I told him and his
response was, "Well, if that's what you are, it's what you are."

ME: Oh, how wonderful.

CHIP: He said he'd known for a few months because of some of the
friends I was hanging out with. He said, "Several years ago I might
have had a problem with it, but now I don't." So he was fine. I told my
one sister in Muncie; she was fine. I never officially told my sister in
Florida. But she found out and she was okay. They were all fine. The
extended family's been fine. You know, you worry about what that
reaction is going to be because you hear people with horror stories,
who've been cut off or who have been treated horribly by their family.

I have a [gay] friend in Pennsylvania—his father was a minister—
and he's still in touch with his parents. He has four siblings, three of
whom have cut him off. They banned him from their kids' weddings.
His family didn't come to his wedding. They didn't want to hear
about it. They didn't want to know about it. I want to say to him,
"Why do you even make the effort any longer? Trying to keep this
going with this much hostility is just not worth it. I know they're
your family …" But you know I'm one of those that's like, "Cut your
losses … no matter what you say, no matter what you do, they're never
going to accept you the way you want them to and they've made that
perfectly clear."

At the twenty-year reunion, we're all sitting around different tables and sharing. One of the questions was, "Who was your crush in high school?" I threw out this name of this guy who was a year above us—actually he was at another table, it was a mixed class of '85 [and] class of '86 reunion. I told one of the other women I went to high school with, who was not there ... I connected with her on Facebook and said that, yeah I had crushes in high school. Like, who doesn't? But you know, I couldn't do anything about it. I couldn't say anything about it. I couldn't give any sort of inkling that I was even thinking that way. She actually said, "That's just not fair ... that's so unfair."

I always say I don't have any regrets in life. Things that happened when I was younger, I think I did the best I could at the time. I don't really consider this a regret, because it was really beyond my control in many ways, but I think one of the disappointments in my life is that I never got to be young and in love.

ME: *Oh, Chip .... Yeah, because you had to hold all that back.*

CHIP: I never got to do the stuff you do as a teenager when you're dating. I never got to do that. Friends of mine who are the same age ... kind of an "older" joke: that's why gay men are so screwed up when they're adults. Because they don't get to do all that stuff as teenagers. When they start dating as adults—when they finally come out—they're like teenagers. They don't know what to do. They don't know how to handle all of this.

Armistead Maupin, who is a gay writer whom I really like, he did the *Tales of the City* series, which I recommend. It's a fun read. It's about a group of friends in San Francisco from 1976 until about 2010. I think there are nine books in the series. They read very quickly .... He did an interview somewhere and he was quoted, something along the lines of, "I gave up my youth to the people who hated me."

ME: *Oh yeah, that summarizes it for you.*

CHIP: Yeah, and in all honesty there really wasn't anything I could have done.

ME: *Yeah. What have you learned through the years, Chip? Is there any advice you might give to a younger person who hasn't come out yet?*

CHIP: It depends. My blanket advice was always "Come on out and enjoy life" and all that. It's so much better and so much easier when you do. But it depends on the circumstances of their life. I read a story—and it was an anonymous-posted story on a gay website. I can't vouch for the veracity of it. But it sounded real enough to be true. It was of parents who found out their teenage son was gay—very religious parents. And they removed the door off his bedroom. They took away his phone. They made him quit the basketball team because they said it wasn't fair to the other boys on the team for him to be on there. They refused to have him go to prom. They basically told him he had to be celibate for the rest of his life. So that's still going on … that sort of stuff is still going on today. If you're a kid in that situation, all you can do is ride that out until you can leave.

My advice is realizing that not everybody's life situation is the same. Find who you can trust, who will accept you in your life, whether it's friends or whatever. If you feel like your family will be okay with it, then tell them. You don't have to make it a big deal. You don't have to have a whole big coming-out ceremony. I've read accounts of people who are just … very nonchalant about it. You just kind of go and that's how it should be. It shouldn't be a big deal. It should just be, "I like him." Then we move on. If you're in that situation, great! Go out, live life, enjoy life. If you're not … oh God … it sucks to be in that situation. It's awful in that situation. But if you can confide in someone, hang on to them and just ride it out until you can leave.

I used to be very militant about it, saying, "Everyone. They should always come out and live their life, and screw who doesn't like them." But if you're in a family situation where it's not going to be good, then you can't do that. In some situations, you could put your life in danger …. Some of the stuff I hear just turns my stomach about what people do to their kids. If you have to ride it out, ride it out. If you can get out of your home and get to a point where you can be yourself, then hold on till you get to it. It's gonna suck until you can get to that point, but there's absolutely nothing wrong with you. You're just exactly who you're meant to be. Don't be afraid of it. It's perfectly natural. It's who you are.

ME: So, Chip, what struggles do you face now? Have you faced some struggles as a gay man recently?

CHIP: Yeah, I got called a "fag" in a deli the other day. Just a perfect stranger. I had my headphones on, I had my mask on, I was not paying attention to anything around me. I was waiting in line. I just happened to look up at the guy who was standing over there ordering and his response was, "Stop looking at me, fag."

ME: Oh my gosh.

CHIP: I have my headphones on, that's all I could hear, he's still talking. I can see he's still talking but I can't hear him. But that hadn't happened in a while. That's a rarity, but it does still happen. You worry about your safety. I don't always think about it, but sometimes you have to worry about your safety. Particularly in certain areas, certain times of day. I don't think I come across as a big raging queen, but clearly people can tell. [Like] when I'm walking down the street or they're just making an assumption ....

I was in New York—this was about four years ago—and I spent the weekend with a guy I met there a couple times before. A really, really nice guy. We were walking. It was Sunday afternoon, we were somewhere in Midtown, not too far from Times Square. We're crossing Fifth Avenue and he reached over and took my hand. And I thought, *Oh, that's nice.* My next thought was ... [Chip pauses and looks around him.] *Who's gonna say anything? Or do anything, or ...*

I know a lot of people, a lot of guys, who have that concern. They want to hold their husband's, their partner's, or their boyfriend's hand walking down the street. That's very natural, but they're concerned what reaction it's going to draw. Still, even here in DC. There's concern. That was in New York—in freaking Midtown, Manhattan—and that was my second response. You worry about that.

I am thinking about moving at some point in the near future, and it's looking very much like my job's going to go largely remote at this point. We'll know later in the year. But I've been thinking about places

I could move to. I've thought about moving over to southern Delaware near the beach town that I like so much.

ME: *Oh yes, you've told me about that.*

CHIP: I've also thought about moving back to Indiana and living in Indy somewhere. I actually was looking at houses in Indianapolis. There were these really cute houses on the Near Eastside. Then I thought, *Wait a minute … I'm going to move into an area like this … would this make me a target? How would the neighborhood, the people, react to a gay man moving into the neighborhood?* Five years ago, I probably wouldn't have thought twice about it. In the last four years, I've thought a lot about it. I no longer trust that people would keep their bad reactions to themselves. I could see scenarios of harassment, scenarios of vandalism. We have vandalism here in DC. Somebody I know had hate speech spray-painted on their garage door here in DC. I can see worse than that. Straight people don't have to worry about that.

ME: *You're right.*

CHIP: It's probably not likely, considering where I would want to go to live, but it's a distinct possibility. I haven't been in Indiana since Christmas of 2019, thanks to the pandemic. I have never, ever felt uncomfortable or threatened or anything walking around anywhere in Indy or Indiana. After the last few months, I don't know if I'm going to be completely at ease. Granted, I won't be out in rural areas for very long. My sister lives way out in the country in Selma, Indiana. I'd be in Indy, in areas that I would imagine would be pretty okay. But after everything that's gone down in the last month [the January 6, 2021 Capitol siege], I don't know what kind of reaction I'd get walking into the mall at Keystone at the Crossing. Would there be someone there who would say something? I don't think there would, but it's possible.

It's something I think that, especially if I went out to southern Delaware … southern Delaware is very rural. That's one of the cons that I thought of when I started the pros and cons of moving out there. There are only three counties in all of Delaware. It's very lightly populated and it's very rural. There's been a slight uptick. You know, Rehoboth has always been like … sort of this "gay haven." It started off very hostile, but over the years it's become, like, the community is an asset here. "They brought a lot here, it's made the city better ...." Blah blah blah. But there's definitely been an uptick in the last few years of harassment going on there that we never used to see.

I would hate to think that living in the city is the safest place to be because you know it's a bit limiting.

ME: *I've never thought about that ... wow. What would you like to tell the world to do differently, Chip?*

CHIP: There's one other struggle, and more of a personal, psychological thing. I mentioned before [that] the start of HIV coincided with my mom's dying and realizing that I was gay.

ME: *Yes.*

CHIP: There's a lot of trauma right there in one fell swoop. To this day ... even though the treatment ... people who are on antiretroviral treatment can't transmit [HIV] to someone else. People go on medication—daily medication—to keep from getting HIV. It's incredibly safe.

To this day, sex is still scary for me. And I'm one of the fortunate ones who didn't have to bury a lot of people. There was nobody I was close to who has died of it. Everyone I knew who died of it is sort of an acquaintance or friends of friends. The guys who are a little bit older than I am run through the list of who they buried. For some, it runs into the hundreds of people.

ME: *Oh my God.*

CHIP: I know people who said they stopped counting after their one hundredth funeral. There's a level of death and devastation in the gay generation just above me that's unbelievable. When they talk about the number of people they lost ... My director, he's HIV negative. He's been negative the whole time. He was one of the founders of an HIV organization. He and thirty others were the founders of an organization in the eighties called NAPWA, the National Association of People With AIDS. He was in his thirties at the time and he couldn't understand why they wanted him to join with them. Well, he's the only one left alive. And he said now he understands why they asked him to be there ... so that someone would be there to carry on the memory. It's astonishing to me to talk to some of these guys who are a little older than I am and talk about the loss that they've had. Just the number of funerals they had to go to.

Then there's—and I'm not going to do this justice—but the last time I went to New York before the pandemic set in, it was almost exactly a year ago. I went to see this two-part play called *The Inheritance* on Broadway. It was a commitment. Each part was three hours long, so you went for the matinee for part one, and then you left and came back for part two in the evening. I actually loved it so much, I bought the play in book form. The whole premise is, it follows a group of gay men in New York and talks about how gay culture and gay history is passed down from one generation to the next because there's really no formal education in it. One of the main themes is how the first generation that dealt with HIV passed that experience on to younger generations. And the younger generations don't really want to hear about it. They think it's ancient history. It's not. It's in the past ... it drives me nuts sometimes. You should know the history of your community. You should know what came before and who came before you and what they did.

There were two scenes in the first act that I think really did an amazing job conveying just the sense of loss that went on in the eighties. One of the guys has this guy over who's in his sixties who lived through the devastation of the eighties and early nineties. There's a scene where he's talking about just the devastation of it. And the younger guy responds with, "I can't imagine what it was like." But the play is staged where there's a great big platform in the middle and the main actor's in the center of it reciting the lines. The rest of the cast is sort of sitting around the platform on the side. So he was trying to convey what it was like in the eighties when it was really, really bad. At one point all the actors get up and they're walking back and forth across the stage really fast, walking by the main character, and they're going "so-and-so is dead," "so-and-so is in the hospital," "so-and-so is infected," "so-and-so lost their job," "so-and-so has gone home to die"

…. And the guy's just trying to keep up with all of them and it just keeps going on. Just back and forth constantly for several minutes. So the guy just gets completely overwhelmed. And he says that's what it was like. I'm sobbing at that point.

And he tells this story about this house in upstate New York that is their getaway, their escape from all the death in the city. And his husband—his partner—goes away to London for a business trip. He goes into the city and he runs into a friend of theirs who is dying and he's basically homeless. [This friend has] been kicked out of his apartment because it used to be people with HIV could get kicked out of their homes.

ME: *Yes, I've heard about that.*

CHIP: So this guy is basically homeless and dying. [The main character's partner] takes [his friend] back to their house in upstate New York to die peacefully—to take care of him until he dies. He talks about how he did that over and over and over again. He'd go into the city, he'd find a friend of theirs who was dying, he'd bring them back. It started with his friends and it became acquaintances, then it became total strangers that he'd bring back to this house to die. And then he would bury them on the property …. [The play represents] the worst part of the epidemic because it's better controlled now and people aren't dying from [AIDS] like they did. It's not the monstrosity it was. But that whole experience of the eighties/nineties still kind of sits on my mind and it sits on them.

I think Steven Spielberg talked about how the Holocaust sort of sits in the middle of the twentieth century. It's like this whole century of progress and advancement, and you have this horrific crime that's sitting right in the middle of it that you can't remove and you can't take away. The whole HIV epidemic sort of sits on the gay male community in a similar way. It's this huge shadow that still gets cast on us, and those of us who remember it, whether we lived through the experience of burying our friends or seeing people die, it's still trauma. It's still trauma to me. It still affects my sex life to this day. I still am running through a checklist in my head ... did we do that ... did we not do that ... it's just sort of like you still have to get everything right.

ME: I never even realized that, Chip. I never even thought about it. So tell me about who you work for, Chip. I think that's a fabulous way to wrap things up this evening.

CHIP: Sure. So the National Minority AIDS Council, or NMAC, was founded in 1987 to address the fact that communities of color were not being included in HIV and AIDS research. All the people who are involved [and] all the medical research was for all White people. There was very little in the way of looking at how HIV affected people of color and how to reach communities of color when it came to HIV prevention, HIV care. HIV affects different communities somewhat differently. So our founder, in a moment of great civil disobedience, stormed the stage at an HIV research conference, grabbed the microphone, and said, "I will be heard!"

ME: Wow!

CHIP: It's a great organization to work for. It's an enlightening organization to work for as a White man. When I worked at Whitman Walker Clinic, which was an HIV, AIDS, and LGBTQ health center here in DC where I worked for fourteen years, I learned a lot ... about the world outside of the White community. I really had my eyes opened a lot there. But it's been a real eye-opener working as one of the only two White men in a staff of twenty. The rest are all African American, Latino, Asian, or biracial, so it's been very enlightening, particularly in the midst of Black Lives Matter and George Floyd protests.

HIV has been largely forgotten by a lot of people. But it's still rampant in a lot of communities and particularly in communities of color, particularly among African American women; young gay [or] bisexual Black men; the transgender community .... Right now, a young gay Black man has a fifty-fifty chance of getting HIV during the course of their life.

ME: Oh my God.

CHIP: Yeah, it's one in two right now. Of course, you talk about issues of access to quality care. There's a tremendous amount of stigma still about HIV, particularly in communities of color. This is an old story, but it's one I always used to tell. Before we had a program for HIV-positive mothers of young children—and most of them had kids who were infants—this program was trying to teach them parenting skills and how to be a good parent, how to raise their kids to deal with being HIV positive at the same time. The program director told me that they had one woman who was not "out" about her HIV status to her family. Someone in her family asked her why she was losing so much weight and she said, "Oh, it's the heroin."

ME: *She said that instead?*

CHIP: She said that instead. So that's still a problem. I think one of the things we found in the COVID-19 pandemic is that there's a lot of mistrust among communities of color when it comes to the medical establishment. The African American community has been treated very poorly by the medical establishment. It's the Tuskegee experiments and all these other things. The Latinx community is suspicious of government anyway ... so that's one of the things we also try to address. It's a big task, and my boss says we're not gonna fix racism and that's not really our job. But we can help with dealing with inequities in people's health care ... people of color who are dealing with HIV, either at risk for it or living with it. They can get the quality care they need.

Going back ... one thing I would ask people to do is approach other people with more empathy. To understand that everybody struggles through life in some way. It may not be an obvious struggle because, like, you had no clue about a lot of this.

ME: *Nope, I never did.*

CHIP: I'd say just more empathy for people. I struggle with that at times myself.

As I did with every person I interviewed, I asked Chip to email me anything he wanted to add that we may not have discussed. Here's what he sent me the next day:

So here's the video link I was telling you about. And here's what I wrote when I posted it for World AIDS Day: Today is the annual

World AIDS Day. While we face another deadly pandemic, there is still one going on well off the radar of most of us.

Back in February, on my one theater trip to NYC before COVID, I was fortunate to see a two-part play called *The Inheritance*. Its premise is how culture and history is handed down between generations of gay men, particularly from the first generation to deal with HIV to subsequent generations.

At the end of Act 1, the character of Walter has a very long monologue about his partner of thirty-six years and how they each responded to the devastation in NYC during the 1980s. It was the first moment of the play that left me near sobbing ... but it wouldn't be the last.

For World AIDS Day, Matthew López, the playwright, had more than thirty-three different actors and other prominent people read passages from the monologue. It's still incredibly moving and I wanted to share it: The Walter Project, Matthew López and The AIDS Memorial, [https://m.youtube.com/watch?v=0Pd77JOgeNA].

Organizations mentioned during this interview:
- National Minority AIDS Council: www.nmac.org

Instructions for living a life. Pay attention. Be astonished. Tell about it.

-MARY OLIVER

MOOKIE

I met Mookie during one of the few times I was truly "punked" (having a major joke played on me) at a local arts center. It was a fun, memorable evening and I instantly liked him. In fact, I became Facebook friends with him to hopefully set him up with my girlfriend! I quickly found out he wasn't single. However, he is one of my favorite social media friends. He's not just a comedic genius but he has incredible depth and wisdom. It was a joy to get to know him better.

NAME: Mookie (Kevin)
AGE: 53
IDENTIFIES AS: Male
ETHNICITY: White
OCCUPATION: Museum Interpreter

MOOKIE: I have a fun job. I get to work as a museum interpreter, which means that I get to try to connect people with museum displays and artifacts. I happen to work in a great children's museum with dinosaur fossils as my subject. So connecting kids and their families to dinosaur fossils—there's nothing wrong with that! It's a lot of fun.
ME: *Yeah, definitely! So let's set the stage so people can get to know you. Tell me about you and your family growing up.*

MOOKIE: I had a pretty normal childhood. I was born in Speedway in Indiana, just outside Indianapolis, home of the International Motor Speedway. I don't remember that house because we moved away pretty quickly. My dad was with IBM Computers, which back in the day, they were *the* computer industry. Dad got moved around a lot as a technician, so I lived in a number of places. Pretty much all over the eastern side of the US—upstate New York, the Chicago area, Tampa, Florida.

Eventually my parents and my brother and I moved to Raleigh, North Carolina, and we put down some roots there. Mom and Dad stayed; they retired. My brother and I at different times have both moved back to Indianapolis. There was something that pulled me back. I ended up doing a little bit of moving around on my own. I've also lived in Richmond, Virginia, and just outside DC.

So I think part of what shaped me was moving around so much as a kid. I always had to go through that process of being the new kid in school, and so I developed social skills based on that. A lot of what I've done since then—especially comedy—but a lot of my personality came from just being able to quickly fit in.

I was never the class clown that does big wacky stuff to make everybody else laugh and gets in trouble. I had a really dry sense of humor, and I would do subtle things that would make other people laugh, and *they* ended up getting in trouble … but I never got caught.
ME: (laughing) That's the way to do it.
MOOKIE: Exactly, yeah!
ME: You also do comedy.
MOOKIE: Yeah, I perform improv comedy theater and have done that also since college. In fact, the nickname … came right around the same time, which was around '91.
ME: Well, now I'm going to move into the more difficult stuff. When did it first hit you that "something's wrong"?
MOOKIE: When did I first realize I might have depression? I was thirty-one. I lost a job and it was one of those things that it wasn't fair. That really hit me hard. Just losing a job in the first place is a blow, but when it's something that is also unjust … it really sent me into a

spiral. I'm glad for it in retrospect, because it was so hard and damaging that I was forced to seek out help, and so that's how I first sought out a therapist.

I first got on medication to help me, and then ever since then it's been sort of a journey of learning more about that and different therapies and tweaking the medication. Always trying to get it just right, things like that. But if it hadn't been for that, I might not have stumbled across that part of me nearly as quickly—and thirty-one is not quick, right?

Then once I knew about it, there was this moment that I always talk about. It's like that moment in *The Matrix*, when the sunglasses come off and suddenly reality is revealed. I suddenly had a clarity about myself, and I was able to look back at my life and say, "Oh, that was depression … and so was that … and so was that." I look back to the moments all the way back to grade school.

There was a lot of time where I was struggling with something that I didn't know I had. I just expected myself to work like everybody else does. On the superficial level, we know that not everybody thinks the same way. But usually when we say that, we're thinking of opinions and things like that, right? But we don't all use the same process in our brains to get to the same end point. I can't see the way you're thinking or the way anyone else is thinking. I can only assume that it must be like the way I operate. And so everything gets filtered through that. But once I figured out that, no, I wasn't thinking and feeling just like everybody else, then it became a whole lot easier to deal with.

ME: *That's a great way to put it. So what struggles did you face?*

MOOKIE: Like right off, the big thing that I was dealing with was a big spiraling depression. I just never wanted to get out of bed for the better part of a month. Eventually I did, but each day I would just kind of hunker down in the covers and try to stay there as long as I possibly could, and hide from the world.

What I've found since then … there's been some struggle with just kind of narrowing in on exactly what type of depression I had. The initial diagnosis was general depression, which just kind of covers everything. So I was working under that diagnosis for quite some time. It wasn't until I was forty-nine when a psychiatrist that I was seeing said, "I think you might actually have something different," and ran me through a battery of tests and said, "Everything you're showing is looking more like bipolar type two—the fun type."

I was like, "Wait a minute, there's a fun kind of bipolar disorder—what?"

He said, "Yeah, you've got the kind where you have lows with your depression but your manic side doesn't go that high. You don't go off the rails with that high mania, but you get the same lows of depression that you already thought you had."

Once I got that diagnosis, and got medication more specific to that, and started doing more research on my own about that condition, then that really opened up even more windows for me.

ME: *What an "aha!" moment!*

MOOKIE: Yeah, but it comes with its own struggles. There are times when I don't recognize right away that I'm slipping into a low or I don't recognize that I'm suddenly going high on the manic scale. Sometimes I'm already in all of that before I realize it and then I have to work to get myself back down to an even keel. Most of the time, though, I'm able to kind of step outside myself and look at things and say, "Ah, you don't want to make these choices. That's just going to lead you here or here." And that just comes with time and kind of studying myself … I expect the rest of my life to be learning a little more all the time. I don't think I'm ever going to completely know myself.

ME: *Do you have a story that illustrates how [bipolar disorder] affected you one time in your life?*

MOOKIE: I think looking back to when I was a kid—grade school age—and moving from school to school now and then. Like I said, I tried to make friends right away. I tried to fit in and, if that didn't happen, it really hit me hard. It's not every six-year-old that is just crying themself to sleep because the kids at school haven't immediately taken a liking to them. That kid was me. I would go from a school where I had made a lot of friends to a new one, expecting to fit in right away. And if that didn't happen, man that depression really hit me. I would overreact badly and, of course, nobody knew why.

I don't mean to make it sound like my entire childhood was all sadness; it was mostly pretty good—but man, I really didn't have a handle on my emotions as much as I should have or could have if there were any way that somebody had recognized it and diagnosed me back then. Things could have been a lot easier but, you know, we can't change time.

ME: No, not at all. What have you learned about yourself because of it?

MOOKIE: I've learned that I have a great range of emotion, and I value that. One of my heroes in life—I went to North Carolina State University—[was the] former head basketball coach, Jim Valvano, back in the eighties. He eventually died of cancer. During his final years, he established the V Foundation for cancer research. He gave just a brilliant speech at an awards show that was named for him.

He knew he was dying. He knew he was in his last months. One of the things he said during that speech [that] really hit home with me was, "If you're able to laugh and cry and love all in one day, you've lived." He was a very passionate, emotional Italian guy, and he let his emotions come out when he was on the basketball court, things like that. But it really inspired me to not try too hard to stifle all that. [Those emotions are] really a part of living, and I carry that with me today, even though I know that I don't want to ride a roller coaster all the time. Feeling those emotions is natural and part of the life that I want to live; that's how we should live.

ME: Yeah, I agree 100 percent. You mentioned that he had cancer, and you battled it as well. Do you mind sharing a little bit about that?

MOOKIE: In 2015, I had what I thought was a lymph node swelling up on my neck, and eventually it swelled up more and more …. It was a cancer which started in my tonsil area and worked its way outward. It was eventually like the size of a small lime and you could see a big bulge there before it was finally zapped away. They couldn't operate on it because it was too close to the jugular, so it was all radiation and chemotherapy.

My oncologist said, "If I do my job right, you're gonna hate me for the remainder of this year, and then you're gonna love me after that." He said, "We're gonna beat you up. It's gonna be rough. The treatment is not going to be easy, but we're confident that you're healthy enough otherwise that your body can take it."

It worked out that way. I had a cancer diagnosis and it was eliminated within a year. It was all like a really weird, short blur. But there were like three or four months there where I could barely get up. I just laid on the couch most days. I couldn't eat for a while. I had a feeding tube.

ME: *Wow!*

MOOKIE: Yeah, luckily they recommended that I get that before I needed it. They said, "We've seen enough people go through this that you don't want to wait till it's a necessary thing." Even that was just a weird thing—to suddenly have an extra navel.

ME: *Sounds like you were in very good hands.*

MOOKIE: I was. I found out later that if you have a head or neck cancer, New York City is the best place to be. Indianapolis is second …. I had a great team. There was never a moment where I didn't trust them to just do what was necessary—what was best—and they got me through it.

ME: *Good Lord, though, I can't even imagine what your emotions were during that time.*

MOOKIE: Exactly. I knew going into it … I really just kind of sat with myself and said, "Okay, you know they're gonna do this work on a cancerous growth, but they need the rest of me to be healthy. And that includes my brain." So I was doing everything I could to stay in as good condition as I could. Even if it meant just getting out and taking a quick ten-minute walk or whatever I could to keep my mind clear and my body going so that there was something to work with.

ME: *I thought [this] was brilliant … a friend of yours created like the Hulk character at that time for you? The Mookie Smash?*

MOOKIE: Yes, exactly. There's a hashtag of #Mooksmash. It was a good friend of mine who, right around the time the first Avengers movie came out, made a drawing—a caricature of me as Hulk—and I sold T-shirts with that image through GoFundMe.

Even though I had great insurance that covered the basics, which were astronomical, there were still odds and ends that insurance doesn't cover that I would have had a really hard time with if it hadn't been for the generosity of friends pitching in. A little here and a little there made a big, big difference.

ME: *Well, that's great. I remember reading your posts and seeing the #Mooksmash at the time, and I just thought,* Wow—this is awesome.

MOOKIE: I wanted to keep people posted and aware of what was going on because it's still kind of a fringe cancer. Oropharyngeal cancer is the technical name and it is the same basic trigger that can lead to cervical cancer in women. It starts with an HPV infection, which is super common. It's everything from warts to much more serious infections, so it's super easy to catch.

Then that can allow this cancer to grow. And for a long time, we've been giving HPV vaccines to girls, and they weren't giving it to boys because they didn't see a need for it. So part of my getting the word out about my cancer was also aimed at my friends that had grade school–age boys that, "Hey, there's a vaccine out there—get it!" You don't want this to be a problem when you're in your thirties that you can't foresee now.

ME: *Right. My boys got it. But you're right, it's not something you and I got when we were kids.*

MOOKIE: That's great. I'm so glad to hear that.

ME: *So here you are, Mookie—the funny guy. Is it hard for people to believe you really suffer from depression?*

MOOKIE: Yes and no. I think it was at first. It's become, sadly, much more well known over the last decade or two how much depression there is in the comedy industry. You know, Robin Williams and hundreds of others. He's just the most well known, but it's really kind of been a window to most people … that people who spend a lot of their time being funny are really often sad on the inside.

While I don't walk around in a perpetual sadness, I would say that my life is not as cheerful and jolly as my everyday face. I struggle with a bad rainy day as much as anybody else does. Sometimes the mask that I'm able to keep up really doesn't tell the whole story, and so it can be very hard for people sometimes to put those two things together.

ME: Have you ever been treated differently because of it?

MOOKIE: Not that I know of, not really. I've always tried to be as open as I could and I think that serves me well. I tend to treat my mental illness the same way that I would treat a physical illness or any other physical health condition. If I broke my leg, I wouldn't be ashamed to tell people what I needed. If I had to get around a little differently, then people need to know that.

Communication—just letting people in on that—really helps. So, no, I've never really suffered any bad repercussions from it. If anything, I feel like people have been very understanding. It's led to other people being a little more open about what they're dealing with too …. I just feel like the more we can knock down stigma, the better it is for everybody.

ME: Absolutely. We shouldn't be ashamed of saying, "I'm struggling with anxiety or depression or whatever."

MOOKIE: Yeah, and it ends up helping me in the same way that it helped me when I was communicating to people what I was dealing with as far as cancer goes. It was nice to hear back from people and share the experience and share the load of that, rather than just sitting in the darkness and going through it by myself.

I feel like whatever people are struggling with, whether it's a physical impairment, a physical illness, or a mental illness or disorder, the more we can let others in and let them share some of that … man it really makes it easier on yourself to let other people in.

ME: Yes, it's not easy for people to do though. It's scary. But I'm learning more and more that it's okay to be a little vulnerable, that people appreciate it. That was scary for myself, so it's nice to learn that lesson from people like you.

MOOKIE: It's okay to share your weaknesses to others, and your struggles …. We live in a world where, especially in business and things like that, we have a culture of—we don't even like to use the word "weakness." You'll hear people refer to it during like a performance review or something like that. They'll talk about strengths and opportunities—like we have such euphemisms for it—that we can't just say, "I'm strong in some areas and in others I'm not."

But the more we are vulnerable, and the more we can talk about it and just realize that everybody has vulnerability or everybody has some weaknesses ... we're not all 100 percent strong in every area of our life, [and] we aren't all weak in the same area.

ME: *So Mookie, what would you tell the world to do differently for people that have depression?*

MOOKIE: Well, the hardest part is figuring out that you have depression, but luckily we live in a time now where there's more resources, especially at the school level. People recognize [mental illness] more. It's easier for somebody to get steered toward resources for that. Then once you're there, once you understand that you have depression, that you have some sort of mental illness or disorder, then just sitting with yourself and coming to grips with that and realizing that this is who you are. It's something that you can deal with and you don't have to live in shame of it.

People are very willing to work with you when they know that you're working with it yourself, and I think that goes for most things. If I had some struggle in my life and all I did was complain about it, it'd be really hard for other people to sympathize and get on board with me. But if they see that here's what I'm going through and I'm fighting this thing and I'm struggling, it's a whole lot easier for other people to say, "You know what? I'll help you. I'll jump in there with you and support you."

So I would say for anybody who's just realizing that they're in this world of "fun"—let other people in, even if it's just a few [people]. You might not be in a position to let everyone you know in on it. You might not be in a position to let your workplace know. You know it's easy for me to say this is what I've done when I have a fantastic workplace that makes it easy for me to do that.

ME: *Not everybody does.*

MOOKIE: Right. So that's a huge privilege for me. But do everything you can to research what you've got. There are plenty of great books out there, and then once you've figured that out and you're going through therapy, whether it's medicinal or just talk therapy, understand that it's never finished. That if your medicine doesn't work the way you need it to, change it. Always keep that communication open with your doctor and don't feel like you have to live with subpar results.

ME: *Excellent advice. Mookie, what organizations do you know that help people with mental illness that you've had experience with?*

MOOKIE: So there are a number of different organizations that deal with all sorts of different mental health issues. Every little specific branch has some organization or society or something or other like that. For me, personally, I find that support groups through social media—whether it's Facebook or Reddit or really any other place—there's always a community out there. It can be easier for a lot of people to talk to faceless strangers who are dealing with the same thing, and then of course there are wonderful resources like the National Suicide Hotline. That's one of those things that if you're depressed and you ever contemplate hurting yourself, having that number nearby is absolutely fantastic.

But the most helpful thing for me that I've kept nearby is a little [sticky note] that I made for myself that I have on the bathroom mirror. It just says, "Life is a roller coaster," and it's kind of shorthand for what I was talking about earlier. That life always goes like this. Nobody's life just goes in a flat line, nobody's life just goes steadily up …. And there's this awful kind of truth that when we are at our happiest moments there's no part of our brain that says, "This is never gonna last, you're gonna be sad again." We just kind of accept that we're happy. But when you're at your saddest with depression, it's very easy for your brain to tell you you're never going to be happy again. Life is never going to be good again, and of course it will. It always goes up and down.

But depression and mental illness in general are about your brain lying to you and telling you a reality that isn't true. So when you're at your saddest, your brain will tell you that you're never gonna be happy again. It's way too easy to believe that, and if you believe that, then why would you stay around for a life of sadness? So getting help when you need it, and especially if you need it that much … if you're at a point where you just don't feel there's any hope, then at least talk to somebody. Get yourself through that one little moment and then build on that.

I've lost people in my life. I've had too many friends who have lost friends and family members. You know we're at a point where teen suicide is a huge problem. Veteran suicide is an even bigger problem, and we can't let people like that fall through the cracks anymore. So anything, any little thing that I can do to help, even if it helps one person, that's great.

ME: *Thank you for sharing everything.*

MOOKIE: It's been a real pleasure talking to you and sharing something that is such a core part of me …. If just talking about what I deal with helps somebody else, great. If it helps a whole bunch of people, even better.

If you, or someone you know, has thoughts of suicide or harming themselves, please contact the 988 Suicide & Crisis Lifeline (formerly the National Suicide Prevention Lifeline) at 988 or 800-273-8255.

"We can't think of changing our skin," he said. "Change the world. That's how we gotta think."

–QUOTE FROM ZACH, A CHARACTER IN
THE SECRET LIFE OF BEES BY SUE MONK KIDD

BRYAN

I met Bryan G. when he joined our group to compete in the All-America City Award competition in 2008. This was back when I worked for the City of Noblesville, Indiana, just northeast of Indianapolis. Bryan was friendly, fun, and outgoing right from the start. I could always chat with him easily and admired his passion in life. He had a conversation with a fellow columnist in town about race, and I knew he'd be a great addition to this book.

NAME: Bryan
AGE: 63
IDENTIFIES AS: Male
ETHNICITY: African American or Black
OCCUPATION: Retired

ME: *Tell me about you and your family. [Can you expand on your ethnicity? And] where did you grow up or move to?*
BRYAN: I tend to say African American when I'm talking about a group of people (noun). As a modifier or adjective, [I] say "Black people." I'll use the two interchangeably, either one, I'm not offended. Some people don't want to be one or the other. I'm comfortable with both.

So I went on a hiatus from Noblesville [Indiana] during a big portion of life. I grew up in Noblesville in what they call the Southwest Quadrant.

If you know something about the Black history of Noblesville, most of the families living in Noblesville during my childhood had been around Hamilton County and Noblesville for a long time. Everyone [locally] knows about the Roberts Settlement up in Atlanta, Indiana, an African American farm settlement that was established in the 1830s. Well, my mother's family and part of my father's family descend from this settlement. So our families have been around [here] from the 1830s through today.

Even though most Blacks in Noblesville lived in the Southwest Quadrant, the neighborhood wasn't predominantly Black. There were plenty of White kids in the neighborhood that we hung out with—played with, rode bicycles with, collected pop bottles, whatever. We played baseball and basketball and other games as kids because we were all in the same neighborhood. Kids were just kids. We did what kids did; we didn't usually notice those things.

ME: *Right.*

BRYAN: Not that you never noticed, or never talked about it, or never heard your parents talk about it. But you're just too busy being a kid most of the time. So observations that I might give you today are really a reflection on times then. Processing it now is not necessarily the way I would have seen it then. I wasn't that wise. I didn't have that kind of wisdom and ability to interpret my surroundings.

ME: *What were some traditions you and your family had and some good times growing up?*

BRYAN: Well, my parents were both working people. I think my parents were probably striving to be part of the middle class, so we didn't have a lot of money to go on vacations and have lots of stuff. We had what we needed and didn't want for too much. So traditions were really doing things with family—[that] was really important.

Weekends would often be spent with our cousins in Indianapolis, or our cousins would come to Noblesville to see us. Family dinners—you know, the holidays—were always ones with sets of grandparents or the others for family dinners. Everybody from a certain driving radius would come and be together. We were always very close as cousins because we all spent so much time together. And that was an affordable way for our parents to offer us a good time.

ME: *It sounds wonderful!*

BRYAN: Growing up, we were given no choice about attending Sunday school. Sometimes that meant staying for church service after Sunday school at Bethel AME Church in Noblesville. That was part of a regular weekly routine. But these were the same families and same kids that we saw all week long. We all went to the same church …. It was a neighborhood church located in the heart of Noblesville's Black community. It was the heart of the Black community, not only worship, but organizing social events with one another.

I wish I had more grand stories to recall. My mother's probably going to say, "Well we did this, we did that, why didn't you remember those things?" We just sort of spent time with our family, you know, cousins and things like that locally.

ME: *There is nothing wrong with that. You were reminding me of all the history that's right beyond the railroad tracks by my house. I hadn't thought about that in so long, but yeah, it's tremendous.*

BRYAN: In the late 1800s, Noblesville [was] beginning to have a sizable Black community—free people of color (never having been enslaved) from the Roberts Settlement and newly arrived Blacks putting down local roots. The Black community of Noblesville, however, was segregated from the White neighborhoods in those days. If you were a person of color—and at that time pretty much the only people of color moving to Noblesville were Black people—the only place you could live was west of the Nickel Plate all the way to the river, and south of Connor Street down to where the foundries were located at the far south end of Eighth Street. Blacks had very few choices where they could live, and it stayed this way through the sixties in Noblesville. The intentional segregation going back into the late 1800s defined the Black community that I lived in as a youngster in Noblesville.

ME: *Yeah. How much did things like that affect you, Bryan? You brought up segregation and you were saying earlier that you probably didn't think about a lot of things as a kid. But now, looking back, what things do you look at and go, "Whoa!"?*

BRYAN: I can probably talk for hours as I think through the things that I see that are so different in hindsight. I mean ... how do I say this ... the use of the N-word when we were growing up. We heard that word directed our way quite often when we were kids. I am sure the first time I heard the N-word I wasn't quite sure I knew what it meant until I went home and asked my parents. And they would say, "The next time someone calls you that, you go and punch them in the face," kind of thing. "You don't let anybody call you that."

You became very aware early on that people viewed you differently, and they knew the N-word was a word they could use to try and hurt you psychologically. I heard it enough. I won't say I heard it every day, but I heard it enough in the schoolyard, on the ball field. And oftentimes I think kids didn't really know what they were saying. I imagine they heard the word in their homes, their family, and they probably understood it was a "charged" word. In certain moments, it was a word that would fit to express something mean spirited.

You begin to realize these things early on in life. I don't know that we thought a lot about the fact that most of the Black families lived within a fairly defined geographic area of the city. Again, there were a couple of exceptions. We didn't necessarily think about the reasons why; we just thought, *Oh, our parents and grandparents chose to live near parents, siblings, cousins, etc.* It wasn't until we got older that we realized sellers and realtors were not going to sell Black folks a house in any other city neighborhood. Even in the 1960s, there were new housing subdivisions that had covenants stating houses were restricted. *Restricted* meant that Black people couldn't buy them. These restrictions were a big reason why suburban cities like Noblesville grew in the 1950s through 1970s. We, my sisters and I, didn't know of these restrictions at the time.

As we got into junior high and high school, we had friends that lived in other city neighborhoods. I can remember my White friends in high school coming to pick me up for weekend evenings of joyriding. I would meet them out front of our house. We never hung out at each other's homes. It seemed like an invisible line we didn't cross for whatever reasons. These guys were my best friends, but—this is early to midseventies—I think we were still trying to figure out how to work this so-called color line, you know? I don't think they were consciously embarrassed to bring me into their homes or vice versa. I don't think I was constantly thinking, *I can't have a White friend come in and play records while we talk or do whatever teenagers do.* We just didn't do it. Perhaps a subconscious social rule. I think we were still subconsciously aware of racial boundaries that had existed for a long time. The "unwritten rules" as my mother likes to say.

My mother grew up in Noblesville in the 1940s and 1950s. It wasn't like the South where there was a sign stating *Colored-only* or *Whites-only* seating. Her generation knew the local unwritten rules that you couldn't sit down at the lunch counter at the corner drugstore and order a soda. You had to get your drink and take it outside while your White friends enjoyed their soda sitting at the counter. Rarely did a local store owner ask you to go outside with your drink, but you know the owner *might* say something, so you avoided the embarrassment and confrontation. It's almost like it was coded into their genetics not to cross certain social boundaries because this might create problems for you and your family.

Social conditions and race rules had changed for my generation, but we, or I, was not quite sure how far we could go. For example, dating in high school ... There were many girls in my class I would have liked to ask to go to the movies or on a date. I never did ask. I felt like, "That's a line I am not sure I should cross." I don't know why ... maybe it will upset my mom and dad, maybe her parents won't like it. I probably didn't want to find myself in an awkward situation, or worse, have my feelings hurt. So I just didn't go there. I think it's very different now. I also think views on race began to change during the time I was in high school and entering college. There's still a lot of work to be done.

Also, I think, culturally, Black Noblesville kids in the sixties and seventies were often looking for Black cultural experiences in this all-White town. For example, when it came to music, movies, and things like that, what we enjoyed, our White friends didn't know about. They didn't relate to it. I don't think they had much curiosity about my culture. I could be riding around with my buddies—and I love these guys—and they're listening to the Doobie Brothers, and I want to listen to Earth, Wind & Fire. Well, I'm sort of outnumbered, you know? I'm not bringing my Earth, Wind & Fire eight-track tapes for the ride because I know these guys aren't going to listen to this music I like. Or at least I [don't think] they wanted to. I could be really wrong.

Once again, I didn't want to find myself in an uncomfortable situation where something might be said that caused a fissure in my friendships. So I found myself often "going along to get along." That is an expression we use—"You go along to get along"—to describe not expressing your true self for fear you won't be accepted. I was naive and unsure of my own identity. I was certainly unsure of my own Black identity. I was simply trying to fit in to a very White cultural existence.

When I left Noblesville and went to other places, I was made to feel as though I was not being Black enough. "Well, you're a little different ... you listen to the Doobie Brothers." A Black friend at Purdue who was looking through my record collection once said, "The Doobie Brothers? Who is this?" He was from Gary, Indiana. His experience to this point in life was a very different experience than mine. He obviously had not been riding around in cars listening to the Doobie Brothers! So I found myself trying to figure out how to fit into a Black identity that was somewhat foreign to me in Noblesville. This awakening to my Black identity often came with challenges for my nineteen-year-old self.

At Purdue, my newly found Black friends pointed out that I spoke differently, I dressed differently, my growing-up experiences had been very different from theirs. I [was] trying to now fit in with a group of people that seemed very different from me. There was a lot to learn when I left Noblesville, like I said, about my own Black identity. I don't think I was pushed to be extremely conscious of my Black identity. My parents did not drill "Blackness" into my development. I feel like I was guided to try my best, fit in where you feel comfortable, and make it work in this community that you live in.

ME: *Yeah. Well, you transitioned beautifully to what I was going to ask. Is what happened when you got to college and then what happened when you got to California … did you awaken and say, "Oh wow, wait a minute …"?*

BRYAN: Yeah, sometimes at Purdue I had my challenges fitting in. I felt more comfortable in an environment where most of the guys were White because that's what I was used to. I often found myself as an outsider with other Black students because where I grew up … some of the kids [at Purdue] had never even heard of Noblesville —and then to learn there are Black people there? "Well, you don't sound like a Black person. You don't look Black."

… Even at this time in my life, I had some understanding of the multiracial makeup of my Roberts Settlement ancestry. At the time, I think I believed that being Black had a lot to do with how you look, talk, and lots of things that don't make any sense now. Maybe I was uncertain about how to talk about my European ancestry because I identified as a Black person. *Will anyone understand this? Free Blacks choosing to have children with Whites? No one will understand,* so I thought. I think I also believed that maybe I didn't possess enough "legitimacy" to identify as Black.

I developed a few good friendships with guys that I started with at Purdue. I spent my time there hanging out with them. It probably was after college, when I got to California, that I really began to think about and understand more about my Black identity, and the way I could define this Black identify for myself.

California was a whole new world for me; I quickly understood that the world isn't just Black and White. Los Angeles was a rainbow of people and cultures. Los Angeles was the most eye-opening experience I could have had at twenty-two years old. The reason I think I stayed in Los Angeles so long, and I know this sounds a little corny, I loved that my friends were all so different racially, culturally, and from many different national origins. I began to learn about different cultures and Black people who were from places other than the United States. Blacks that were not African American, but possessing of a rich Black culture I knew little about.

I realized quickly that I had a lot to learn and experience. LA turned out to be a great place to expand my cultural competency. LA may be politically a very liberal place, culturally very diverse, but Los Angeles grapples with many of the same issues of racism and bigotry I found in Indiana. In the professional world, I heard the N-word used by my colleagues in office settings in Los Angeles just like I heard it as a kid growing up in Noblesville. No one should think that prejudice and bias don't exist in Los Angeles. It does indeed!

Sometimes I think outsiders believe Los Angeles is this weird place where everybody is at the beach smoking weed, playing volleyball, and listening to street musicians—that Venice Beach is Los Angeles! Because of its diversity, there's a lot more cross-cultural interconnectedness that may be responsible for that "something" that felt good to me about Los Angeles. But I still had experiences that made me sort of, you know, scratch my head and wonder, *Maybe I didn't leave hostile attitudes behind in Indiana.* It turned out that there are a lot of changes that need to happen anywhere one might live.

ME: *What examples can you share of that, Bryan? Is there any story—one or two—that stick out?*

BRYAN: I worked in a Big Eight CPA [certified public accountant] firm, and we had a client in Compton, California—a mostly Black and Brown community. One of my White colleagues had asked a Black employee working for our client for some information. I don't know what transpired, but my colleague returned to our office upset about the encounter. His first words entering the office, after closing the door, was, "That N-word so-and-so said ..." Realizing I was in the room, he said, "I'm sorry, you're not like them. I don't mean that about you ... I meant that about—"

ME: *No, no, no, no, no!*

BRYAN: It was too late ... he had already said the word ... and I think my internal reaction was, *Wow, how easy it was for my colleague to respond with that word in a situation that made him upset.* It happened more than a few times. Not all the time, but it happened enough. Sometimes my colleagues thought they were being funny with their racist humor. They expected I would laugh right along with our White colleagues. It seemed unreal to have to tell your colleagues that racist jokes are not funny!

When you get to the top of a Big Eight CPA firm, you become a partner—like a law firm, you're a partner. And these partners always belong to social clubs. They have memberships at different clubs. It's one of the perks that go with the position. Los Angeles has the Jonathan Club, which is like the Indianapolis ... what's the one downtown?

ME: *The Columbia Club.*

BRYAN: That kind of a place—at the time, mostly White men. Back in the 1970s, it appeared to be almost exclusively a membership of White men in different professional endeavors. A partner lunch was often at one of these social clubs. I believe many of the partners at our firm were members of the Jonathan Club. The Club was a popular lunch spot. Most of my White junior colleagues loved to lunch at the Jonathan Club, but for me it was a cringeworthy experience. The only Black people I saw in the Club, besides me, were the waiters.

... My observation was that the club members had this insincere first-name relationship with their waiters. There was just something about the relationship that made me uneasy. Honestly, it appeared to me to resemble a servant-master relationship ... a Black man taking care of a White man's requests. I don't know if the members consciously examined the dynamics of their relationships with the waiters. It was part of a system of practices that existed for a very long time and was never given much thought as to its meaning.

Today, when I think back about those lunches, it reminds me of Black men in Noblesville in the late 1800s. Black men could only get menial jobs or jobs servicing White people: a "shoeblack" at the barber shops in downtown Noblesville, or barbers for White men only. They might have their own business as a barber, but it was that personal service that they could deliver to White men that made them acceptable.

I didn't want to go to those lunches. I hated going to those lunches, because I was usually the only Black person in our group, and maybe there was also one woman. We stuck out, you know. I wish I could ask some of those women how they felt during those experiences. What was going through their heads when they were often the only woman at the table?

Monday-morning coffee talk often brought about surprises too. I remember conversations about things that coworkers did over the weekend with one another. *Why wasn't I invited to that?* We're working on the same client engagement, we're all doing the same thing. I wasn't invited to the Dodger game. I would wonder why, but I would never say anything. It's similar to what I said about hanging with my high school buddies. Maybe they didn't think I would enjoy their brand of fun. I also felt that these after-work opportunities for scoring points with the boss advantaged some colleagues at the expense of others.

Having cited these examples, I think it is only fair that I acknowledge that my employer's efforts toward diversity were sincere and earnestly pursued in the late 1970s and early 1980s. Hindsight suggests that simply hiring for diversity wasn't enough for sustainable change. For example, I don't believe that company leadership was looking at systemic racism and gender bias, or implicit bias of individuals, etc., within the organization. So everything I said previously and I am about to say should be placed in that context, and with the understanding that some of my negative professional experiences may have resulted from good-intentioned folks just not knowing better.

At the firm where I was employed, there were no Black partners, there were no Black managers, so we didn't have mentors who looked like us. This time in the seventies was a time of change. Employers were implementing affirmative action programs. I don't think the women had many or any mentors who were women. As I look back on it now, some of those experiences were downright uncomfortable and sometimes distasteful. I will never know how it may have negatively impacted my career development. My career turned out okay. Things worked out. But you wonder how they might have been different if the environment had been more inclusive.

Today, the awareness of equity and inclusiveness in companies has come a long way. I believe it has improved but still has a way to go. I realize there's always some fitting in to do no matter what you're doing, but there's also this idea: Let's expand on our diversity. Let's make sure all voices are truly being listened to, make the table a little bigger for more people—from who we ask for ideas to solve problems on the job or to where we go for rest and relaxation after a hard day of work. Be more inclusive.

It would have been more inclusive thinking to consider what others might find enjoyable, or want to talk about, or where they want to go—that sort of thing. I don't think my supervisors and coworkers did the inclusive thing very well during that time in my career. Not in the same ways we try to be more inclusive today. Then, you would just have to fit in. So those are the kind of things that I remember. I think these kinds of experiences would have been the same or similar in any other city I might have picked to begin my career. The issues are very much universal.

ME: *What did you learn through all this, about yourself or about society as a whole ... their treatment toward Black people and African Americans?*

BRYAN: I like to think that I learned that, if I [am] in a position of power or decision-making, that I think about including ideas from everyone in the group. As a hiring manager, I'm pretty proud of the fact that the first staff I ever had—and I inherited a lot of staff diversity—I was responsible for making it even more diverse. I tried to be conscious of having diversity within my group. I don't think I understood this whole idea of equity and inclusiveness the same way I do now. But I was beginning to think in these ways.

I was always thinking of equity in terms of performance reviews, promotions, salary raises, bonuses, you know, trying to figure out how can I set my biases aside and be fair and equitable. There were staff members that I was closer to than others, but I tried to disregard those close personal relationships and find more objective ways for evaluating my team. I tried to keep in mind those past experiences that I thought were unfair to me.

I see myself as a consensus builder, so that approach to my decision-making made me want to be a better listener. I wasn't always successful, but I tried to be a good listener and consider all ideas. Maybe I was this way because I felt that my voice had been silenced at various times. I realized there were probably people, like me, who felt silenced. I never sat down and thought about them. It's easy to view my actions with complete hindsight, but I do think that's where a lot of that came from. I have also learned a lot about my own biases. I know that I will always have biases. I know I always have to work on eliminating my biases no matter what. None of us can easily rid ourselves of biases; we're human beings .... I think I've just tried to become more and more aware. When I'm not getting it, somebody will tell me and I'm okay with that. I don't know if that's a very good answer.

ME: Oh, it's a great answer! And I agree with you because, from the beginning, I've told everybody, "I'm going to screw up. I'm not going to say things right. I need you to gently correct me." Everybody's been so gracious so far, and I'm really grateful. So I think it's important to be like, "Hey, I'm human. Help me out." Don't be afraid to say something that's really important. So, to back up a little bit, did you come back here to Noblesville for the liquor store? It was a partnership, right, with your family?

BRYAN: Yes, it was. That business was started by my father and my uncle and their father in 1977. When they started that business, there were no Black-owned retail businesses in Noblesville. And there aren't many today.

My family started Mr. G's in the 1970s. Some people in the community, I can't say I ever knew who they were, doubted that a Black-owned retail business could be successful in Noblesville. My grandfather was a very stubborn and confident man. When a new carryout liquor license became available in the mid-1970s, my grandfather, father, and uncle said, "We're going for it." And they did. They had their challenges along the way, but my grandfather made it clear that he was not going to be deterred. If they didn't get it, he was going to make a "stink" about it … read: challenge the unfavorable decision through legal action. They were awarded the license, opened the doors in 1977, and forty-two years later Myron—my uncle—and I sold the business in 2019. I think forty-two years is a long time to be in business—a retail business in any community. I am very proud of our successes.

I didn't come into the business until I moved back to Noblesville in 2007. [After] my experience in public accounting, I went into the entertainment business. I worked at Universal Studios and at BMG Music Publishing, one of the major music-publishing companies. Between Universal and BMG I had the good fortune to work at a start-up business in the technology space. A very good friend of mine launched his own online record label and direct-marketing business. I went to work with him for about two years. This was 1999, during the early days of music downloads and file sharing, booming days of the dot-com space. So most of my career was spent in the entertainment business in some way, shape, or form. My role was always in financial operations.

I was usually one of a handful of Blacks in middle to senior management. When I looked around the room in all of these companies, I couldn't help but be conscious of the fact that I was maybe the only person of color around the table. That's the way it was. There was not a lot of diversity, even in the entertainment business. You still read about it now, especially with the creative side where there's been a lot of criticism about who is making the decisions about entertainment choices. Who are the people making the decisions about what films and

TV shows are going to get the green light? We have seen many changes in the last several years. Women, men and women of color, etc., having a lot of success, and that's great for opening the door to more change.

It has changed so much since I got into the entertainment business in the early eighties. By 2007, I had reached a point where I was ready to leave corporate America. I had been away from family for a long time. Maybe my parents would come to visit Los Angeles every couple of years. I might come to Noblesville for a visit once a year or every other year. But a couple days here, a couple days there. After a certain point, and due to several other circumstances, I began to rethink what was most important to me. So moving back to Indiana seemed like a good move, the right move.

I'll never forget when I first moved here—and I knew a little bit of Spanish from being in California ... a customer was asking me about a certain kind of whiskey. He pointed at my Scotch-whisky section and said what sounded to me like the word *bukanas*. I had never heard of this particular Scotch. He asked me again a few weeks later. Finally, I asked him to write it down. He wrote the word *bukanas*.

One day, a woman came in the shop and I overheard her speaking Spanish. I thought she might be able to help me. I asked her if she had ever heard of *bukanas*? She laughed and she said, "Your customer is looking for Buchanan's Scotch Whisky." She explained to me something I did not know about Mexican pop culture and how Buchanan's Scotch Whisky became popular. We added Buchanan's to our product line and the next time the customer came in, he was so happy to see it on the shelf! I felt very good about that. He even asked if we could get the more expensive eighteen-year-aged Buchanan's, which he liked to enjoy on special occasions.

ME: *Yes! I love your story! Fantástico! Yo estudio español ... por un año—teléfono! [Fantastic! I study Spanish ... for a year—telephone!]*

BRYAN: Well, the good thing, we have [the internet] now. It's funny because after she told me, I realized that's silly. I should have typed it in phonetically because I did find it [online] under "bukanas." I could have figured it out three months, six months earlier had I just [looked up] what he said phonetically. I do this all the time. I've got a friend who is studying to improve her French language skills. She will send short readings in French. I usually [look up] the translation. I'm learning and starting to retain a few things ... As we are talking, I am thinking about the importance of speaking more than one language. As Americans, we often think we're the center of the universe; it's up to everyone else to learn our language and not the other way around.

When you travel abroad, you realize that, "Wow, this person can talk to me in their language and in my language, but I can't reciprocate." I'm in France and I can hardly speak a word of their language. Why am I yelling at them in English, shouting, because they don't understand me?

ME: *Right. It's such a shame. So many people speak two or three languages outside this country.*

BRYAN: I only know a few words or phrases in other languages, but I could go so much further if I only had the ability to speak and understand in at least one other language. This may be part of what you're writing about. People don't make the effort to understand or put ourselves in someone else's shoes ... we don't ... we just expect everyone to come around to who we are, what we think, what we need or desire. It's one of the biggest challenges that we have with everything that is going on now with diversity and inclusion and equity. A lot of people are uncomfortable with change. "Well, I've been doing it this way forever. Why do I have to change? Why do I need to think about this or that?" Unfortunately, I think we do.

ME: *Yeah, I agree. [At the time of this interview, the year] was 2021, with 2020 being just the most God-awful year. For me, it was the year where I finally woke up and said, "We are a mess!" I kind of thought in the late sixties/ early seventies that we took care of all this. People aren't hurting Black people anymore. Then you see all this police brutality and all the things that happened last summer. What are the things that you're facing now, personally, in the last couple years, that you can share?*

BRYAN: Personally, I think it's about some of the things I'm currently involved with in the community. Our Noblesville Diversity Coalition

[NDC] is currently rolling out a program of community conversations. We are also working on our own personal development. [I'm] learning about my implicit biases that influence me. In very small ways, I think I have been engaging in conversations about equity even before I got involved with the Diversity Coalition.

Our local coffee shop is a great environment for conversation. I never know who will be at the table and what subjects may come up for discussion. There are times viewpoints are expressed that should be challenged. I can't ignore the elephant at the table. The idea of "going along to get along" no longer works for me.

My first approach is to make sure I understand what has been said. I usually like to know what are the facts that support a viewpoint. When it's my turn to talk, I give my viewpoint and the facts I have to support my statements. I am slowly learning to share my views without trying to change someone's mind. Let the conversation flow until we find some common ground. Just having a civil conversation is something I now consider a victory. I realize that we all change our minds in our own time and not when someone else tells us something. I can't tell you how many of these difficult conversations came up during the last two presidencies.

I'm not this twenty-year-old youth anymore that is going to suck it up, try to move on, and get along. I'm going to speak up and say something now. But I hope I've gathered enough wisdom to know how to have a hard conversation. I try to probe a person's way of thinking. Asking why they think what they think. Hearing their perspective. I like to share the facts that underline my thinking. I realize people change their own mind when they are ready to change. The best I can do is give them a different perspective and hope they will consider what I have to say. If it is an honest conversation, I hope they believe I am giving their view equal consideration.

It became clear to me in 2020—and really this all started in 2016–17, well, even 2015, as the political campaign ramped up—maybe we wanted to believe conditions regarding racism had gotten better in our country. In the last several years, it has become clear to me the level of bias, intolerance, and unwillingness to acknowledge the truth about race in

America. The views ... the things that I hear people saying. When I hear people speak about Black people or economically disadvantaged people as "those" people, that is very demeaning in my opinion. It is as if "those" people are not also Americans. Tell me about "those" people. What do you know about "those" people? My questions have often been met with a response, "I don't mean you, Bryan. You are not like them." This kind of thinking has been around for a long time. We've got real problems in America, and these problems can be found right here in Noblesville.

We had a local youth wrap a swastika flag around his neck and shout the N-word on social media on Martin Luther King [Jr.] Day in 2018. Racist comments have been found on bathroom walls in the schools or on buildings in town. Thankfully, good people in the community condemn these actions. This is encouraging to me. What discourages me at the same time is reading letters to the local newspapers or social media posts that suggest we have a long way to go before the voices for equity overwhelm the voices satisfied with the status quo, or worse, a return to a bygone era. I see it, I read it, and I feel like, *You know what? This is 2021 or whatever it is ... why? Why is it?* I've come to this conclusion that we have never had a true reckoning on the topic of racial injustice in America. We can't agree on a collective truth. What is a fact? Facts are no longer facts.

You've heard that word "alternative facts." The facts ... they're black and they're white. They're facts! What makes coming up with a collective truth so difficult? I feel like we don't know each other. We live in silos. Our neighborhoods, our social circles, are still very segregated. There are changes, but I think, for the most part, where we go to church or where we hang out in our neighborhoods or other places, we tend to stick with people that are like us. We don't make the efforts to learn about each other, or each other's community or culture or experiences.

Amy, I cannot separate what is happening in our national and state politics and how politics is influencing and stoking division in our society. Leaders who play on peoples' fears to maintain a system that is biased to favor a group of people over others, [they] keep the fear and distrust going, however it has to be done, because it's a good way to maintain the status quo. When state legislatures changed the voting rules to disenfranchise voters who look like me … that's taking away my power and my voice. It maintains the divisions and distrust between people, which means people stay apart and fight like hell to maintain the systems and structures that make equity possible.

We can build bridges. We can figure these things out. We must talk about difficult topics. I think we're trying to do that at the NDC. We're trying to have these conversations and encourage folks to have difficult conversations within their own social circles. I want to believe I am taking my lifetime of experiences and attempting to apply these experiences and the training I have received to be part of the efforts to bring about change. I think our city and county has so much it can do to come alongside what we are doing as a diversity coalition. As I said before, it means confronting some stuff that we've never really dealt with. Voices of color, women's voices, LGBTQ voices—I think [they all] are speaking out more. I think we're all done being quiet. Twenty twenty was a watershed year and that's [made] a lot of people uncomfortable with the changes that are demanded.

I can't say it's someone else's problem to fix it. I've got to do some things differently. We all have to take responsibility for influencing change. There are a lot of people who are doing the work, but I think a lot of people think that it's somebody else's problem to deal with. Those who do not engage either don't want to change or think it's someone else's job to do.

I hope we don't want to just sit back and say, "Well, let's just wait for it to happen organically." No, we've got to do something to get things moving—stir the dust up a little. And hopefully get things moving in a drastically different direction because the place we are in right now doesn't seem to be good. We seem to be growing more divided as a nation. We've got to find a way to solve problems, not just bridge differences. We need substantive change.

ME: *Yes! You've mentioned the Noblesville Diversity Coalition. I think that'd be a great way to end. I want to let you know, too, Bryan, that I am going to include a link about the Roberts Settlement in here because I think that'd be* *interesting to readers. But let's hear about the coalition. When did that start here in Noblesville, and what's it all about?*

BRYAN: I think we started in 2018—that sounds about right—right after the Martin Luther King [Jr.] Day incident in Forest Park ... when the young man took to social media parading around with a swastika flag and shouting the N-word. Beth Niedermeyer, our school superintendent, decided this is not what we want from our Noblesville student body. The incident needed to be denounced and we needed to bring greater awareness of the wide diversity in our schools and community.

We probably spent the first few months getting to know one another and figuring out our mission. Our first program at the high school highlighted the diversity within our schools. Not only racial diversity, but gender identity, ethnic and national origin, and other aspects of our diversity people needed to know. For me, it was a really powerful program. Listening to each person share their story of coming to America, and their individual experiences—good and bad—as students in Noblesville was good stuff.

We've got these things coming up soon, Amy, called Community Conversations, where we're getting groups together, like six or seven people, to begin to have hard conversations that you and I just talked about. The city's going to lead conversations, so is the chamber. Maybe you'll be part of one of them. Our hope is that church leaders, neighborhood associations, civic organizations, etc., will all agree to participate in conversations that build the inclusive and welcoming community we envision. Talking and listening—that's our plan to keep the dialogue moving in a forward direction. If we get a critical mass of community members engaged in the work, it will be possible to bring about change. I truly believe this.

ME: Right. I am excited to hear that. I'd like to be in on those personally, but also professionally. Well, Bryan, we could probably talk for another two hours, but I try very hard to give everybody equal time. I'm going to stop for now, but if you think of anything, just send me an email! You know where to find me.

BRYAN: Bye, Amy!

Organizations mentioned during this interview:
- The Roberts Settlement: http://www.robertssettlement.org/

I can never truly walk in someone else's shoes, but I can walk closely enough to pay attention and believe them when they tell me what it's like to be them.

-JUSTIN McROBERTS

ANNE

nne reached out to me six years ago through the Grant Professionals Association, a group we both belonged to. I almost didn't meet her for lunch because I was so busy at the time. I thank God often that I did. She is a strong, remarkable soul who makes everyone feel good when they are around her. Though we've been close friends all this time, I've never asked about her mental illness until now.

NAME: Anne
AGE: 57
IDENTIFIES AS: Female
ETHNICITY: Caucasian
OCCUPATION: Professional Fundraiser

ANNE: I was raised in southern Indiana, down off the Ohio River, and I'm the middle daughter of three. Raised in the sixties, obviously. My mother just sold the house [we grew up in] four years ago. Our childhood memories through our fifties are wrapped up in that one house. Not too common these days. We grew up in what you would call a normal household, I think.

ME: *I believe you battle depression and anxiety?*

ANNE: Yeah, I've struggled with depression most of my life. In fact, when I was around age fourteen, my mom recognized it in me. Mom actually suffered from depression when we were kids. There were times when she had a hard time getting out of bed.

She really was, I would say, a pioneer. She was prescribed [antidepressants] back in the day when no one talked about this stuff, and you were considered crazy if you were taking [them]. But she did it for herself and she did it for us. Because she was depressed ... that led to some problems [for us] as kids. I think that's part of why I have depression now.

I do think it's a chemical imbalance, but also because of Mom being depressed—she had her own issues. She was a rager. Once you set her off, she was raging for the day. There was no turning her around. Everything just turned into full-blown yelling, all-day screaming.

I think it impacted me in two ways: I inherited the imbalance of chemicals because it does run in families, [and] by having somebody with depression raise me. My mom was the person with the power in the household, and when you have somebody raging who has all the power, you want to run and hide.

[From] mid–elementary school—maybe even earlier, I can't remember—all the way through high school, that's where I learned to love reading. I would go to my room and I would hide. I would just hide and read and stay out of the way. This way, I didn't cause—and I avoided—the wrath.

Also, when Mom raged, your thoughts, feelings, opinions didn't count. You couldn't have an opinion as a child or express your own feelings because she would overpower you. Basically, I kind of lost who I was. I grew up without knowing what my own true feelings were—what my true opinions were. I always had to waive them to her.

Even picking out clothes in the store, I could be so excited about a cute top and pull it out and show her. If she didn't like it, she would roll her eyes and say, "Put it back, no way, never." I felt invisible .... There was a perception that we were just in the way as kids. We were always told, "Get out of the kitchen." Mom never taught me how to work around the kitchen or how to cook. I was in the way. Again, I think it comes back to her depression. She just needed to get through the day. And keeping us quiet and out of the way helped her maintain some sense of control, peace, or something.

I look back now as an adult, and knowing depression myself … the poor woman. She had to have been in a great deal of mental/emotional anguish. She just was struggling to get by day-to-day and there was no one to talk to back then, other than her doctor. You really didn't tell your friends about that kind of stuff. I have a different appreciation for her and what she went through, in my life now. But I still struggle today with the results of being raised in that type of household. I know people are raised in a household of addictions like alcohol and drugs, things like that. Not sure how this compares.

And then I was dealing not only with a mother that was depressed, but a father that didn't like to deal with conflict. He was a quiet man—a very smart man. A kind man. My mom ran the household, and he left the household to her. She ruled the roost, as they say. Every once in a while when she would get a little out of control—and that would mean, like, coming up in the middle of the night and get us out of bed to come down and empty the trash, stuff like that—those were times when he actually would stand up and say, "You've got to cut it out. You've got to lower your voice. You've got to go take a break."

She would break down and cry and go into her bedroom and just sit for a while. But there was rarely an apology or an explanation. I think that's what bothered me … and maybe why I have my depression today. There was no closure or explanation as to why she acted the way she did. Why didn't she come back and just talk about it and just say, "This is where I am. I feel awful that I've yelled at you." She must have learned along the way how to shove down the feelings as well. There was never that sit down on an eye-to-eye level and discuss what was really going on. We just existed. In isolation and in pain.

ME: *That just breaks my heart, Anne.*

ANNE: That's kind of what makes me who I am today, though. I'm a people pleaser. I had to … back then. I had to do everything I could to keep the peace in the house, and so that's who I am now. I am a people pleaser.

Being a people pleaser isn't all bad though. Sometimes I can help people a lot, but other times I have a tendency to get walked on. I allow people to abuse me in that way because that's the love I've known. That was the love I was raised on and so ... I guess I recognize it more now for what it is. I've been through some therapy, some counseling. Some good, some not so great. But mostly counseling has helped me.

ME: *When [your mother] did get on [antidepressants], I assume she got better?*

ANNE: It helped, but the raging didn't go away altogether. It was almost like a reaction to any frustration. I think it did help level her out a bit. I think she started taking the [antidepressants] when I was in high school.

ME: *And there you are at age fourteen, starting to realize maybe you had it.*

ANNE: Yeah, Mom recognized it in me. So many parents back then probably couldn't have recognized it or simply would have denied it because it was so taboo. I give her credit for having it diagnosed back in the late sixties for herself. That she was able to recognize it in me was helpful. That was one thing we could actually talk about ... easily. With her, I didn't have to be ashamed about it. We actually could talk about this in a pretty intimate and positive way, unlike so many other conversations [that] were so surface or full of criticism. I think she felt she could really help and guide me and, in turn, she felt useful and needed. I don't know.

ME: *Your sisters—did they have it?*

ANNE: Not like me, at the beginning. With my younger sister, I think Mom had loosened up quite a bit by that time. I had been experiencing Mom's depression in a different way than her because she was about four years younger than me. My other sister, who was only nineteen months older than me, I think she did feel the heaviness of my mom's depression and anger. But we all reacted to it in a different way. I think my older sister, Sue, just completely ignored it. She had some ability to just walk away. I absorbed it. I think all of us are affected by it today, though.

ME: *Do all three of you have depression?*

ANNE: My older sister does, and I do. My younger sister really isn't plagued by depression.

ME: I was just curious when you said it could be inherited, it could be passed down, and that there were three of you ….

ANNE: My older sister may not have recognized it till later on. But I think if you have the tendency in your family, at any point it could get worse if you're going through some really bad transitional periods in your life. It can trigger those brain chemicals.

ME: So if your mom recognized it when you were fourteen years old, what happened? Did you go to a therapist?

ANNE: Actually, yeah, I saw a therapist. They prescribed me [an antidepressant]. It took a little while to work, but it wasn't quite the right drug for me. I think I was on [the medication] for a couple years and then they had some new drugs coming out that they thought would work better.

I don't know if you've heard about this, but you have to be careful about taking any new antidepressant and the possibility of feelings of suicide. On occasion, they can take you in a totally opposite direction … really dark. Most of them will help you get better, but some of them—if they don't mix with your brain chemicals right—are going to take you down to a dark place. I remember I was a sophomore in college and I was definitely having struggles. I remember staying in my dorm room a lot and just being so depressed because [the medication] spiraled me so deep and fast and hard. I'd never experienced anything like that before. It was almost like the world was closing in on me. It felt like I was literally falling apart, and it took all of my mental energy to hold myself together.

Thank goodness, I called my mom when this was happening and she told me to call the doctor right away. She was very helpful in that situation. I do want to mention something here … about God in all of this. He has the power to make good come out of any bad situation. I feel this is true in my case.

ME: You were in your twenties when you met a gentleman from England?

ANNE: Yeah. Right after college, I [took] a position in England at a small international university. When I was there, I got to know the community quite a bit. One family in particular took me in and so-called adopted me. I got to know all their kids and we hung out and did a lot of things together. And I got to know Nigel …. Honestly, I don't remember being depressed in England. All I know, all I remember, is that things were exciting there and there was nothing to be gloomy about …. All together, [I was there] a little over two years.

ME: *And you and Nigel got close.*

ANNE: And we got close.

ME: *It sounds to me like maybe your depression kind of ebbed and flowed?*

ANNE: It did. It ebbed and flowed at different times and in different situations, especially through my twenties and thirties. I was [still] single, you know. I was back home from England and was dating. Nigel and his family were over in England, and so I thought that life was gone. And now I was thrust back into a life of wandering and apathy. I wasn't really thrilled with the direction I was going. I didn't know where I was going. No direction. No passion. I started doing marketing and writing newsletters for a video promotion and duplication company. But my life just didn't seem to be going anywhere. So, yes, depression was really hard through those years. Everybody was getting married, having kids. What was wrong with me? I didn't even know what I really wanted to do. I don't know if depression causes lack of direction, brain fog, and apathy—or is depression *caused* by that type of thing? I'm thinking one feeds the other, and it goes round and round …. I just didn't know who I was and what I wanted to do. Part of that could be from my being raised and growing up and having to shove my opinion down—my thoughts about who I am. I didn't get to really explore what my likes and dislikes were. Am I rambling too much?

ME: *No, you're doing great. I know you've had some pretty traumatic times … you lost Nigel, right?*

ANNE: Nigel got in contact a few years after I had come home. He came here for about, I don't know, six months the first time around and then came back a second time. We were just really dancing along in a relationship, an intimate relationship that was possibly going somewhere. We were talking engagement at the time. Although I was excited for him to be back, he was not acting the same. Something wasn't right. He was just not as upbeat—as happy. One day, when we were planning to head out for a fun travel weekend, he suddenly fell into a full grand mal seizure and just hit the floor. I'd never witnessed a seizure before.

I immediately called 911. He's raced off to the hospital in an ambulance. I follow him in my car. They wouldn't let me ride since he was thrashing so much. Within two hours, we were told that he had a [glioblastoma] tumor in his brain. The doctor, who was completely insensitive and lacking compassion, told me straight-out that there's no hope for him. "He will be dead in a year. Send him home, back to England." I was shocked. I was devastated … I was told that the medical resources would be better in England. He would also have his family there to take care of him. At the time, I'm like … I don't know what to do. I couldn't take care of him just myself here. I didn't know how long his insurance would last here in the US. [The doctors] put him on steroids and an assortment of other drugs. I flew with him down to Atlanta to get him on a plane directly back to Heathrow. His family was waiting for him there. I talked to him frequently, but sometimes he couldn't talk as the headaches were so debilitating. I went to England to visit him a couple of times when I could afford it, to see how he was doing.

Within one year and one week, Nigel was gone. He actually died during my visit. It was almost like he was waiting for me. He was awake the first day I got to see him and then faded into a coma the next day. He died three days later. It was traumatizing.

ME: *I'm so sorry, my friend. So I'm guessing your depression probably worsened then?*

ANNE: Yeah, after that it was tough to move forward. Where do you go from there? I mean, he had been back in England for a while, so he had been distanced from me a little bit. But still, the whole idea is, here's your best friend who you were making future life plans with

... and now he's gone. I don't even remember a whole lot that year. It's almost just like that year disappeared. So that was probably in my late twenties, early thirties, something like that.

ME: *So after that year that disappeared, you feel like you started to feel a little better?*

ANNE: Well, that's when I actually was starting [to grow] into myself. After talking with peers and doing some interviewing, I found fundraising to be an interesting field. I finished my master's degree in public administration with the concentration in nonprofit management and fundraising. So that was really helpful and good for me. It propelled me forward into new and exciting work and adventures ... I ended up working with an international conservation organization. I was so thankful as it gave me the opportunity to travel abroad—especially Africa—as it was a place I had always dreamed of traveling to.

ME: *Cool! I forgot about that—you going to Africa—those were big highlights! So things started to look up with this new direction in your career. Did people know that you had depression, and were you generally supported? Or did you run into people who, like you described with your mother, were like, "Oh, she's crazy, I'm not going to get near her"? I'm curious how you were treated.*

ANNE: I always put on a good face. Most people didn't know that I was dealing with depression even through all the fundraising and travel. You just learn to do that. I had to learn to do that at home with my mother as a child. You have to put on a good face—no crying, you know—you just get over it and you move [on]. But here's the kicker that I've learned as I've aged: Even in my work, depression has impacted me ... because I'm always somebody that felt that they needed to stay behind the scenes and in the shadows. I couldn't expose myself for fear of enraging somebody and the shame that would cause me.

In my mind, authority figures—i.e., my supervisors/bosses—were always an image of my mother. The authority is always the one with the last word and you always bow down to what the authority says. So whenever I took a position, I always stayed out of the limelight. I always made sure that I was the supporting person—never the lead. I think that, in a lot of ways, impacted my career. I just wanted to hide.

I wanted to stay behind the scenes. It was safe. Here is my thought process: If I exposed myself, I would do or say something foolish and embarrass myself. The shame would be unbearable. I assumed people would yell at me.

I think I've worked my way through [this way of thinking] as years have gone on, and recognized it for what it is. Today, I'm much more willing to kind of step out and risk more. However, this tendency to stay in the shadows led to some conflict with my mentor, Gail, because she would always take the limelight. I would think, *I'm doing all this work behind the scenes, but she's always taking the credit and attention.* I was always the person that everybody would be like, "Okay, step aside. I want to talk to [Gail]." It wasn't her fault; it was me. But I blamed her sometimes because I *could have* stepped away. I didn't *have* to be her shadow but I felt that was the safest, most comfortable place for me, even though I didn't like it.

ME: We need to get to the big recent story in your life. You were working at the local animal welfare agency and that's where you met Jesse?

ANNE: Yeah, he worked security at night and managed the kennels during the day. He was a vet tech and Mr. Animal Guru. He also had his own business, rescuing … bats in your belfry, raccoons in your attic, snakes on your dock, and other animals in fun predicaments. He took pride in no-kill, free release trapping …. I was director of development at the same agency and he was, you know, the nice young guy down with the animals. He was six years younger than me. I was, what, maybe thirty? Fifteen years later, [we were] married! Oh my gosh, who would've thought? Not me!

ME: When was he diagnosed with cancer, Anne?

ANNE: So he was diagnosed in February 2014. We were married in September of 2009, so we only had four years and about five months without cancer in our marriage. I had been encouraging him to have a colonoscopy for a while because he was saying his abdomen had hurt. He felt that there was a blockage somewhere. Men just tend to put off those doctor appointments …. So anyway, that's how we found it. And he had surgery within that next month and a half. He was on and off chemo for the next six years.

It went from his colon, to his liver, to his lungs, and then finally to the vertebrae in his back. He was such a trouper, such a fighter. Eventually one of the tumors pressed against his spine, which then made him lose the function of his lower body, basically from his chest down during that last year. So it was just quite a roller coaster ... and believe me, I was on antidepressants through the whole thing. And there's some anxiety medication, and a little bit of sleep aid too. But it couldn't be too heavy because I had to be able to hear him and get up in the middle of the night to help him.

The thing is, when your partner has cancer, you do everything for them. You put your own desires away, as you know their time is short, and you will have time later. I have no regrets about that at all. But the reality is ... life, my life, [was] put on hold for six years. You can't think about yourself anymore, it's all about what can [you] do for them that's gonna give them the most life. Whatever's comfortable—what are their desires, what are their wants and needs. Where do they want to go? Where do they want to spend their time when they're feeling good? So your life does get put completely on a shelf. I wouldn't change it, I mean, I love the man. I would do it again in a heartbeat. But it is six years of my life that completely stopped. That basically disappeared ... All your dreams disappear—the ones with your husband, your partner, your love. You don't have the privilege of thinking ahead and planning out life together anymore. You must live day to day, in the moment. That's all you have. And that's taught me a lot.

ME: *How can people best help those with depression, and how can people best help people who are dealing with cancer?*

ANNE: For those that have depression in their lives—sometimes it's hard to recognize it in people, but I think there are signs that you can see. When people withdraw, when they commit to things, but then they back out. And not just one or two times but, you know, consecutively or often. It's hard because people can hide it so well. But I would say ask questions and just be a really good listener. I think so many people forget to shut their mouths. They just talk and talk, and they need to listen. It is just huge.

And maybe just asking a few questions and not pinpointing exactly, "Do you have depression?" Because they may not even know they have depression. But just recognize maybe some things that you're seeing. Saying, "I recognize that you've been backing out, that you haven't been reaching out to me lately, what's going on?" so that they don't feel uncomfortable.

Sometimes people are uncomfortable even talking about the word *depression* or *anxiety*, right? It's mostly dancing around it and saying, "Hey, I recognize this about you. I see this stuff going on. Can you tell me more about what's happening, what's going on with you? Because I care." You know, that kind of thing.

ME: *I wish I'd done that [for] my friend years ago. She pointed out that her husband kind of took over and everybody was going through him. None of us fought to reach out to her and just listen. I thought I needed to leave her alone. Unfortunately, I was in that thought a lot of us have in society,* Oh, she's depressed, she's kind of crazy, I'd better leave her alone, *when what she needed was somebody to listen and give her that safe space.*

ANNE: I think all of us can think back on situations like that. We're like, "Oh man, I should have reached out to her or him."

ME: *But that's why I'm writing this book. We can all learn how to do better, as [you] said, how to make us more understanding of one another. So that leads me to one of my last questions. Do you know or belong to any organizations that support people with depression or support people going through cancer in their family?*

ANNE: Okay, the Cancer Support Community are a good outreach group and have all kinds of things going on. Everything from massages all the way down to yoga, to counseling, to cooking classes. They've got groups for the families going through it. They've got groups for the actual patient. They've got kids groups, all kinds of stuff, so it's wonderful.

I actually see a counselor—I don't know if it's grief counseling, but she's just a counselor that I love. Everybody needs a good counselor in their life … it's nothing to be ashamed of. It's right to think about those deeper things. If you can work through those deeper things, you can excel and get beyond those walls. But you have to get with a good counselor. If one doesn't fit, it's not going to hurt their feelings. You need to get to one that's going to work for you. Believe me, I've been to a couple that didn't work for me and I had to move on.

One thing—physical fitness—getting to the gym at least two to three times a week for a half hour or doing something in your home … the adrenaline and all the chemicals that you get in your system when you're physically moving and working out … walking outside, whatever it is, that helps tremendously. That's tremendous for me even when I'm not with a counselor.

[Another] group that I want to talk about is Ignite Transform. It's located here locally, and they help women going through any kind of trauma or even post-trauma. They have a three-pronged approach where they address the physical, the mental health, and the emotional/ spiritual side. You don't have to do everything. You can do some things, but it is a year-long program and everything is paid for. So your counseling is paid for, your physical fitness is paid for. They take you step-by-step through whatever you're going through to help you get to the other side.

Then even when you're on the other side, it doesn't all just disappear. You have peer groups. You still have people you can talk to. There's huge support behind it. It's an organization that I just love tremendously. They've helped me a lot. I don't think I could have made it as far as I have mentally, spiritually, physically without their help. It's been huge because it started before Jesse passed away and it continued after.

ME: *I'm excited [Ignite Transform] will be [mentioned] in this book. I want people to understand how they can help others. [Others] may read your story and it may touch them and they may think,* I want to get involved with some organization that helps. *And so here we go, let's spread the word about Ignite Transform.*

Anne, I'm honored you took this time to share your story.

ANNE: I feel it's a privilege for me to be able to share my story if it is going to help somebody else. I thank you for asking.

Organizations mentioned during this interview:
- Cancer Support Community: www.cancersupportcommunity.org
- Ignite Transform in Central Indiana: www.ignitetransform.org

There are only three prayers:
Help, Thanks, and Wow!

-ANNE LAMOTT

GLORIA

I *actually had never met Gloria before. She was referred to me by Patricia and her husband, Carlos. They said I'd "love Gloria instantly." That I did! Gloria and I went off on several tangents during the interview. She's smart, funny, and one tough cookie. I'd love to join her at temple someday.*

NAME: Gloria
AGE: 57
IDENTIFIES AS: Female
ETHNICITY: Jewish
OCCUPATION: Project and Production Manager for an Advertising Agency in Zionsville

ME: Well, Gloria, this is exciting because I literally do not know anything about you! So tell me about you and your family growing up. Where were you born?
GLORIA: I live in Zionsville [Indiana] and have been here for fourteen years, but I'm from Indianapolis. I grew up at 57th and Ralston in the Broad Ripple area until I was eight years old. Then we moved up to 86th and Ditch to a townhome and lived there [until I was] fourteen years old. Then [we] moved to 79th and Lieber Road.

I'm from a family of six—my father, my mother, my two sisters, and my brother. When we lived at Fifty-Seventh and Ralston, we lived in an 860-square-foot house. It was a little tight, but I have fond memories of our time there. My oldest friend, Maggie, lived across the street, and I still talk to her to this day!

ME: *That's rare!*

GLORIA: Yes, it's lovely. She's been a very good friend.

ME: *With the siblings, where do you fall?*

GLORIA: I'm the youngest of four. My sister Gina is the oldest; she's ten and a half years older than me. My brother, Larry was nine years older, then Debbie is six years older. I have eight nieces and nephews. All lovely kids. Unfortunately, we've had a lot of tragedy the last few years. My mom passed away on October 31, 2018, and my brother passed away fourteen months later. It's been a very trying time. I lost a friend of forty-eight years September 21, 2020. And many other family and friends have passed as well. Massive life changes, and then there is COVID.

ME: *Wow!*

GLORIA: Most of us live here in the Indianapolis area. We have a very tight-knit family … very, very close extended family. Second and third cousins are close. We're Sephardic—I don't know if you know what that is?

ME: *Some readers may not either ….*

GLORIA: I'm a Spanish Jew. We originated from Spain. When the Jews were expelled during the Spanish Inquisition, my ancestors landed in Greece, traveling through many regions to get there. My grandparents—my father's and mother's parents—were from Salonika and Monastir. They came over in their teens. I'm second-generation Sephardim. The majority of the Jewish population in Indianapolis are Ashkenazi Jews, who speak Yiddish. And then there are the Sephardic Jews, which is comprised of a much smaller group. We speak Ladino, which is a form of Spanish.

My temple that I attend is an Orthodox Sephardic Synagogue at Hoover and Seventy-Third Street, and was formed by the immigrants from Greece, including my grandparents, between 1911 and 1913. There are approximately three hundred families that belong to the synagogue. There are fifteen thousand Jews in Indianapolis.

I truly love being Sephardic. We have such a rich history. I did an Ancestry.com DNA test recently, thinking it would come back that I was 100 percent Spanish, knowing full well I'm not. I'm 36 percent European Jewish, 31 percent southern Italian, 23 percent Middle Eastern, 7 percent Cyprus, and 3 percent other regions. I love the fact I'm 31 percent Italian though. I love Italy and the food! My father's mother's maiden name was Modiano, which is an Italian last name. Our food is different than Ashkenazi food. I don't know if you've ever been to Shapiro's; have you ever been to Shapiro's?

ME: *Yes, years ago.*

GLORIA: Okay, so that food—you know, the corned beef, pastrami, matzo balls, the potato pancakes—is Ashkenazi food. I grew up with Sephardic food, which of course has Greek influences. My mother was an incredible cook and baker. We grew up eating all different kinds of food. She used phyllo dough in many dishes, grape leaves, olives, feta—no lamb. Our matzo balls are even different than the Ashkenazi's; they're more like dumplings. I grew up on a Mediterranean diet. Everything's different. We have different customs and traditions. We have prayers in Ladino as well as in Hebrew.

My mom was eighty-nine years old when she passed, and so much of the history passed along with her and that generation. We have a cousins' group text going, where we all talk about many things, but specifically about our parents and grandparents. We send pictures, recipes, etc. We're trying to keep it alive.

When we moved to Seventy-Ninth and Lieber, I was the only one left in the house. It was my dad, my mom, and me. I played softball starting at eight years old and spent most of my time at the ball field at Seventy-Third and Hoover. We were the first girls' Delaware Trails Softball League, and I spent most of my preteen and teen years playing there.

ME: *It sounds amazing to me and wonderful! But I'm sure it wasn't all hearts and flowers.*

GLORIA: Oh, of course it wasn't. Not at all.

ME: *Well, did you encounter any issues as a Jewish family? Were you accepted overall, or did you have some struggles?*

GLORIA: Things have been said over the years ... people make stereotypical comments, which is unfortunate to hear. We had anti-Semitism in our neighborhood in Broad Ripple, which was very difficult for our family. I was young, so I was not as aware of it as much as my parents and my older siblings were. They dealt with it all the time. I talked to my sister; she said she wouldn't say a word when things were said; she would just internalize it. My cousin and I were the only two Jewish kids at our school. When we moved north, there were a lot more Jewish families and the schools I went to were diverse. As an adult, I purchased a home at Sixty-Fourth and Hoover, where many Orthodox Jews live. In that neighborhood, where my home is, it had all Jewish families living there at one time. I was told the neighborhood was built by a Jewish builder because Jews could not live in neighborhoods that were being built north of Seventy-Third Street. So they built their own. This was in the early 1950s. But overall, I never felt a lot of anti-Semitism.

Back to your question about things not being all hearts and roses ... I know you want to know more about my life as a Jewish lesbian.
ME: *There's the other thing ... when did you have that, "Wait a minute ... I think I like girls"?*
GLORIA: I was twenty-six when I met a woman that was a lesbian and became friendly with her. Our relationship developed over a period of time and became romantic when I was around twenty-eight and a half years old. I had dated men. I had decent experiences with men, but I just connected on an emotional level better with women. I was very lucky when I came out. My family, friends, and the community were very loving and caring. I didn't have a bad experience. My family was a bit shocked. My dad passed away when I was twenty, so he was not alive when I came out. My mom was upset, but not upset with me, just sad. My siblings were sad because they thought I was going to have this other life. They basically were mourning the life they had envisioned for me. With that being said, my mother was upset, but then she quickly embraced it. I'm sure there was gossip ... "Oh my God, Gloria is gay." People were talking, but it wasn't hateful.

ME: I'm glad you had that support. Not everybody has that.

GLORIA: Yes, even my strict Orthodox temple had no issues with it, and they still don't. What I explained to my mom was … I don't lead with gay. It's just a part of me. I'm an American, I'm Jewish, and gay. It's just a part of me, and that's what I told my mom when she found out. She was upset, but I explained to her it's just one piece of who I am. Nothing has changed; it's just another facet of my life, and she quickly embraced all of me.

ME: One thing I wanted to ask you, what is it like being in this world—in the United States—that's Christian, Christian, Christian? Especially at Christmastime? How do you feel surrounded by all that?

GLORIA: I have a strong faith and a strong sense of identity as a Jew, so I never felt like I was missing out. If someone says "Merry Christmas" to me, I just say "Merry Christmas" back or say, "No, I'm Jewish." You know what I mean? It's a Christian world, definitely. There are only, I think, about fifteen million Jews in the world. Which, if you think about it, is crazy.

ME: Only fifteen million Jews in the world?

GLORIA: Yes. I think Christian ideals drive our country, so when those Christian ideals cross over into laws, etc., I do find that hard to tolerate. But as far as how I maneuver in the world, it's never been a problem. I love Christmas. My girlfriend is not Jewish; she celebrates Christmas. We've been together since 2003—seventeen and a half years. I celebrate all of her holidays with her and her family. When I was younger, our family would go out and look at Christmas lights and listen to Christmas music, but I grew up in a Jewish home.

I do have a few examples of situations I found difficult with people I engaged with that tried to convince me I should believe differently. I was walking down the street one day, when I struck up a conversation with a man who was a "born-again Christian." He saw my Star of David that I was wearing and tried to convince me Jews need to believe in Christ to get into heaven, and that I needed to be saved in order for him to get into heaven as well. I was mainly annoyed because I don't think we should impose our beliefs on others.

Another example, a woman I worked with was a "born-again Christian" too, which I don't even know if people say that anymore, but she would pray for me to be saved. I cared about this person and I loved her. What's so funny, she would also pray for me because I was gay and that was a sin in her eyes. So it was a double whammy!

ME: *Yes, lucky you!*

GLORIA: Yes, lucky me. She was the receptionist, and one day when I came into work, she was crying. I asked her, "What happened?" She said, "I just found out my sister is gay." So here I thought, *Wow, isn't it funny how God, or the universe, works?* Her sister fell in love with her best friend—both were married to men at the time. All I could do was sort of laugh. I wasn't laughing at her, but at how crazy life is. I said, "Oh, I'm so sorry, but God handed this gift to you, so you can have a better understanding of others." It's fascinating how things work out.

So it does bother me when someone imposes their belief system on me, but if they're not doing it in a malicious way and their intent is good, then I don't let it get to me. I'm not combative. I listen and also explain my beliefs to them.

ME: *So you mentioned recent years—what's that been like? As a gay Jewish woman, how have you been feeling lately?*

GLORIA: Being Jewish and being gay and what's been going on? It's been really hard to hear all the anti-Semitism, the hate being spewed about people of color, minorities, etc., the struggles in the LGBTQ community. I don't think it's a perfect world, but I do think it's better than it was when I came out.

Talking specifically about being gay, we can get married—that happened so quickly. My girlfriend and I are not married, and we don't plan on getting married; however, it's just incredible to me we have that choice. Again, I surround myself with people who accept me for who I am. I'm in advertising. It's a very welcoming environment. They're a very open-minded group, even if they have a different belief system, so I haven't encountered a lot of discord in that regard.

As a Jewish woman, I do have to say I don't know what's happening with all the anti-Semitism and hate that is on the rise. Many people haven't been educated about what happened during World War II and the Holocaust. I think about that. The overall current climate to me is stressful. You hear all these conspiracy theories about Jews. It's difficult to combat the beliefs people have.

As for being gay … it's everywhere—in advertising, television programs. I think it's a good time to be gay. You have this next generation that views it entirely differently. I'm not naive, I know people struggle in the LGBTQ community, have families, friends, or communities disowning them when they come out for being who they are. I didn't have that experience, but I do know others that have, and that's devastating.

ME: My gosh, in my own city—you probably knew about this—the young man from the high school a couple years ago that went into our main park and had the swastika. I couldn't believe it, and my sons know who he is.

GLORIA: That's so upsetting. In Zionsville there was a picture of a soccer team doing the Nazi salute. It was two years ago.

ME: I missed that!

GLORIA: They were kids from Zionsville but not a Zionsville-sanctioned team. Yeah, that happened, but then on the flip side, you have this woman that lives in our neighborhood, who we're friendly with, who started crying after she heard this happened. She gathered her kids in the house and sat them down and said, "Don't ever forget how wrong this is and that the Holocaust happened. Don't ever forget what happened to the Jewish people and to other minority groups." I have faith in the process.

Also, the synagogue down the street from me—you remember— it was Shaarey Tefilla on 116th street. The burning swastika. It was horrible. And everybody came together, all faiths came together. That was a tough period, but inspiring too.

ME: So what have you learned from your experiences—either Jewish or being gay or both? What would you tell others?

GLORIA: Just embrace who you are, who you are meant to be. Be comfortable in your own skin. Be authentic. As long as you know that you're doing these things and you're living life successfully, then hopefully, life will be a little easier.

ME: What would you like to tell people to do differently? To help change things?

GLORIA: That's a big question. That's hard to say. I mean, it goes so deep and there's so many levels to it. On an overarching level, we just need to be kind. I'm not getting that from Ellen [DeGeneres]. You need to be kind. You need to respect people's beliefs, respect who they are as people, respect where they've come from and where they are now. My mom taught me—this is a huge thing—you really never know what people are going through in life, and if someone is treating you a particular way, you might think it's about you, but oftentimes it's not. If someone is cross with you or they cut you off in traffic … you need to think outside yourself, put yourself in their shoes. I try and live by my mom's words. She always used to say if someone came up to her and said, "You short little Jewish blah blah woman," my mom might say, "Well, what's going on?" instead of her internalizing it. "What's going on with you? Can I help you?"

ME: Good for her.

GLORIA: Yes, she was amazing. I'm not saying that she didn't have her flaws, we all have flaws, but she really was an exceptional person. She accepted all walks of life, and that's pretty much how I think I live my life, and it's all because of her. She was a friend of the friendless. She always tried to see another point of view. Often, we only see our point of view and it's all about "me." We need to get away from that. We need to embrace each other and look outside ourselves because [to do otherwise is] damaging, so damaging. We have to learn from others, listen to what they have to say, what they're experiencing. Listen to them and learn about their struggles and triumphs. You hear this often, but we all bleed red. We're more similar than not.

ME: Yeah. I have enjoyed this process because I've gotten the chance to ask questions and to learn about different people. Would you be open to that? Like if somebody were like, "Oh, you're Jewish?"

GLORIA: Oh yeah, people asking questions? Completely! I'm an open book. I would be more than happy to talk to anybody interested in learning more about Judaism or me being gay.

ME: It seems like most everybody that I've talked to so far has been like, "Yeah, just ask me questions." But I think a lot of us are scared. I know the very first interview I had, I was so nervous. I was like, "What am I doing?"

Well, I'm going to go right to my last question: Do you belong to any organizations that kind of do what you advised us to do earlier? Or do you know of any organizations that do that?

GLORIA: There's the Jewish Community Center.

ME: Yeah, I don't even know what that does.

GLORIA: It's like a YMCA for Jews. But every walk of life is represented there.

ME: Oh, okay. Are there community centers—something like that—all over the country?

GLORIA: Yes. I belong to the Etz Chaim, which is my synagogue. I would be more than happy to take someone to visit if they're interested in learning more about Judaism.

ME: Well, it's been a pleasure talking with you, Gloria! This is not easy for people to do, so I really appreciate your time.

GLORIA: Great, have a good evening!

ME: You, too! Nice to meet you.

Organizations mentioned during this interview:
- Indianapolis Jewish Community Center: www.jccindy.org

There is no such thing as a single-issue struggle, because we do not lead single-issue lives. Our struggles are particular, but we are not alone. What we must do is commit ourselves to some future that can include each other and to work toward that future with the particular strengths of our individual identities.

—AUDRE LORDE

DAVID

avid is a part of "Our Gang," a close-knit group of my friends that gets together every month for dinner and games. I've known him for twenty-one years now. We are quite different from each other, but that makes things lively and interesting! He's been there for my family many times, and we appreciate him. David is one of the sharpest guys I know, despite us teasingly saying differently! We love him very much.

> **NAME:** David
> **AGE:** 61
> **IDENTIFIES AS:** Male
> **ETHNICITY:** Jewish
> **OCCUPATION:** Senior Deputy Prosecuting Attorney and Adjunct Law Professor

DAVID: I was born in Detroit and lived in Livonia, Michigan, my first two years. I have no recollection of that. We moved to a town called Southfield, Michigan, which is suburban Detroit. I lived there until I went to college—from two to about seventeen.

ME: So your family didn't move around?

DAVID: No.

ME: Nice.

DAVID: So just an ordinary, middle-class Detroit suburban neighborhood.

ME: Okay, and siblings? I think I know this, but I'll let you describe.

DAVID: Siblings—two brothers, one sister. One brother is deceased, one brother is older by four years, and a sister is my junior by ten.

ME: So they are also still residents of Michigan? Gotcha. Are you comfortable sharing ... when did your brother pass?

DAVID: In 1979. So I would have been nineteen years old; he would have been twenty-one. I was the third of three boys.

ME: And what happened, David? I can't remember.

DAVID: They don't know. He was either murdered or he died of an overdose of PCP and other narcotics that were in his blood system. But there were signs of a struggle at the hotel room where they found them. So they never really found out.

ME: Oh my God.

DAVID: It doesn't matter, quite frankly.

ME: No, it doesn't change anything. Wow, that must have been incredibly hard on your family.

DAVID: Hard on my parents ... a lot of guilt.

ME: Yeah ... yeah.

DAVID: They dealt with that for a long time, really until their death. Any parent probably would. They did a spectacular job in trying to really turn his life around. He was a sweet guy, a very compassionate guy, a highly intelligent guy. But he had a Dr. Jekyll/Mr. Hyde kind of thing going. There was the side of him that hung around with the wrong people and got into trouble. That ultimately got the best of him.

But our parents did a phenomenal job in trying everything. Unfortunately, they still felt guilty about it, which I think is natural for a parent. But in my view, they did a spectacular job in trying to turn his life around. They certainly gave him every opportunity to fix his issues. This just happens. If he had maybe lived a bit longer, maybe to turn life around ... but it didn't happen that way.

ME: Yeah, same thing with one of our family members and his daughter. He spent ... I can't even tell you how much money and resources to try to help her, and it just didn't work.

DAVID: I have a friend of mine whose parents are both physicians. She has a sister that's a physician and another one who's homeless.

ME: Yeah ... Well, I'm curious, did you grow up in a Jewish community? With lots of people around you Jewish?

DAVID: There were a good number of Jewish people, but I would say it was actually quite diverse. A lot of Christian people ... When we walked around the neighborhood at Christmastime, which was one of my favorite things to do, we looked at all the Christmas lights on all the houses. You could always tell where the Jewish families lived by the absence of Christmas lights.

ME: Yeah, it sounds like it.

DAVID: For the early part of my schooling, I would say in the elementary school maybe up to seventh or eighth grade, there were some times when we got the Jewish holidays off, Yom Kippur and Rosh Hashanah. Just some of the years, because we had a decent Jewish population in those schools at that time, but it changed.

ME: One thing I need to ask—what kind of Jewish person are you? The lady I interviewed last week is a Sephardic Jew, and I'd never heard of that. I don't think you are because that's Spanish, right?

DAVID: Yeah, the Sephardic Jews are mostly from the Mediterranean. The Ashkenazic Jews are more from Eastern European/Russian descent. That's my family line. My mother's family is from Poland. My father's family was from Prussia and some from Russia as well. So I would say [I'm] Ashkenazic rather than Sephardic.

ME: I've actually looked that up now and I know how to spell both! It was very enlightening. I'm learning so much doing this book. It's been tremendous.

DAVID: There's quite a difference between the Ashkenazic Jews and Sephardic Jews, even with regard to their dietary restrictions on Passover. There are certain things that Ashkenazics feel that they should not be eating versus what the Sephardics do. But to me, it's interesting.

ME: *Yeah, that's kind of what Gloria said, too, that what everybody eats is different.*

DAVID: Mm-hmm, yeah. There are slightly different rules of what's called *kashrut*, the rules governing what is kosher, depending on whether you're Sephardic or Ashkenazic.

ME: *She was making it sound like there are not as many Sephardic Jews, that they're kind of the minority.*

DAVID: Do you mean globally or in this country?

ME: *In this country.*

DAVID: I would say that's accurate. Globally I don't know what the demographic numbers are. In Israel, I think presently there's probably more Ashkenazic than Sephardic. It might be closer than it is when you compare it to the demographics of the United States.

ME: *Gotcha. So, growing up, before you went off to college, did you encounter any issues being Jewish? Anybody give you a hard time?*

DAVID: Sure, I mean, it wasn't uncommon to be called "dirty Jew," to be made fun of, but people get picked on for all kinds of reasons. It didn't really bother me.

ME: *Good. I'm glad to hear it. You have to, though, share the Christmas story because that's such a good one ... the one where you and your brother woke up that one Christmas day.*

DAVID: I was a little kid—probably no more than eight years old, he was ten. This is with my brother Marty. And it was a beautiful, postcard-snowy Christmas morning. You look out the window and the snow was falling, the trees were covered, it was beautiful. We stood on one of the beds and looked out the window and he said, "Well, everyone's going to have a great day today except us."

ME: *That's hilarious!*

DAVID: Yeah, but we discounted, of course, Hanukkah. By that time, even back in the sixties, it had become somewhat commercialized. We didn't do the eight gifts—that never happened in my household. It's a big myth that every Jew has eight gifts on Hanukkah. We never did. We got gifts the first night and so we felt like we were able to keep up with our Gentile friends. Ultimately, it doesn't matter.

ME: Okay. How do you feel at that time of year because, geez. I mean it's getting, in my opinion, worse and worse as far as the commercialization of Christmas. Are you ever just like, "Whoa," or are you like, "I'm Jewish, I don't care."

DAVID: Do you mean about the holiday itself or about [it being] kind of "shoved down your throat?" I think that's just a product of the commercialization of it. I don't know that I have any resentment of it. It is a Christian holiday, it is Christmas, no question about that. But that being said, that's okay. What's wrong with that? I never felt, like, excluded in some way because I wasn't celebrating the religious holiday in the way they might.

ME: Good.

DAVID: Mostly, you know, it was a nice time. The snow, the lights, there is a feeling of a little bit more camaraderie among people at that time. It was a little bit more festive. Of course, there were vacations—that always helped—from school and elsewhere …. My feeling about it is no different. I like the holiday season.

ME: Great. I asked that for a reason … I don't know if I ever told you this story, but when I was a little girl, I was talking to another little girl and had no clue. I had not been exposed to any Jewish families. And she was Jewish, and when she told me that they didn't celebrate Christmas, I burst into tears. I didn't understand, and I was brokenhearted for her.

DAVID: I have to say that's a rather condescending view, isn't it? That's like saying, "Oh, I'm so sorry. You don't accept Jesus. Too bad for you."

ME: True. I was little and clueless.

DAVID: This is not something that I haven't come across in adulthood, you know?

ME: Oh, really?

DAVID: Yeah, people will condescend in that way. They'll say, "You're a good person, it's too bad you're going to burn in hell. I really feel badly for you; there is a way out for you if you accept what these other people believe." But that's a rather condescending statement.

ME: Mm-hmm.

DAVID: This is not to cast [aspersions] against you or even to impart any kind of evilness to anyone, but it's just a way of looking at the world. "There are consequences to you not believing what I believe. Bad things are going to happen to you. You really should believe what I believe." To me, this is maybe farther down on the list, but that is a relatively close extension to, "I'm going to force you to believe what I believe, or at least practice what I'm going to make you believe." You look at autocratic nations ... this is what happens if you're in Iran and you don't want to practice Sharia law ... or Saudi Arabia. You're going to have some trouble. I suppose there's a big difference between someone trying to convince me to adopt their point of view religiously or politically, whatever, and somebody exercising force, particularly through the state or federal government. There's a line there. But it's a stone's throw from one to the other in my opinion.

If you look at the history of the Catholic Church, the influence of Rome and the power that they had and wielded ... look at the history involved. It's all about the exercise of political power—the Crusades, the Spanish Inquisition—the exercise of political power to serve a religious agenda. Nothing new in the world, same thing that's going on around the world in other contexts.

ME: Yep, very true. So you had people throughout your lifetime trying to force their views?

DAVID: Of course, yeah. "It's such a shame what's gonna happen to you."

ME: Wow. Damn.

DAVID: If you go to church on Sunday, in many churches around the world, Catholic or Christian churches, you will hear, "There is one way to get through the pearly gates: Accept Jesus as the Messiah. If you don't do that, regardless of how you behave in the world or what merit you brought to the planet, you're going downstairs." That's nothing new. That's thousands of years old.

ME: Yep, sad to say. You know, you're one of the few people who have lived in different places that I've interviewed. You didn't stick around the Midwest. Tell us about where you went to college and then some of the places that you lived.

DAVID: Well, here in the States, I lived in New Mexico, I lived in Texas for a little bit. I then moved to Santa Fe, New Mexico, and was a state trooper out there for about a decade. Then [I] wound up here in Indiana and got a job, and my life was over!

I've [also] spent a considerable amount of time in Israel—lived on a *kibbutz* and was a volunteer in the army for a little bit. I worked on a *kibbutz*, which I don't know if you know what those are. It's basically like a farming collective, kind of an experiment in socialism, rather interesting.

ME: Yeah, so how long were you in Israel doing that?

DAVID: Well, I've been there, I think, ten times now. I did part of my law school there, so, many months at a time. But it's been a little while since I've been there, unfortunately.

ME: So, [when you lived outside of the Midwest] in those different places, was it pretty accepting? Did you just get the harassment of, "Oh, you're Jewish. Shame on you"?

DAVID: No, I don't perceive myself as a victim. I don't walk around looking at myself as somebody that gets picked on. Are there instances I could point to where there was patent discrimination against me as a Jew? Sure. Can I point to discrimination against me because I'm White? Absolutely.

This is a classic example of religious discrimination: when I applied to the Texas Highway Patrol. I was about, what, twenty-one years old. I finished college. I was living in Dallas with some buddies of mine. I applied to the Texas Highway Patrol and I had gone through all of the phases of recruitment—the physical agility test, the psychological exams, the written exams, all of that. The last phase before getting accepted to the recruit school was the oral interview.

There were about ten guys who were sitting around me in a half circle while I stood answering questions. They asked me a bunch of questions about how I would react in situations. They would throw hypotheticals at me. One of the questions that they asked me was about capital punishment. They said, "Well, how do you feel about that?" And I said, "Well, there are pros and cons. On the one hand, you never want to execute somebody who was factually innocent. There is that danger. On the other hand, I think it's a political judgment that people can make when someone commits an act so heinous as to say that, "You've now lost your license to participate in society or even to enjoy a game of checkers in prison." I think the government can—society can—make that call. They can also make the call not to impose such a sentence or to have that system. But it's a judgment that society can make."

[The interviewers] asked, "Well, do you know what this provision is in the Bible, what the New Testament says about this?"

I said, "No, I'm not familiar with that passage."

They asked, "Don't you go to church every Sunday?"

I said, "No."

They asked, "Aren't you religious?"

I said, "No."

They asked, "What religion are you?"

I said, "I'm Jewish."

They looked at each other with disapproval, their eyes dropped, and that closed the curtains on the interview. The main interviewer said, "Okay, I have no more questions. Please wait in the hallway, and we will give you our response in a moment."

I stood out there a few minutes. I got called back in. They said, "Thank you for applying to the Texas Highway Patrol. We've decided not to promote you to the next phase of the recruitment process."

And that was that.

I remember driving away from there thinking two things. One, it's probably good that that came out in an interview because if that's a representation of the agency, that's not an organization I want to work for. Two, the guy in particular who was leading that charge ... I said, *If I ever do become a police officer and he comes tooling through on my highway, he's mine!* It happened. It's one of the two hall-of-fame tickets I ever wrote as a New Mexico state trooper.

He and a bunch of buddies were on their way from Texas to Colorado—speeding. This was about three years after the Texas interview and about two years after I had joined the New Mexico

State Police. I stopped him and I recognized him instantly. I don't think he ever recognized me. He's like, "Hey, this is my badge, Texas Highway Patrol."

And I said, "No, today I'm checking driver's licenses. Yesterday I was checking badges, but today I'm checking driver's licenses. So I'm going to need to see yours."

I don't really think he knew what hit him. I figured I was going to get a complaint on this and I never did. I put the vehicle that they were in through a complete inspection—turn signals, lights, windshield wipers. I even tested the lug nuts on their wheels; there's a certain torque that they had to be. The car was tip-top. I couldn't write them for anything, but they must have wondered, "What in the hell happened?"

ME: *Yeah, awesome!*

DAVID: I told my father about it. I called him that night and I said, "You will never believe who I stopped today."

My father said, "Well, wait for him. See if you can catch him on the way back." But I never did.

It's Texas. Texas, I think, is a great state in so many ways. Everything's big, and I think a lot of people are very independent there. There's less of a reliance on government, more of a belief in the individual. I'm in favor of all those things, but I think that in certain areas of Texas, they tend to be a little bit more closed minded. There's a whole section there of Southern Baptist or whatever. It's just really not consistent with Midwestern or Eastern Jewry.

That was about the only patent example that I can really point to. And, again, I didn't feel like, *Oh my gosh, I'm a victim, and here it is again. They need to accept me.* This is the way people are.

The opposite can also be said. When I was in New Mexico, there was, for a long time, only two Jewish troopers on the entire force—me and another guy who was in Albuquerque. He eventually left and went somewhere else. So I was the only guy. I think being Jewish gave me an advantage on at least two occasions. One in particular was when the Israeli ambassador from the United Nations was coming through New

Mexico. I was assigned—because I was Jewish—to escort him around. We went to fabulous places and great restaurants. I had so much time to question him and talk about life, and politics, and Israeli life. Had I not been Jewish and celebrated for that fact, I don't think I would have had that opportunity. So I'm very grateful in that respect.

For every story in my life that's out there—that I was picked on or called a "dirty Jew" when I was a kid or something like that—I could point you to experiences where it's been great.

ME: *Well, that's good to hear.*

DAVID: [My religion has] been embraced by my non-Jewish friends. Professionally, if I wanted to take Passover off or Yom Kippur off— never an issue. Although I know there are probably laws that require my employers to make accommodations and so forth. But it's never even an, "Oh my God, I guess I have to do this, so let me go ahead and do it."

For every struggle that I had, I could point to opposite examples. My parents and my grandparents had a different experience, especially my grandparents, and many of their family members were rounded up and killed. There are bad people out there, but I haven't faced that kind of action. They called me things, but I don't consider myself to be a victim.

ME: *Some people do feel that way. What advice would you give them?*

DAVID: My advice is stop emphasizing the fact that they have *otherness*. People get picked on for all sorts of reasons. I got picked on because I was short. That's just the way it is. I think that what we have done— certainly in the last ten years and probably more—is to exacerbate, to emphasize the differences between people and focus on what people demand of other people. You need to accept me because of "X." I think that promoting the differences by demanding acceptance rather than saying, "Here is the value that I bring to your life in this way," actually [is] a disservice to those people that many are trying to aid. It's a stone's throw between saying, "You need to accept me for what I am," and me saying, "You know what? Even if you don't accept me, I'm gonna go get somebody else to ram it down your throat whether you like it or not." I think it actually produces the opposite result that those minorities—whether they're Jewish or Black or others—are really trying to accomplish. You're taking people's ability to be people out of the equation, and you're simply using force to promote an ideology.

Discrimination is wrong, and it doesn't matter who the winners and losers are. As Justice Roberts famously said, "The way to stop discrimination on the basis of race is to stop discriminating on the basis of race." I think that when we emphasize these differences between people, it's a stone's throw from using political power to start regulating what people can and cannot think. Certainly what they can and cannot say.

Economically, there's a myth that Jews are—

ME: *I was going to ask about that.*

DAVID: Jewish people in this country had a history of discrimination against them where they were precluded from universities, they couldn't hold many positions. This is nothing unusual, historically, for Jews. This was true in Europe and elsewhere. They were precluded from engaging in many occupations—one of the exceptions being merchants. Which is one of the reasons they used that to their advantage.

I remember as a kid, my father—once he started becoming successful—wanted to join a country club. There were several that he could not join because they were restricted to Jews. What is the response there? Do you say, "Oh, we need to go to the legislature and force these edicts upon these people"? Or do they say, "Okay, we'll buy our property; we'll create our own"? So I think that there's a kind of a self-sufficiency that goes with Jewish ideology. But it, anti-Semitism, is not really related to the success of Jews. This is a relatively recent phenomenon and it's localized to a certain portion of America.

When you look around the world, many Jews are very poor. But in fact, where there are no Jews, anti-Semitism flourishes. The problem with Jews is that they're Jewish. They don't accept the edicts of Christianity. We don't accept the [Muslim's] Ascension of Muhammad. So at its core, that's the real problem; the rest is exposition.

Nevertheless, there are good people and bad people everywhere. In these times I see all this racial tension going on in this country. And I think we can get past this …. The mob mentality of some groups is the greater danger.

ME: How have you felt about things that have happened around here in the past couple of years—the kid in Noblesville with the swastika and the team in Zionsville that was talking about "Heil, Hitler"?

DAVID: That's kind of been on the rise the past couple years, things like that. According to several organizations, there's a lot more anti-Semitism in the United States and a lot more in Europe … a lot more.

ME: How have you been feeling about all this lately?

DAVID: Do I worry about it in terms of personal safety? Generally not. Will I get to a point where that happens? Maybe. Other countries have, certainly. I don't feel like I'm deprived of the ability to run my life and to capture opportunities that may be available to me. There are people that hate; they're just out there.

I think that the world is better served by appreciating individuals for the value each person brings to the world, rather than by mandating which group is legally preferred today. We're not all homogenous. I want to appreciate and enjoy all the differences between people. I don't want to be ordered as to how and what to think. I think that's dangerous and actually, in my opinion, creates far more harm than good.

ME: You've kind of expressed things pretty well already, but there might be something that we didn't cover. What have you learned in your lifetime, being a Jewish man?

DAVID: When I was about thirty, I was in law school—I did part of my law school in Israel—and one of the research projects that I engaged in there was "What does it mean to be Jewish?" I was especially interested in Israel's "Law of Return." It says that if you are Jewish, you have the right to return to your homeland, Israel, and declare citizenship there. Now, if you are not Jewish, you can still declare citizenship there, but it's a much more difficult process. It's a more time-consuming, onerous process, much like what it is here if you want to do so legally.

So what does it mean to be Jewish for purposes of this law? What is Israel? Is it a Jewish state—a religious state—or a state for the Jews that was born following the Second World War when Jews had nowhere else to go? There are good examples from the Old Testament about how it's actually both, about how Jews are bonded both by a theistic belief, more or less, and as a people. Did Moses really spend forty days and forty nights a couple of times up on Mount Sinai? I don't know. But is it possible that former Egyptian slaves galvanized as a people with common ethics, morals, and values somewhere in the desert? Sure. The extent to which the theistic belief intersects with Jews as a people led me on that exploration.

I'm not a religiously observant person. What I discovered in my exploration was there are many good things that Judaism offers the world. It is family oriented, it is justice oriented, it is rule oriented in terms of the right thing to do. The payoff for doing the right thing is the benefit that you receive today by doing the right thing. It's not a payoff that you'll get after you're dead somewhere.

Judaism has an emphasis on education, responsibility, cleanliness, and a bunch of other things that I believe are excellent values. So much of Judaism I really have come to like. But there are religious zealots as Jews, just like anything else. They exercise political power just like the Roman Church did. They are hostile to those who do not practice as religiously observant as they do, and so forth, and so on. I think that they are problematic in all of the same ways that religious zealots and other disciplines are.

The question is, again, what do you do about it? There's a Jerusalem neighborhood called Mea Shearim. It's a very Orthodox area of Jerusalem. When it's starting to head toward sundown on a Friday and the Sabbath is approaching, you see all these people wearing their Hasidic garb and they are getting ready for the Sabbath. They're going to the market, getting the fresh bread and the wine. It's like you are watching *Fiddler on the Roof.* Most Jews around the world don't live that way, though, for better or worse. This is not to disparage their thinking. Many parts of Israel are highly technically advanced.

ME: *Wow, I had no idea.*

DAVID: I haven't been there in a few years, but when it's Passover, for most of Israel, it's tough to get bread. You're going to find matzah everywhere. And on *Yom Hashoah*—the day of remembrance of the Holocaust—there's a period there where, just for two minutes, basically everything stops. Traffic stops, everything stops. People have this moment of silence for the Holocaust.

There's a certain social affinity that I share when I'm in Israel. I feel at home socially. I feel like … you're walking down the street in Tel Aviv and everyone's Jewish. It's a feeling unlike I get anywhere else. I'm not a very religious person, but there's still this Jewish connection there that I guess ultimately is rooted in some agreement on theology.

ME: *What would you tell the world to do differently for people like you?*

DAVID: Nothing. What I would tell people is that they are going to be better off as well as I am if they create a world in which people can exercise their separate interests.

There was a great essay called, "I, Pencil," written by a guy named Leonard Read in 1958. It's about all of the cooperation that it takes to make a simple item like a pencil. About the people that have to cooperate to produce the graphite, the brass, the wood. All the people that have to invent the machines, and distribute the machines, that will mill the wood and produce the graphite, the brass, the rubber, and so forth. And how they were all able to cooperate without any government direction through something called "the price system."

The people who are harvesting the trees that are going to eventually be made into pencils don't really care that they're going to be made into pencils. All they know is they're in a position to produce them at a price that somebody is willing to pay. When people start relating this way on an economic level, it bypasses many of the obstacles that people have in life.

My advice to people is to stop thinking of yourself as a victim. Just get on with your life. When I was turned down by the Texas Highway Patrol because I was Jewish, I applied somewhere else. If I go to a bakery and they don't want to serve me food because I'm Jewish, I'll go somewhere else and they won't get my business. Maybe I'll try to convince my fellow man not to eat at that restaurant.

Get on with your life. Make the most of the opportunities that are afforded you. Stop looking at yourself as being a victim, being special, being entitled to certain protections. Disadvantaged groups will prosper—if only we stop treating them as inferior and incapable of success.

I think women have faced the same thing over the course of years. It used to be, for example, that prenuptial agreements were totally unenforceable because the law presumed women to be incapable of bargaining. The law ensured that the wife was protected with a lawyer and that the husband paid for it, even if the wife was wealthy in her own right. The law required the bargain be reasonable, not unconscionable, and so on. That's a very condescending statement toward women—that they're not capable of exercising equality if given the opportunity. That's like saying they're stupid and naturally delicate and the law therefore needs to protect them. I'm against those kinds of things, so my advice is stop promoting a society in which we live this way.

ME: *Well, gosh, David, you hardly said anything tonight! Come on! Do you belong to any organizations? I know there's the Jewish Center at Seventy-First and Hoover.*

DAVID: I used to for the gym. Who was it that famously said, "I wouldn't belong to any group that would have me as a member"? I'm kind of like that.

There are a couple of groups that I do support. One is the Cato Institute, which is a libertarian think tank who's had some success. The other one is something called EdChoice, which is a renaming of a Milton Friedman educational foundation, which promotes freedom of choice in education as a means of elevating poor people.

So those are my thoughts, Amy. I just think that my biggest advice to people is not to say, "Oh, he's a Jew. Let's give him preferential treatment." Instead, it's to appreciate people for their differences and the value each person brings to society.

ME: That's a good way to end this evening. Thank you so much for this! I hope to see you next month.

Organizations mentioned in this interview:
- Cato Institute: www.cato.org
- EdChoice: www.edchoice.org

"I see no color" is not the goal. "I see your color and I honor you. I value your input. I will be educated about your lived experiences. I will work against the racism that harms you. You are beautiful. Tell me how to do better." That's the goal.

-CARLOS A. RODRIGUEZ

THE BANDA FAMILY

I met the Banda family thanks to Andrew, my son Jacob's close friend. Andrew and his entire family light up a room whenever they enter it! They're warm, welcoming, and fun to be around. I had always wanted to learn more about them, and this book gave me the wonderful opportunity!

> **NAME:** Laurie and Patrick and two of their three children, Maria and Andrew
> **AGE:** 43 (Laurie), 53 (Patrick), 13 (Maria), and 19 (Andrew)
> **IDENTIFY AS:** Female, Male, Female, and Male
> **ETHNICITY:** Patrick is Malawian, born in Africa in Malawi. Laurie is Caucasian.
> **OCCUPATIONS:** Laurie is an instructional assistant in special education for Noblesville High School, and Patrick is a nurse, currently delivering for a pharmacy.

ME: *Most of the time I interview one person, but since this is going to be the four of you, we're going to talk about the start of your family. So let's hear a little bit first about where you both grew up, and I'd like to hear how you met.*
PATRICK: I was born in Malawi in a really remote area. Part of Malawi, like in the sixties, was very undeveloped. I actually was born and raised, up to age six, in a village more like what you'd see on TV

if they show you [African] villages or something like that. Then at age six, I moved to the city to live with my oldest sister in Blantyre. That was like the biggest city then in the country. So I grew up there; that's where I was most of my life, in Blantyre.

ME: *Why did you move in with your sister?*

PATRICK: Because my sister and I are, like, twenty-three years apart. She's older. Her first [kid] was older than me and then her second one is younger by, like, forty-three days. I'm just forty-three days older! And at the time I was born, she was in the United Kingdom studying because she's a nurse too. So she was studying then in the UK, and then she didn't want my mom to raise me. She was like, "You have grandkids ... and you have a little one. You're gonna raise him like a grandkid, so you're gonna spoil him. So instead I wanna take him and raise him with my two girls."

She took me in and raised me, and so most people didn't even know that she was my sister. They thought they were my parents because, you know, my nieces and I are the same ages and growing up in the [same] household. They just said, "Oh, they've got two girls and the boy."

ME: *Interesting! Well you're [not the only] person in this book that's got such a big gap between siblings. And my brother is fifteen years older than me, and my sister is sixteen years older, and it's the same thing. I've got nieces and nephews very close to my age. In fact, I grew up with two of them and so I'm always fascinated to hear others who kind of had that same thing. Okay ... so you grew up and became a nurse there?*

PATRICK: No, I wanted to go to college, but ... it's hard to explain what really happened, but secondary school—which is high school, like, from grade nine to twelve—is very competitive over there. I should say "was." You had to score like a 100 percent almost in everything just to get into high school, or else you had to redo eighth grade again and try again the next year ... and then the next year. Some people ... I know friends that were in eighth grade for like seven, eight years before they actually made it into secondary school.

ME: *Oh my gosh!*

PATRICK: Yeah, that's how competitive it was. And so I went through the same problem. I was a smart kid, but maybe I didn't get 100 [percent], you know. You know, it was like, "Maybe I didn't make it." Because there were just very few high schools. The other option was you just learn on your own. The high school material there used to be called Malawi Correspondence College. So what you did is you got materials for, like, ninth and tenth grade because we would do ninth and tenth, which is ... we call it "form one" and "form two." And then you would write an exam and you'd get a junior certificate at that time. Then eleven and twelve were, like, form three and four. You would study for that for three years and then go write an exam. If you pass that, then you got your high school diploma or whatever you call it. We call it a certificate over there.

So that's the option I did because I was like, "Well, I can't get into high school." I literally just started on my own and just took tests, and I passed both the junior and the high school. The only problem is, it's so hard after passing the high school from just learning at home to actually go into college. That was another hurdle, to go into college. Because at that time, maybe you're looking at twenty thousand to thirty thousand people competing for maybe just two hundred to three hundred spots.

ME: Oh, yikes!

PATRICK: I found a really good job with World Vision International. I didn't have expenses ... everything I made, I just saved most of it. I was able to save enough and apply for my college year and pay my deposit. Later on, when I quit, they gave me whatever my end of the contract was, so I had enough money to come and start college here.

I came here and did marketing because my intention was, I was going back home. Marketing was one of ... I shouldn't say the hardest ... but you are guaranteed that you're gonna have a really nice job. Especially if you did marketing, because most people were marketing managers over there [in Malawi]. They had, like, a bachelor's, some business studies, or administration. But they would put them in there because they do a little bit of marketing on the side. I wanted to just do the actual marketing that was my major. So I did that and I graduated in '98 at SMC [Southwestern Michigan College].

ME: Okay! Laurie, what year did you come to Southwestern Michigan?

LAURIE: I came in April of '94. So I grew up in Cassopolis, Michigan, from the time I was born until I graduated high school and moved to Elkhart, Indiana, where I started working. I went to school at Indiana University of South Bend for two/two and a half years for business administration. During that time, Patrick and I met. We had known each other through friends and my sister and her husband and stuff for a while.

But when we started [dating in 2000], Patrick was at the end of his nursing education; I think he was taking his exams in the next month. I worked at a health-care company doing marketing and admissions for long-term care patients. He was a CNA [certified nursing assistant] at the time there but going to school for nursing. We started dating in October of 2000 and by February of 2001, we knew! We started making plans for the wedding. Then, before you know it, I'm pregnant with Andrew. [Patrick's] family came for our wedding that summer in July from Malawi. We invited all of his siblings; he's the youngest of nine.

ME: Wow!

LAURIE: His oldest siblings that currently live in Texas—his sister and her husband—are my parents age ... or older?

PATRICK: Older.

LAURIE: So yeah ... you have that. So they came. We brought several of his siblings over for our wedding. I think only two of the eight of them were unable to come. Then some of them stayed after our wedding and some of them went back home to their jobs or businesses or whatever. I was in a very good job at that time and so I didn't finish college. But here we are, fine!

ME: You did okay!

LAURIE: I had Andrew, and that kept us just busy between working full time and having a newborn. Education was kind of put on the back burner, I guess.

ME: So you guys met in the midnineties, it sounds like?

LAURIE: Yeah, it was probably like 1997 when we first met each other through working together.

ME: Okay, well, I have to ask the tough question. How did people react to you dating?

LAURIE: Some people were fine with it. I feel like the interracial relationships were kind of, like, becoming more familiar to people at that point in time. I have an aunt that was very supportive, but as far as my parents, they were hesitant at first. I had other aunts and uncles, and the same with Patrick's siblings and his nieces that were living here … they were also very hesitant of what that was going to look like. Was I going to "Westernize" Patrick? My parents [were] just unsure and thinking about, "What are other people gonna think?"

For me, the town Cassopolis that I grew up in, it was very diverse. We had, I would say, fifty-fifty of African American to Caucasians that I went to school with all my life. So it didn't look different to me. I had even been in other interracial relationships in high school. It didn't bother us the way it bothered other people. Even today, we don't let other people's feelings affect how we live our lives. That's on them and sorry that they have to, like, burden themselves over our life. Do you want to say anything?

PATRICK: Regarding that point in time, on my part, I just remember how most African American girls were so mad at me.

ME: Really?

PATRICK: Really, yeah, just for choosing a White girl over them.

LAURIE: A girl that we worked with and we were around daily was very angry, very upset with Patrick. They [the girls] would ask questions, "What does she have that we don't have?" Stuff like that.

PATRICK: I'm like, "I just fell in love with her … that's what it is." I don't see color; I just see her as a person, and I fell in love with her. I remember this so vividly. We were in a restaurant eating, and across the table from me was an African American family—women, it was all women. They all stared at me and wanted to make a point like, "We're staring at you. How dare you."

And I told [Laurie], "Those guys over there are wasting their time. I don't know why it's hurting them …. This is our choice—my choice, your choice. I wonder why they are the ones that are suffering over there."

I think, initially—like the first five years or so—we had more people be very direct with us about their disappointment or anger toward our relationship. Some of it would bother us—not like it's gonna change anything for us, because it wasn't—but bother us like, why? Why? It's just our lives. What does it have to do with you? It's not affecting you; it doesn't affect what you're doing with your own life. But the looks that we would get and the mean comments from people …

LAURIE: Like at my five-year high school reunion … even though I had dated African American boys in high school, one of the African American girls when I showed up with Patrick was like, "I had no idea that you would do anything like that." What does that even mean? Like, "I never saw you dating or marrying somebody like that."

Patrick and I talk about it a lot and feel like we have a good life. We live our life for ourselves. Our kids live their lives for our family and for themselves. We're not worried about what other people think around us. We don't know if that vibe puts off this … makes people feel, like, envious of that. We're not sure. We're just trying to figure it out, I guess—why people react the way that they react to us … like with such shock. Because to us, it's just normal.

At that time, Patrick and I got married in Elkhart, Indiana, and that was in July. In March of 2002, Andrew was born. We were both working. Patrick was working as a nurse full time. I was still doing marketing full time for the health-care company that I worked for. Then, two years later, Samuel was born, and three years after that Maria was born, in 2007. We just were living the best life we could for us and our kids.

We had family members say hurtful things about us and about how we were raising our kids throughout that time. So we just made different choices for our daily lives. We're not the kind of people that like to be around drama and the unnecessary or the bad vibes. We just started to avoid that and just live our own lives. Then we moved to Noblesville in 2011, and we've enjoyed our time here since.

People have come around. Even our family has come around more. My parents ... after we got married, it was like an instant change. Patrick has this draw to people that sometimes I don't think he realizes it. Even the most racist person could come and talk to Patrick like Patrick is just another Caucasian person standing in front of them. He just has this aura about him that makes people comfortable. It's easier for them to talk to him.

[One day] we met some of Patrick's work buddies at this event in downtown Indianapolis and even they were like, "Wait, what?" Like they couldn't believe what they were seeing—that Patrick's wife was a White person, and they were White people.

I just feel like we're in the year 2021 ... why are we still talking about race? I've said it for the last four years—or even all of our twenty years being together—why is this still ...? That is the number-one question, that's for sure.

ME: *Yeah, I don't understand it either, and that's kind of the purpose of this book ... is to try to help ... build a little more understanding, for gosh sakes!*

LAURIE: It's crazy. Like as far as the kids, I honestly never worried about them getting any pushback growing up. They're just normal kids. They're our kids ... we love our kids ....

ME: *I don't know ... the jury's out on Andrew as far as normal. [I was joking here, as my son and Andrew are best friends.]*

LAURIE: I know ... throwing his back out doing a dance video challenge!

I think that the boys [Andrew and Samuel] first started seeing people stereotyping their hair as they became teenagers and that maturity point. We have a lot of people that stereotype Patrick and the boys because of their hair. Patrick has had people ask him if he has any ganja.

PATRICK: Yeah.

ME: *Oh my gosh ... because you all have dreadlocks?*

PATRICK: Yeah, just assuming stuff like that. It's like, "Oh, he's got dreadlocks, so he must smoke weed." There's ... one time I was at the truck stop. I just stopped there and I'm outside my truck. This truck pulls up—it's a husband and wife. And the wife is just so excited looking at me and I'm like, "Do I know that person?" Then they parked and she comes running. She's like, "Man, it's been like three days, I haven't had anything to smoke. Come on, do you have anything?"

ME: *Oh!*

PATRICK: So I started talking and then she hears the accent, she's like, "Definitely he's got some stuff."

I'm like, "No, I don't do that."

She said, "No, no that can't be. You shouldn't have that hair if you don't do that."

I said, "I'm not what you think. I am as clean as they come when it comes to stuff like that. I'm not into that at all."

She walked away really disappointed. That's nothing I've ever been interested in, never, even from when I was young, not even when all the kids around me were doing it. I was like, "Nope!"

LAURIE: We feel very blessed that our kids have not been involved in any of that. I feel like they've learned from our leadership, or guidance, or how we live our lives, I guess, about those kinds of choices. They've heard us talk stories about similar things.

The last few years [have] been sad for me because as Andrew has become, like, an adult, we've tried to guide him on things. We've had to remind him with everything in this world that's going on around us ... we've had to remind him numerous times, "You are not a Caucasian boy. Your hair, your skin complexion—you're not going to be treated the way that other White kids would be."

Look at everything happening around us ... that breaks my heart that I have to, in 2021, teach my grown son something like that and draw attention to who he is because people are segregating, you know? People are pointing things out. I don't know ... it just kills me, you know? All three kids—they are so comfortable. This is all they know. It's like, to them, Black ... White ... gay ... it doesn't matter.

PATRICK: Whoever you are, you're gonna live your life. It doesn't even faze them. We have to remind them, like she said. I was just talking to Andrew the other day, trying to remind him that chances are likely you may be pulled over for nothing sometimes, just because of who you are. Just remember to be polite and don't do anything silly or whatever, because of who you are. You may be light skinned, but once they look at you or see your last name on your driver's license, they're gonna know you're not Caucasian. It's sad that you have to say that.

LAURIE: Samuel, he's going to be seventeen in a couple months. We've had some tough conversations. He's very free spirited ... just speaks whatever is on the tip of his tongue, it just comes out of his mouth. He doesn't care who's around. We've had harder conversations with him, talking about who he is because he's like, "I'm Samuel."

You're not Caucasian, but you're also not African American ... we don't even know how to explain it. There is a difference in the culture of African Americans and Africans, like where Patrick is from. It's been very difficult to explain that to somebody [Samuel's] age, at his maturity level. Teenagers want to think they know everything. He draws the race card. He's like, "You're just being racist."

I'm like, "No, that's not what this is about." He's not at that point in life where he gets what we're saying. He's not had enough life experiences to understand it.

PATRICK: One of the main things ... I was born and raised in Malawi. Malawi was under the British so we're mostly, like, British stuff. We don't have, like, racism over there. I mean—there are more Black people than White people, and we just live our lives. It's just as normal as can be. So coming to America was like a big shock for me, looking at how race mattered for a lot of people. So it's the different thing about me not being born in America and raised here.

I don't look at race—Black, White—the same way people that were born here look at it. The Caucasians and African Americans born and raised in this environment, in this culture of racism ... when I came here [I was just] one of the human beings on the planet experiencing life. Just having fun or whatever. Then I started noticing how life was here between the Blacks and Whites, and I'm like, "Oh boy." You never know when you're on the other side, until you're living here, that it's an issue.

LAURIE: I remember at one point—I don't even think Andrew was born yet—really early on in our relationship, that somebody commented to Patrick about the way that Patrick and I were living. That Patrick didn't have to worry about what they were worrying about because his ancestors weren't brought here on ships as slaves. So that made him more privileged than they were. That didn't make sense to us. I'm sorry that that happened to your ancestors, but that shouldn't affect your behavior toward fellow Americans or fellow human beings now. Treat everybody respectfully as humans. You want to be treated as a human—that's all we're asking.

PATRICK: There's definitely that divide. Here we are the land of the free, you know, in America, and I think we have more division as far as racism than anywhere that I've heard around the world, which is so disheartening.

ME: I have never thought about that—about how it is in other parts of the world. We are especially bad in that area, it sounds.

PATRICK: My sister, she's in a PhD program on the island of Cyprus in the Mediterranean. It's very diverse there. They're just people living with other people. They don't experience any of that. They have friends that are of all nationalities that come to this university over there and that they are with on a daily basis. They treat them respectfully and vice versa. They don't see any of the hatred that we see here. Even in Malawi, if we went there, I don't think that we'd get the same reaction as what we get here. Unfortunately, twenty years this year, and [Laurie] hasn't been to Malawi yet.

LAURIE: Right, I'd love to go. It's just a costly trip, and if you add three kids into that picture …

PATRICK: If we went home, it'll be nothing but celebration and happiness. That's all it is. Nothing about like, "Oh, White or Black or whatever." None of that would be there. Because that's not how we are over there. We are just people. That's it. Malawi—if you [look it up online] … it'll say it's called the "Warm Heart of Africa."

ME: *Oh yeah?*

PATRICK: Because of how nice the people are over there, they just labeled it the "Warm Heart of Africa." Chances are likely that you're always going to meet somebody that's really nice and wants to be helpful. That's just how it is.

ME: *Yeah. Let's have a little fun with that topic for a little breather here. I understand that some people know you there, Patrick, because of your music, right? ... Just a few people? [I ask this sarcastically.]*

PATRICK: Yeah! Well, it started in eighth grade. My brother was in a choir ... he taught me just a little bit on the accordion, and then the rest I figured out myself. And then I'm like, "How do people write songs?" So I started writing songs, and I only had three songs written. I would play them, you know, and there would be like a Christian gathering. I said, "I got a song! I gotta play!"

So I go there with my accordion and play. Then this band saw me and they're like, "Oh, he plays the accordion—keyboards!" They wanted somebody to play for their group. But at that time, I had not joined their band yet. They said, "Dude, let's strike a deal! We have this huge crusade coming in. There's this international German pastor that is coming to the country. We're having auditions to see who's gonna be performing. Can you come and play the keyboards or accordion for us for our band?"

I said, "Sure!"

Then we're there and they're like, "Hey, we know you've got those songs that you like to sing. We can practice those too and back you up so you can also audition."

I said, "No, no, no, no!"

But the head of the band just went back there and put my name in too. Then they called my name and I said, "I didn't put my name in there!"

They're like, "Come on, we already know your songs." So I did a song and then I got picked to be one of the musicians, the singers at this thing. It was a two-week thing. Every meeting, every night was over a hundred thousand people attending, and that's how I started with a huge audience.

ME: *What kind of music, Patrick, did you play again?*

PATRICK: Mostly Christian music. I became really big when I was a solo artist. Then I joined with one of my friends, they were the same age, we just started performing together. It was a duo, Patrick and Jim, all the time. We became really big at that time. Even the time I was coming here was when I was probably at the peak.

LAURIE: I think it has just been two years ago that you went home to Malawi, Patrick? Two years ago he went home—he was trying to keep it a secret. He was not going home for shows or performing or anything. People got wind that he was coming there even though he had tried to keep it a secret. So he had to go in the airport. He had to get picked up through like the VIP private entrance. His family is part of the government, like presidency over there in their country. So he got picked up by their escorts, their staff over there, if that gives you any idea.

PATRICK: I don't know how it'll be when we go to Malawi, all of us, because they probably won't remember me by now. It's been a while ....

ME: *Well, since I see Andrew, let's bring him in here.*

LAURIE: Maria's here too. Even though she hasn't made her appearance, she's been here the whole time.

ME: *Hey, guys! Andrew and Maria, I want to really thank you for being a part of this interview today. I was telling your parents that I wanted all ages in this book. So having teenagers' voices here, I think, is going to be really helpful. I wish my questions were going to be super easy today. But I'm going to probably ask a couple difficult things today. I'm trying to have people tell their stories so we can increase understanding. So I'd like to hear your experiences growing up as biracial kids in the Midwest. What are some good things and bad things about it that you've experienced?*

ANDREW: I actually don't think I've ever experienced anything bad about it, which I'm thankful for. I mean, there's only been, like, one instance where I think maybe something was not right, which was at school my sophomore year. I remember me and my friends were in the back of the class. The teacher thought that we were being suspicious or something like that, even though we were just talking. That was the day that I got sent down to the office and searched. Of course I'm the only "different" one there … I was the only one who got sent down, which made no sense to me.

LAURIE: I didn't go into all the details when I talked earlier about the stereotypes that you guys get over your hair. People assuming things that are not accurate because they simply don't know. They're just looking at your appearance. Some of those came up during that Diversity Coalition "come together" meeting that they had at the high school after those racial slurs were in the bathroom, on the bathroom stalls, at the high school. They brought in anyone that was not Caucasian to discuss with them what experiences they had had. We talked earlier about that, Amy, that the boys—maybe Samuel was still in middle school at that time. I'm not 100 percent.

ANDREW: I was in my junior year; Samuel was a freshman.

LAURIE: Yeah, that's right.

ANDREW: I didn't participate in that [conversation about the bathrooms] because it was optional. I just felt like it was weird that they were splitting everyone up for something that we needed to come together for. I've had it really good. I really can't name anything where I've been targeted or it's actually got in the way of something that I want to do. I think I've been lucky.

ME: Do you get nervous though sometimes, Andrew? I know your parents have cautioned both of you to be careful … you guys have to be more careful in certain situations.

ANDREW: Yeah, the other day, actually, I was driving. I got pulled over for something minor. That was the only thing that I can think of recently where I was actually afraid, while I was getting pulled over. He was a nice guy, so I was safe. I've heard a lot about these incidents. I just kept my cool and was respectful. I used what my parents have taught me in that situation, which I'm thankful for.

ME: *That is good. Maria, how does it affect you? Have you ever had any instances where you were like, "Oh my gosh, what are these people doing just because of what I look like?"*

MARIA: Not really. But one time before one of my friends met my dad, she was asking if I was adopted. We'd just became friends and she didn't know my dad yet. She'd only met Mom.

LAURIE: She didn't know because your skin complexion is so much darker than mine. She only had seen us together.

ME: *Right, yeah. But you feel like growing up so far things have been pretty good?*

MARIA: Yeah, I think we do live in a better time, though. When you think about how things were even one hundred years ago, or even fifty years ago, it's really crazy to think how far we've come. I feel like nowadays, the majority of people are really good people. There's always going to be messed-up people, but with the internet and just showing how cruel a lot of people are, I think we've gotten a lot of people on our side. There's definitely something to still worry about, and there's always room for improvement, but I feel like we're at the best we've ever been. I feel like everyone's really coming together, especially this last movement. I like to see that really the majority of people are with each other. We all just want to be equal.

ANDREW: There are always going to be some weird people out there who don't believe that stuff [about wanting to be equal], but seriously, as generations go on and on, I think it's starting to come down to a [reality.] At this point, you see that people who believe those things, those are the new minorities. It's like we're the majority now—we're all the majority now—so it's all of us versus that small group of people. We're really moving forward; it's the best way to look at it.

PATRICK: It seems like our kids—these newer generations—you can see most of them hanging out together more than it was during our generations. They're having it a little better than what we did.

LAURIE: Yeah, I definitely think so. It is something that depends on where you're from. I bet some places it's still a lot more, like, rough than we have it here. But I feel like here in Noblesville, I've pretty much had almost nothing but good experiences and nice people.

ME: So I'm thinking about what you said about how, for you guys, it seems like things are better. You're young, with your age group, you're thinking things are getting better. One thing that I thought of for you, Maria, I heard you dance?

MARIA: Right.

ME: It was like a ton of bricks were dropped over me a couple weeks ago. I was on Facebook, and there was a young lady about your age and she was a ballerina. She had gotten a pair of ballet shoes that matched her skin color and she was crying with joy. I thought, Oh my God ... never in my fifty years have I thought about that. I just thought ballet shoes were pink! But that's "flesh toned." And there are all different colors of flesh! So ... when that happened at the high school a couple of years ago, how did you guys feel? When that writing was on the bathroom wall?

ANDREW: It was gross. The person was never named, thank goodness, because that would have just given them the attention. I'm sure they've got something else going on at home to be thinking that sort of way and doing those sorts of things. Because it was just messed up. But I'm glad, honestly, of the response that the students had, because the response was entirely negative. Everyone knew that it was wrong. Everyone came to an agreement that that was messed up. I think it did change our school and how we've functioned from that point on. We definitely became more progressive after that. I guess, for me, it's just the way that I look at it. I try to look at things positively because it's the best way that you can look at everything.

ME: In that moment, what was your feeling?

ANDREW: It made my stomach drop when I first saw it because I actually saw the stall, it had already been reported, I had seen it, and that was disgusting. At that moment, I remember, I texted my mom about it because I was horrified. It was a real threat; it was definitely not a joke the way they wrote that. It just scared me because it made me realize there are still always going to be those types of people. It's really just something going on mentally for them that I don't understand. Somebody just needs to sit down and talk with them—like a therapist or something—because it's really just something wrong in their head to even be thinking like that.

LAURIE: I think for our kids, we've been far more protective of them, to not expose them, or expose them as little as possible, to all the hatred around us. I think that the town that we live in is more forward thinking in that regard. Maybe if we lived in a more rural community …

We even talked about, when the kids were younger, we took a spontaneous trip to Myrtle Beach. My dad was freaking out about us traveling through some of those towns down there … you know, a mixed-race family. I think depending on where we go, like when we go up to the Upper Peninsula … we have experiences up there, where it's remote that they're not used to. We have people that are wide eyed or cautious—even though it's so remote, we go into the grocery stores or whatever. So we just try to protect our kids from it because we don't want them having the experiences that we've experienced throughout our early relationship.

ME: Well, what would you tell the world to do differently for people and families like yours?

PATRICK: Honestly … be the better person. But always stand up for yourself. Only give love back because, you know, in reality, it's sadly just what they've been taught. People can change. So you just gotta look at things more open minded. Don't cause a war. That's kind of what I was seeing this last year was that it was almost causing some sort of war between people. Instead of becoming something where we wanted to be equal, it was something more like we wanted to be above them. Like above everyone else, which was really weird to me. Because I think that's not even what someone like Martin Luther King Jr. stood up for. He just wanted people to be equal. He wanted everyone to love as people.

Just love everyone no matter what. Everything goes both ways. You can't give people the same energy back if it's negative. More negativity just adds up. So just be the best person that you can. Unless it's affecting your life seriously. If it's affecting your life seriously, always do something about it; stand up for yourself. You're a person and there are lots of people who are with you. That's what I'd say.

ME: Great answer, great answer. I know you mentioned the Diversity Coalition earlier. Are you involved with that or any organizations that kind of help?

PATRICK: I'm not involved with any of that. I support their message. It's something that we just all need to come together and talk about, instead of not talking.

LAURIE: We are not directly a part of any group, Amy. My problem with the Diversity Coalition at the high school or wherever it originated from, is that when they're meeting, it's in divided groups. Like, "Okay, African Americans, go here. If you're Indian, go to this place. If you're Caucasian, go here." The point of diversity is not to separate or to segregate, you know? What's the point of talking about coexistence when you're separating us at the same time? The purpose of it, the concept is great, but how it's being handled is going backward, if that makes sense.

ME: Yeah, that's odd.

LAURIE: Maria, when she was in fifth grade … this elementary school that she was at every year did yearbook-cover contests. She won the yearbook-cover contest that year for doing a cover that was called "Unity and Diversity."

ME: Yeah! Would one of you send that to me? Could I put it in the book?

LAURIE: Sure! People went gaga over it. She was at Promise Road, and in their cafeteria, they have all the flags that Promise Road represents. I think there were like fifty-two different countries that were represented. So they would put up the flags for those countries in their cafeteria. She incorporated those flags, but now that she's in the middle school, they are painting her art—a huge mural on one of the walls at the middle school.

ME: Very cool!

LAURIE: And that's just one thing. We've tried to raise our kids that way—to come together, not to separate. Like I said earlier, we are just living our lives. We're not worried about who you're married to, or are you straight, are you gay, what you want to be identified as, what color your skin is. We honestly don't care how you live your lives. Just live it the best you can! That's how we wanted to raise our kids.

ME: *Well, I think you're doing a pretty darn good job!*

LAURIE: Thanks.

ME: *Is there anything I might have forgotten about today that you might want to add?*

LAURIE: I can't think of anything right now but if we have something, I'll make sure to let you know.

ME: *I know Samuel's got his competition, which is why he couldn't join us, so good luck. Enjoy your day! I really appreciate this, and good luck to the [Noblesville] Millers!*

Maria's award-winning yearbook cover and Noblesville East Middle School's mural representation of it.

When you debate a person about something that affects them more than it affects you, remember that it will take a much greater emotional toll on them than on you. For you it may feel like an academic exercise. For them, it feels like revealing their pain only to have you dismiss their experience and sometimes their humanity. The fact that you might remain more calm under these circumstances is a consequence of your privilege, no increased objectivity on your part. Stay humble.

—SARAH MADDUX

AMY

I met Amy when I watched her oldest son in my day care days. She and her family were such a delight that I wanted to keep watching Luke even when I closed operations! But Amy and I had never talked about her disability, even though we've been friends for years now. I've watched her overcome a lot recently and couldn't wait to talk to her and learn more.

> **NAME:** Amy
> **AGE:** 46
> **IDENTIFIES AS:** Female
> **ETHNICITY:** White
> **OCCUPATION:** Mom, Advocate, and National Ambassador for the Muscular Dystrophy Association (MDA)

AMY: I grew up here in Noblesville and we actually lived in town on Harrison Street, not too far from my elementary school, which was North Elementary. My mom was a second-grade teacher there. I lived with my mom and dad and my sister, who is two years older than me. We lived there on Harrison Street until I was in sixth grade and then we kind of moved out to the country. Well, at the time it was the country—it's not so much the country anymore. There are houses and businesses and all that around, which is kind of nice, too, because my sister and I built houses behind my parents, so we all kind of live around each other still. Growing up, that wasn't really a goal or a plan, that was just kind of how it happened.

So I went to school here in Noblesville—North Elementary— and then Noblesville Junior High and Noblesville High School, and graduated in 1992. I don't know if you want to know more about my childhood?

ME: *Well, I've seen pictures that you've posted on Facebook of you as a little girl … pictures where you had braces on your legs. So you knew from the beginning that, "Hey, wait, something's going on here." I don't know if you want to start with that.*

AMY: Yeah, I can. So my parents told me that I started pulling up on things and walking—like holding on to things—around nine months or so, but they would notice that I just would never let go to walk independently. So around seventeen months, when I still wasn't doing that, they got concerned and took me to the doctor, and that kind of started this whole journey that I've been on.

I went undiagnosed, even though I had my condition since birth, until I was forty-four. I'm very newly diagnosed. Pretty much a lot of my childhood was spent searching for answers and going to different doctors and wearing the leg braces to help me walk. Then, eventually, I had some surgeries that helped me to be able to get out of the braces. They were big, heavy, metal leg braces, and my mom really wanted me to be able to walk without those. So these surgeries allowed me to do that, which was good. I still needed some supports throughout the years, but the surgeries really helped a lot.

ME: *When did you have those, Amy? Were you a teenager or younger?*

AMY: I think my first big surgery was right before I started kindergarten. I had some casting of my legs and stuff before that time. I started kindergarten on crutches with two casts on after the surgery. Then I had several others in elementary school, one in junior high, and one in high school. And then one during college and then one after I graduated college, like, the big surgery.

ME: *Wow!*

AMY: Yeah, it was a lot. But [I] had a lot of good support and good friends that helped me out at school. That's just kind of how people knew me, you know, that was just me. Of course there were some bullies like there are still. I mean, people get bullied for all different kinds of things. There were a few of those, and I made my way through that.

ME: *Good. Well, that was one of my questions … what struggles did you face growing up with this?*

AMY: I think one of the biggest struggles was just, even though I had a lot of good friends, great friends, my lifelong friends I still have … I didn't have any friends that were just like me. Like I didn't know anybody that walked like I did or had the same struggles that I did. I think just that feeling of being alone in that was really hard. That's probably one of the hardest things is making your way through. School is hard anyway, and then to add that on top of it where you kind of … even though you were accepted, you still kind of felt like an outsider. A lot of that I put on myself, probably, but it was just hard not knowing what I was dealing with. That too. I had this physical disability that affected everything that I did and I didn't really know what it was. I didn't know if [or] how quickly it would progress, or if it would get better. When you don't know what's wrong, you don't have any answers.

ME: *For sure. You said it affected you in a lot of ways—I know, obviously, walking. What other ways did it affect your life?*

AMY: Just keeping up with everybody, or like on the stairs at school. Small things that most people just don't think twice about. There were huge obstacles. If I was at school and I knew that I was going to have to go upstairs at some point during that day, I would stress about it. You just sit and think about how that's going to go and, *Is somebody going to knock me down?* It was a big stressor to just think, *How am I going to conquer that?* That would happen every time I'd have to do it.

ME: *So back then, people weren't thinking about making things accessible. So no elevator, I'm guessing?*

AMY: They got the elevator after the surgeries.

ME: *Oh, I see.*

AMY: But a lot of that was probably me too. I think I did my best to just try to act like this wasn't going on, if that makes sense. At the time it was hard to accept something when I didn't even know what it was.

ME: *Over the years did your physicians say, "Oh, it could be this, it could be that?"*

AMY: Yeah, a lot of that. And a lot of, "Oh, you're a really interesting case. I just don't know." A lot of people tried to figure it out and my parents were told at times that it looked like muscular dystrophy, but it didn't look exactly like any of the types that they knew of at that time or that they were familiar with. When I was diagnosed, I went to see one of the best neurologists around for neuromuscular disease. He happened to say, "Do you want to do a genetic test?"

And so I said, "Sure." I was always like, "Of course!"

It turns out the one that he thought he was doing, he didn't do, and instead it tested me for neuromuscular disease. He thought I had neuropathy, so they really did the wrong test and that's when it showed my diagnosis.

ME: *Oh my gosh, that's wild!*

AMY: Yeah, it's just like, "Wow, finally!" It took a mistake to get an answer. He still wanted to know what the neuropathy genetic testing said, so they did that and that didn't show anything. Then my parents were tested, so that kind of helped solidify the results. It really was just a lot off my shoulders and I was able to refocus. You know I'm passionate about helping others that are like me. I always wanted somebody to talk to that could relate to me, whether they were older, whatever. I needed that hope and I didn't get that. So that's a vision of mine that I'm working with MDA on—creating this mentor program just so that no one ever gets left behind. My focus is muscular dystrophy because that's what I know and that's where my passion lies.

ME: *Do you know how many people have it in the country or in the world?*

AMY: I know that my particular disease is like one in two hundred thousand, my type of muscular dystrophy, which is called bethlem myopathy. I can't even tell you off the top of my head how many types there are. There are a lot of types of muscular dystrophy that are way more severe than what I live with. I really consider myself lucky because I've walked, and I'm continuing to walk, even though it's always been a struggle and a fight. I'm still able to do that, and a lot of people don't ever walk, or they need assistance breathing. Muscular dystrophy has a wide range of how it affects people.

ME: I don't think I ever realized that. I thought more of the wheelchairs. And let's face it, a lot of people's experience is the telethon.

AMY: Yeah.

ME: Yep, Labor Day weekend. Many of us have those images, and not a lot of them fit the image of what you struggle with, from what I recall at least. I'd see you in the grocery store, you know, and walking along. I mean, no, you're not running a race, but you were walking in there.

AMY: Something like that, going to the store, that's a huge physical toll. That's a physical task for anybody. But that would be something I was able to do and I enjoyed doing it, but it might wipe me out for the rest of the day, you know? I just see those things as small victories to push myself. To stay where I'm at, I've got to just constantly keep growing and pushing myself the best that I can. I feel fortunate to have the gifts that I do, like walking and being able to take care of my family. That's important to me.

ME: Speaking of, I was going to ask you about how your family started and when you met Jamie. I would love to hear about that.

AMY: So I met Jamie in high school. It was my freshman year, his sophomore year. So we dated for a couple years, and when he was a senior, at spring break time, he broke up with me. Let's just be honest: he kind of dumped the junior. That was horribly devastating but now, looking back, we're both glad that it happened. We stayed good friends, and he went to Purdue for college and I started out at Purdue. So we still talked then, but we both went our separate ways during college. Then he graduated and moved to Memphis, Tennessee. When I graduated college, we were continuing to talk. He was like, "Hey, why don't you come visit in Memphis?" So I did, and then we got back together.

I moved there like a month later. We lived in Memphis for five years, but we both decided that we wanted to be closer to our family when we started our own family. So we moved back to Noblesville. Then it's not long after that we had Luke in 2003. And then we had Jack.

The pregnancies were hard. I didn't even really know if I wanted to be pregnant or even [if] I could carry a pregnancy. But we just kind of relied on God to make that decision, and He saw me through both pregnancies with not really too many issues—other than I couldn't walk easily toward the end of each one. But I love my little family of four.

ME: *That's great. They are awesome young men, and you have the most supportive husband. I saw that years ago when we saw each other on a daily basis, and I see it now with all that's [happening on] Facebook. Could you share with the world how he supports you and the things you're doing together to spread the message about muscular dystrophy?*

AMY: Yeah. You know, in high school, when you meet somebody, you don't really expect to date someone with a disability, I guess. That always stood out to me. I just think that ... I don't want to say that it takes courage to do that, but it's definitely another level of dedication that you're looking at. You're helping that person physically. I just think, at that age, that was just awesome that he was up for that. And he continued to, just even as a friend—that's what he was—and now he's my husband. He kind of took the baton from my parents after we got married, and he continued to go to all those doctors' appointments with me to get the diagnosis. So it was pretty cool when I finally got [it]; it was a relief. Jamie very much has a servant's heart, I would say. Not just for me, but he does a lot of kind things. That's a true servant, when you don't need recognition for what you've done.

ME: *Definitely.*

AMY: He was just really on board with me, when we got this muscular dystrophy diagnosis, to jump in. The whole goal with muscular dystrophy is to find a cure, and with the Muscular Dystrophy Association, that's what they're raising money for. A good part of their money is for funding research to help find treatments and cures for all types of muscular dystrophy and ALS.

We wanted to do our part. Jamie's a runner, like our boys. He was a soccer player in high school, but when Luke started running so much, he wanted to go on these long runs. We didn't want him to go by himself, so Jamie started running with him. Then he became kind of bitten by the running bug too. He's really gotten into it and started running some smaller races, then some half marathons, and then marathons.

I'm trying to think about how we even came about the whole duo-bike, which is a bike that he pushes me in when he runs. He knew that I always wanted to run. That's another thing, when we were talking about struggles growing up; I could never run or jump or keep up with the crowd in the physical sort of way. He knew that I always wanted to be able to do that and do one of these races. At that point, we had gotten involved with [the Muscular Dystrophy Association] and then we had seen, on probably Facebook or something, that they had this team called Team Momentum. It was a team of people that runs to help raise funds for the MDA.

Jamie was already set to run the Boston Marathon a couple years ago. So we reached out to the national director for Team Momentum and he said Jamie could sign up. He then kind of teamed up with Team Momentum and so that's how we met them. And then some point along the way, the director reached out to us. We had looked at those bikes before. At the Boston Marathon, they had an expo and they had this bike there that I was able to sit in. And Jamie tried pushing me and we were like, "Oh, that's interesting! I wonder if we could ever do a race or something?"

That kind of started it. And then we told the national director that we were interested and asked, Did he know where we could get one of those bikes? He knew this gentleman that had pushed his wife who had, I believe, ALS, and they ran a marathon together with the bike. She unfortunately passed away after that, and so he donated it. Several other people have used that bike too. So we went and picked it up in Chicago because it was available, and we were just gonna try it out and see. You can imagine running a marathon—and then running a marathon pushing these bikes! They're big and they're heavy, then you're putting a person in there, right? So he's Superman. I don't even know … somehow he was able to do it and we just started running together some. Then we got the idea that we wanted to run the Chicago Marathon—that would have been 2019.

We started training in June or July, I believe. He would train all throughout the week, and then Saturdays were a day that he would do a really long run with me and the bike. So we had that training schedule. Early Saturday mornings, we'd go to the Monon Trail and usually he would do like ten to twelve miles.

ME: *Wow!*

AMY: We would just keep working up from there.

ME: *Did you have people waving and cheering you on?*

AMY: Oh yeah. That was so great for both of us, but especially for him because it's what kept him going, and I wanted to show people what that journey looked like from my perspective too. I started videoing those runs, and seeing the beauty of it from my perspective and how that was happening for me. Because, at times, it could feel like I was running too.

We did the Chicago Marathon with Team Momentum and that was just really awesome. The crowds there were just unbelievable … just lining the streets. MDA had these cowbells they handed out and were just ringing the heck out of them. I would ring it, people would go crazy, and that really helped Jamie so much to motivate him. My mom, and sister, and Jack, and a couple of my best friends and their husbands came to Chicago to support us too. That was really cool seeing them along the route of the marathon!

ME: *Awesome! That's certainly a boost.*

AMY: Yeah.

ME: *You mentioned it's a bike, but yet he's still pushing you—so he's not behind you pedaling?*

AMY: He's not pedaling, he's running and then he kind of leans on the bike. There's like a place for his forearms and so he kind of leans and runs. The bike has three wheels, two big wheels in the back and then one on the front. You've probably seen pictures of it.

ME: *Maybe, yes, online. I'd love to share one in this book.*

AMY: Probably the coolest thing about all of that was, after we did that marathon, we had a lot of different ways our story got told. These people that worked with Jamie, they heard our story, and they were so moved by it that they offered to buy us our own bike and let us design it and everything!

ME: *That's so cool!*

AMY: That was really just kind of one of those moments in life. I mean, that was just very generous, it meant a lot to us.

ME: *That's really something!*

AMY: I'll share that picture with you of the new bike. We got to pick out the colors and, of course, on the handlebars we did the blue and gold for MDA. Our goal was to do more races with them but then of course ... COVID. So we didn't nail it in 2020.

ME: *Right. Do you still kind of train or maybe do anything virtually since we've got COVID in our world?*

AMY: You know we did a little bit with the muscle walk for the Muscular Dystrophy Association. That's one of their big fundraisers that they ended up doing virtually this year. So we did take [the bike] out. I'm kind of a fair-weather bike rider. The cold's hard on my body, so I would rather we don't take it out a whole lot in the winter. If we do so, it's a warmer day. [Jamie] certainly would. It's me ... that's it, you know, when you're not moving and you're just sitting there ... But we'd love to get out in it more. Our next goal is to do the New York Marathon. We'll have to see.

ME: *When does that take place?*

AMY: November. Of course they don't know if that's gonna happen, so that could be our next one or maybe that would have to be the next year. *(Amy and her husband did go on to participate in the New York Marathon in 2021, along with their son Luke.)*

ME: *Right. So, Amy, how come we get to see you on billboards? Tell us that story.*

AMY: Well, one of my best friends is one of the big reasons for that. She works for a company that does these billboards. Immediately after being diagnosed, I wanted to get connected with MDA, so that's what I did. I signed up to be a volunteer and a local ambassador. Then I found out they were looking for a state ambassador, so that's something that I applied for. I found out in February that I had been chosen to be the state ambassador.

ME: *Man, I was just so excited about that!*

AMY: Something I didn't tell you … growing up in elementary school, I was the Easter Seal child. I don't know if you've heard of the Easter Seal.

ME: *Yes, absolutely.*

AMY: I was first the Hamilton County Easterseal[s] child and then after that, for two years, I was the Indiana State Easterseal[s] child. I enjoyed that. I got to do lots of fun stuff and meet fun people. At that time, I was around some other kids that had disabilities [for] a little bit at these events, so that did help, although they weren't really like me. I knew I liked doing that and so I knew I'd like doing the state ambassador thing.

I will say, it wasn't something that came easy because … you're standing up and speaking and telling your story in front of different groups of people, which I only barely got started with before COVID and all that. So I didn't get to do all that I was on the schedule for, unfortunately, because I was really looking forward to it, even though it was something that certainly pushed me outside of my comfort zone with the public speaking. I've grown with that and I wanted to stay with that. I felt like it's such an honor to be chosen, and that's probably when I started sharing more on social media because that was a way I could get the word out about MDA and what they're trying to do. All while telling my story, which is not something I would have always done. I was not always so open about it. It was hard to share something when you didn't know exactly what you were sharing. I feel like [I've] really come into myself. When you get older, anyway, you become more comfortable with yourself.

ME: I have said so many times, I absolutely love this stage of life. Your confidence grows, and, let's face it, our kids are older. It just really helps you be like, "Yeah, I can do this."

AMY: Yeah.

ME: I like your blog ….

AMY: Yeah, you know, I thought about that for a while and I was like, "Oh, I don't know if anybody's going to read it." But I've grown in that way, too, because even if they don't read it, that was good for me to write it. Maybe one person will read it that needs to read it. So I think when you look at things on … a scale like that, where it doesn't really matter if you've got thousands of people that care about what you're doing, or if you have a handful of people, or just one that you're helping, then to me, that's worth it. It's worth it.

ME: Yes, it is. I agree, Amy. One thing I like to ask people is, What have you learned through all of this—through battling muscular dystrophy—either about yourself or in general?

AMY: Oh gosh, I feel like I've learned so much. I've learned patience. I've learned that, for me, the way that I look at things now, I really lean into God's timing. He truly knows what's best. All those years, they used to feel so wasted, forty-four years of all that. And now I know that they weren't wasted at all. That was the journey I was supposed to be on. I think, even when I was trying my best to ignore my disability, it was doing things for other people that I didn't even realize. I've had a lot of people—teachers, or just people that I knew growing up—that have said things to me like, "You don't know how much you helped me or inspired me." I had no idea that was even happening. I've learned that just by living your life and living it well, you're probably inspiring other people to do the same.

I learned that people are kind, and most people want to help and understand. And that most people are going to be cheering you on when you're trying to do something that's outside of your comfort zone. The people that really care about you—they're gonna be there for you. Luckily, I have a lot of those people that have been with me

... a lot of my life. My family and my good friends, they're just very supportive people—and my husband, of course.

With my boys, I used to worry a lot about being a mom with a disability. You worry about being able to do everything to care for them. And then you worry about if they are going to be affected. Are they gonna have this disability? Then you worry about if they're going to be embarrassed by this, or is that gonna hold them back. I think all of those things. Luckily, both of my boys ... neither one of them have muscular dystrophy, at least at this point that we know. I think they're pretty good since they're both runners and very physically capable.

ME: *So I take it that it runs in families sometimes?*

AMY: Yeah, and both of my parents had genetic markers. The whole genetics thing is so complicated. I couldn't even begin to tell you, but it was even more rare the way that I got it because we don't really know of anybody in my family ... neither one of my parents could think of anyone that had anything like this. Kind of the way the gene thing worked out—it took my parents meeting and there was a 25 percent chance that I would have muscular dystrophy, and my sister too. She does not have it either. So I think it was just meant to be.

My boys ... well, we've talked openly. But who's not embarrassed of their parents, right? I mean, that's just growing up. I think that happens for different reasons. Luke seems to be turning that corner. They've both always been very helpful to me when I need it or ask, but I never wanted it to be a burden for them. I really try to do my part just like any other mom would do. It just might take me longer, or I might do it a different way, but I try to keep my disability separate from being ... their mom, if that makes sense. Not that I'm not asking them to accept that part of me. But I think that's good that they see somebody that pushes through that. I think they certainly drive themselves in different ways to achieve higher goals. I'd like to think I played a little bit of a part in that by persevering through a daily struggle.

ME: *I bet you have, Amy. It's great you've had all this support, but we do know the world, like you mentioned earlier, has some bullies that probably need a little* *bit of a wake-up call. What would you love to tell the world to do when they encounter somebody with any kind of physical disability?*

AMY: Don't judge a book by its cover. If I pull up at a store or whatever, I do have a handicap tag because it's hard for me to walk distances. I can't tell you how many times I will pull into that space and be stared down by somebody that doesn't think that I should be parking there … even though I clearly have my tag displayed. They're just looking at me and I haven't gotten out of the car. And I guess they're looking at my age—I look younger—and I do have a scooter, but I often don't use a wheelchair or a scooter. But I get out of the car and start walking, and then my disability, as you know, you can visually tell that there's something wrong because I walk with a pretty significant limp.

I think I would rather someone just asked me, rather than judging me or just staring. And I don't fault people for that. I think a lot of times it'll happen with kids, too, like I'll hear, "Mommy, what's wrong with that lady?" I'm sure that we've all been there with our kids when they are little and they say things. It's okay to ask. I think most people would rather be asked.

Another thing is not to say, "What's wrong with you?" because nobody wants to hear that. There's really nothing "wrong." I'm not doing anything wrong. It's just that my muscles don't work. It's a pretty simple explanation: they don't work like most people's, and they are weak, and they cause difficulty walking. I think people are afraid sometimes of people that have disabilities because they're not familiar with it and they don't want to offend. Or they just don't have any experience with somebody with a disability, so they have these preconceived notions of what that looks like.

A lot of times people assume that with a physical disability comes a mental disability, and that's not always the case. Sometimes they go hand in hand and sometimes they don't. Unfortunately, there are a lot of people that don't accept people with disabilities or wouldn't be someone's friend that has a disability. That's just the truth. I know that. I've dealt with this my whole life, so I can tell when someone's not comfortable. I can immediately tell .... It's all in their demeanor toward me and the way that they talk to me. That's just something I just know about people. But that's not to say that I couldn't change their point of view or, personally speaking, I'm always open to talking about and educating others.

There are lots of types of disabilities. I can only speak from the one that I live with and the way that I choose to handle it. And for me, that's looked different throughout every stage of my life .... There was a time in my life where I wouldn't have even felt comfortable sitting here talking to someone saying "my disability." Those words probably wouldn't have come out of my mouth because it just was something that I hadn't fully accepted about myself.

ME: *You know, it's funny. All those years I watched little Luke ... I know when I worked with the other home day care person—I can't remember what she said—but she kind of set the stage for when I would meet you. I think she said something like, "She's got a limp," or something like that. I don't think I ever really asked you about it. I think I was just maybe nervous in the beginning, and then we kind of got to know each other and I didn't think about it anymore. [But] I never asked you.*

AMY: Well, like I said, I don't fault anyone for that. I just want people to know that I think a lot of people that live with a disability are okay with being asked. But I don't ever think badly of someone if they don't ask. A lot of people—that I got to know and that I'm friends with—tell me that they don't even notice that about me, which I struggle with a little bit. I've had several conversations with my family about it. They're like, "They mean it as a compliment—that's not what stands out about you to them."

ME: *That's exactly right.*

AMY: Yeah, and to me I feel it ... everything I do ... it's always there. So I think that it's hard for me to hear when people say that they don't even notice it about me, even though they're not saying that in an offensive way.

ME: *I think looking back for me ... my life at the time, I had two little boys— teeny boys—and I was run ragged. I probably just wasn't able to breathe and* *take the time to chat with you like this, and just kind of get to know what you're going through. So maybe others have that too. I don't know ... excuses ... but that might be what's happening with them too.*

AMY: I'm trying to remember ... I know when you started taking care of Luke at your house, I remember your front stairs would be a source of stress for me. But I feel like we worked together on that, but I don't remember exactly.

ME: I don't know either. They are bad.

AMY: They were just hard; I don't think there was a rail. I did work for First Steps. I did all those home visits, and there would be all those homes that didn't have railings and all those stairs. But I feel like you were very accommodating. I never felt in any way not accepted by you. I've had lots of friendships where we have been friends and we've never even had a conversation about my disability.

ME: I'm thinking about you conquering stairs and I can't help but bring this up—this treatment that you're getting. I thought that might be interesting to share a little bit about that, what's been happening with you.

AMY: For my type of muscular dystrophy—and most—there are no treatments and certainly no cures at this point, even though they're getting closer by the day, I think. I really do feel confident in that. So this has nothing to do with—I like to make that clear—it has nothing to do with MDA. I met this doctor on my own. I was seeing him for a completely different reason. I was having a different procedure done and he happened to say, "Do you have any medical conditions that I need to know about?"

I said, "Well, I live with muscular dystrophy."

He said, "Oh, I'm treating a young man with limb girdle muscular dystrophy right now, with stem cells."

So I'm thinking, *Well, let's just see.* I had never even heard of this. I always thought stem cells were very controversial, and I didn't know that you could get stem cells from your own body, which is what this treatment was. They take your fat and they're able to harvest stem cells from that.

ME: Wow, I didn't know that either.

AMY: Yeah, they inject them back into you. It was just weird because I was not there for anything to even do with my disability. So he gave me this book and said, "No pressure. Check it out, see what you think." It's all these stories about this treatment and people with all different kinds of [disabilities]. There was a chapter in there about a girl that had muscular dystrophy that this treatment had helped. So I reached out to her and she said that the treatment did help. She wasn't doing it currently because she had had a baby. I just kept researching it—Jamie and I both for a couple months—and then we went back and talked with this doctor about our questions. We finally just decided that it was low risk and we felt like it couldn't hurt to try it.

It certainly is not a cure. It's something that he thought, at the least, could maybe stop the progression of my disease. My disease is slowly progressive. I have gotten worse, as does aging coupled with a progressive disability. That's kind of a recipe for disaster and that's what was happening. I was struggling a lot and, in my mind, I was very near maybe using a wheelchair even in the house. That's how much I had just started to go downhill. We just felt like we didn't have a choice but to try this. To be honest, I did not run it by my neurologist because I knew he would tell me not to do it. I knew it was a risk that we were taking to throw away money because it was not guaranteed to work. [But] on December 8, 2020, I did this stem cell treatment and I've noticed lots of improvement. I don't use my walker that I was using every day. It sits and collects dust now!

ME: *Thank goodness!*

AMY: I know you've seen I can go upstairs a little bit easier. These things are still hard, but I don't even have that thought right now of if I need to get a wheelchair that works inside the house. That's not even on my mind anymore. So even just going from that ... it's not some big cure. I was told it wouldn't be. But we certainly have documented improvement and just my overall sense of not feeling like I'm drowning currently.

ME: *I'll tell readers right now—it's amazing. She'll post a video of how she used to do an activity and then she posts one after this stem cell treatment. It's weeks later and you can truly tell there is a difference. It's not huge, but it is a* *difference. You could tell that you're more fluid and it's a little easier. I cheer whenever I see one of those!*

AMY: Thank you. I do too. One day—I think it was a week or two after the treatment—I stood up off the couch and I just felt so much straighter. Then my parents saw me and they were just like, "Oh my gosh, that's just a huge visible difference!"

I know that that helps me to be able to stand better and just get around better ... just being more balanced. I try to take good care of myself and exercise in the way that I can. I eat healthy and do my part, which only helps the stem cells and their progression. I plan to do another treatment, hopefully in April. If you're gonna do it, and if you're noticing that it's helping you, you have to keep doing it. It's not something that you can only get done once. For some people, it might be, but for something like a genetic condition, I plan to keep doing it as long as we're financially able to. As long as I'm seeing progress. I'm looking forward to the next treatment to see if I get even more benefits. I'm honestly okay with the progress. If this is the new normal, that would be great.

ME: *Excellent! I'd love to share your blog with people.*

AMY: Yeah, that would be great.

ME: *Is there anything else you would advise people—whether it's somebody with a physical disability or to help those with disabilities? Any other resources you could recommend?*

AMY: I think it depends on what your disability is. I know that, for me, once I finally got diagnosed, I was able to connect largely on Facebook with a group of people that have my exact type of muscular dystrophy. I know those kinds of groups exist for all different kinds of disabilities. That whole making a connection with other people that have lived with the same struggles, I think there's no better way to learn than to connect with people like that.

You kind of help each other out and you can get ideas from somebody, then you're like, "Huh, maybe I could try that!" It's families that get involved because it's families that truly have an interest in helping and being part of this—helping to find a cure. So I would suggest just getting connected with somewhere that it feels like you're helping not just yourself but other people. And if you can do that as a family thing, that's even better. I guess my number-one answer would be connections. Just making sure you're connected with the right people.

I think oftentimes people get stuck. This is not anything against doctors—I've been helped by many doctors—but I think doctors are busy people and they don't often have time to connect on a personal level. When you are dealing with a disability, you're often in with doctors, and seeing doctors, and it can feel very disconnected and cold. You kind of feel like nobody cares.

That's the beauty in connecting with other people with the same struggles, [it's] that we have time to connect with each other and help each other. Just that feeling of being less alone when you're struggling—and that could go for anything—but a lot of times when you are living with a disability, it's hard to connect because there's not a lot of people just like you right around .... Social media and all that has been fantastic in that way. There's good and bad about it, but I talk to people all over the world that have had the same struggles, and that's just really neat, I think.

ME: I agree that is a very good thing about the internet and social media. Is there anything else you'd like to share today?

AMY: It's hard to kind of put out my forty-six years' worth of my story and to condense it down. Like everybody else, I'm on this journey. Mine just happens to include muscular dystrophy, and I'm embracing that and just living out God's plan for my life.

ME: Well, I am proud of you and so pleased to call you a friend.

*Amy and her husband Luke on some of their
duo bike adventures.*

Organizations mentioned during this interview:
- The Muscular Dystrophy Association (MDA): www.mda.org
- To learn more about Amy, please visit:
  - Instagram: @ashinneman
  - Blog: https://humblycourageous.blogspot.com

If I am wrong, educate me.
Don't belittle me.

—UNKNOWN

RIMA

I was so thrilled to work with this next lady. Rima is a powerhouse and a force for great change for thousands of women. I thoroughly enjoy talking to her about many topics. Getting to know her has been a joy, and I'm thankful she is a client!

> **NAME:** Rima (Arabic for "white antelope")
> **AGE:** 37
> **IDENTIFIES AS:** Female
> **ETHNICITY:** First-generation Asian or Pakistani
> **OCCUPATION:** Executive Director,
> Women4Change Indiana

RIMA: I was born here in Indianapolis at the Saint Vincent Hospital on Eighty-Sixth and Ditch. I grew up in Carmel, Indiana. My brother is two years younger than me, and my sister is three years younger than my brother. We're a family of five.

My father is a business owner. He started his business out of our garage on Cooper Street in Indianapolis the year I was born. So I kind of saw, from a child's perspective, how much he poured into his business. His business wouldn't be where it is today without my mother's support and without our larger family supporting him. I remember his first office building was down on Morris Street in

Indianapolis, and he and my mother used to stand outside and convert the parking lot so people could pay to park there when they were attending Colts games.

ME: Smart.

RIMA: Being there as a child was like, "Why do you have to spend Sunday standing here?"

ME: Yeah, not fun. May I ask what the business is?

RIMA: It is a textile business. He imports textiles from Pakistan—the majority of his textiles—but also from Bangladesh [and] Turkey. The reason why he wanted to start this business was, although he moved out of Pakistan, he wanted to do something that would invest in the country where he was born and help create jobs and give back to Pakistan. Although we're very proud Americans, my parents taught us how to speak Urdu. And so we would only speak Urdu in the house. They also taught us to be very proud of who we are.

ME: That is awesome! You led me to my next question. I was curious if you grew up bilingual?

RIMA: Yes, we grew up bilingual. It was very annoying when I was a child because they would not respond if we talked back in English. But they always instilled that we should be very proud of who we are, and that's something that I carry. I'm extremely proud of who I am as an American, as a Muslim, and then of Pakistani heritage. That's something now that I'm instilling in my children.

ME: Good for you! So you grew up in Carmel ... you didn't move anywhere else as you grew up?

RIMA: Nope, I grew up on 106th and Shelbourne, and then we had like a huge move where we moved like three miles down the road ... it was like a really big deal. [*Rima and I chuckled.*] I went to Carmel Schools throughout, and then I actually went to Cathedral High School and I graduated from Cathedral in 2002.

ME: Interesting .... What were some traditions when you were growing up? What were some unique things that you did as a family?

RIMA: So my parents, because of my father's business, he would often have suppliers that would come and stay in our home. I cannot really remember a time where it was just the five of us living in our house. There were always cousins in the house. There were other family members—aunts, uncles, suppliers … our door was always open. My parents had an open-door policy.

My cousins—quite a few of them went to Purdue—they would bring their friends home to celebrate the Muslim holidays with us. I remember [being] like, "Mom, why are you cooking so much?" She's like, "Because I don't know how many people are going to be here!"

So going to the mosque as a child, we would have to go to the mosque in Plainfield, but that was something very important to my parents, for us to go. When the mosque opened on Thirty-Eighth and Cold Spring, we started to go there. My mom, [when I was] growing up, was very heavily involved, as was my father. My father was actually the treasurer of the mosque for maybe fifteen to twenty years. My mom was the vice principal of the Sunday school for quite a few years. They always taught us to be engaged with community, and not just with our Muslim community. We would sometimes end up sitting in a synagogue, listening to the service, or going to church because there was some sort of service or something else happening. Volunteering at a food pantry … that was a big part of our house growing up.

ME: *I love that; that's so important. It's what I've tried to instill in my boys as well.*

RIMA: Yeah, that's huge.

ME: *But I have to ask … you went to Cathedral, which is a Catholic high school. What led you in that direction?*

RIMA: Interestingly enough, in Pakistan, and I believe in some parts of India, Catholic education is actually the best education. So Muslim families will seek out Catholic schools and send their children there. My parents, they're very big on religion, but that's not to say that they were closed minded at all. They thought, *It's a religious place,* and that's where they chose to send both my brother and me. My sister went to the International School because she's always been the smartest of the three of us. She speaks four languages.

ME: *Oh my gosh, your family's kind of brilliant!*

RIMA: Well, I'm the least smart out—

ME: *I think you have your own talents, from what I've gotten to see over the past few months.*

RIMA: Thank you.

ME: *That's so intriguing to me. I don't think I've had the experience and exposure you have, but I remember taking a class about different religions in college and it was so cool because I was like, "That's how that works; that's how this works." So I visited a couple of different places and kind of explored for a little bit in college. I loved that ... I think everybody should do that.*

RIMA: I remember there would be times when people would ask my mom, "She's going to be reading the Bible?" And my mom was like, "So what? That's another book from God." That's what we believe in our faith, that the Bible was sent from God, just like the Torah. She's like, "I don't understand the problem here." My mom was like that. She's a very direct, to-the-point kind of person. She actually encouraged us to read it and to understand other faiths. If anything, actually understanding other faiths makes you respect other people more, I believe. It also brought me closer to my own faith.

ME: *That's incredible. I like that. That's what this book is all about, Rima, it's about opening ... understanding. I love that we're starting off this way with this interview. It sounds like lots of family and some pretty cool times growing up. But I'm guessing that you might have had some struggles because of who you are ... maybe your last name ... anything that you are comfortable sharing? Any struggles you all faced growing up?*

RIMA: There are a few moments that really stand out. One in kindergarten. We used to visit Pakistan quite regularly. I remember in kindergarten I was *so* excited. I went and told my teacher that we're going to visit my family in Pakistan. The teacher thought this was a great teachable moment and so she shared with the kids, "Rima is going to be traveling, so she'll be leaving school a little bit early this year." And the kids were like, "Is [Pakistan] another planet? Where are you going? Are there aliens there?"

I just remember this sense of shame and I was like, *Maybe I'm doing something wrong. Maybe I'm not supposed to go there. Maybe it's not a good place to go.* Again, because of my parents, I was so proud to go and so excited because of all the love that was always showered on us when we went—from my family and my grandmother, who's now passed. As a kindergartner, that shame that I felt … I still remember that.

Then in seventh grade, I remember on … one of the Muslim holidays, some people in some cultures will put henna on. Now it's very cool—they call them henna tattoos—but at the time, not many people knew about it. I went to science lab and my science teacher yelled at me. He said, "What do you have on your hands?"

I was like, "No, this is henna."

He said, "No, that's the school policy, you're not supposed to draw on yourself."

I told him, "I didn't do this! First of all I'm not artistic; I can't even draw a stick figure (which still is true today) but I couldn't have done this."

He's like, "Well, you're not going to participate in science lab. You need to wash your hands."

He made me stand there, washing my hands over and over and over. By the seventh or eighth time, he was then convinced it was some sort of permanent tattoo and sent me over to the principal's office. He had no idea what henna was! Shame on him, because as a science teacher, you should know better. Part of me was mortified … imagine going through puberty, a seventh grader, being called out, standing at the station washing my hands seven, eight times. Then part of me was like, *I don't even like your class! I don't want to dissect this frog anyway …* *I'm out of here.*

Then, of course, when 9/11 happened I was a junior in high school. I was one of two Muslim students—the other Muslim student was my brother. It was just the two of us. I remember I was walking from one building to the other at Cathedral, and I looked up and the TV was playing. I thought there was a movie on—that's what I thought. I was wondering, *At 8 a.m., why are they playing a movie?* Then I soon realized—it kind of gives me the chills today—I soon realized it wasn't a movie. Before we understood what was happening, before the second attack on the Pentagon, people already had jumped to conclusions. "Do you know anybody that's behind it?" "Are you involved?" "Do you know anyone?"

ME: *They're asking you as a junior in high school?*

RIMA: Yes, asking me as a junior in high school.

ME: *Oh my God.*

RIMA: I tell you, it really brings out a lot of emotions. My first thought was, *I need to figure out where my brother is.* I've always been very maternal with my brother and sister. I didn't want kids asking my brother the same question.

ME: *Right.*

RIMA: At the time, the Father of the school, his name was Father Kelly—he's now passed—he came, and he said, "I think it would be best for you and Amar—that's my brother—to go home." And so Amar and I got into my car—my Jetta, which is my pride and joy—and we were on the highway ... and there are no cars on the highway. Then we were stopped by a policeman and he said, "What are you two doing out? There are not a lot of people out right now." And I said (and he could see we were both in uniform), "Well, our Father of the school—Father Kelly—asked us to go home."

Looking back as an adult, I understand why Father Kelly asked us to go home. It was to protect us. But at the time, it felt like he was singling us out.

Then the next few days after the horrific attacks ... questions ... "Are you related to Osama bin Laden?" "Are you his wife?" "Are you his daughter?" "Are you a part of this network?" The questions kept coming and coming. Then finally I went to the principal and I said, "I can't do this."

I have so much respect because he had a school-wide assembly in which he said, "If anybody has a question for Rima and Amar, ask it right now. If you have something to say, you come to me. If any single student is going to say anything like that to either one of them, you will be expelled from the school." And the questions stopped.

ME: *I was hoping, as you were talking, that something like that happened finally ... oh my gosh ....*

RIMA: I also remember—I think I was in third grade, because my brother was in first grade—my brother came home, he was so excited. He was like, "Look, Mom, I got an A on this quiz."

My mom said, "That's not your paper, that's Mark's."

He said, "No, my teacher said my name is too hard, so in school my name should be Mark, and at home it can be Amar."

My mom replied, "What did your teacher say?" I told you she's very frank and to the point. She called the school and she's like, "There's a reason why we named him ... this is his name. Do not ever get that twisted."

To this day, I sometimes joke with him and I'll be like, "Hey, Mark!"

ME: *That just seems crazy to me.*

RIMA: There are so many other things I could tell you right now. I remember every single year in Ramadan being told, "You can't eat or drink? But you're gonna die ... but you're gonna starve ... but what's gonna happen? You can't even have water?" To this day. "You can't even have water?" Nope. "Can you chew gum?" Nope. "Okay, here's a bag of chips, nobody's watching." I'm not doing it for people; I'm doing it for God. To this day, I remember my school nurse and counselor called me in middle school and they said, "Are you doing this because you're anorexic?" I'm like, "Wouldn't I be anorexic the other eleven months out of the year?"

ME: *Right! Exactly. Oh my heavens. You could probably do a book on yourself here.*

RIMA: Maybe ... yeah, I'm just not a very good writer.

ME: *Did things improve, like, a year or so later after 9/11?*

RIMA: In 2003, I actually moved overseas and I lived there for eleven years. I didn't come back until November 2014, I believe.

ME: *Okay. And then you met your husband?*

RIMA: I met my husband actually when I was at Cathedral—much to my parents' horror [he is six years older than me]. We actually got engaged when I was a junior and got married two years after.

ME: So you both went overseas?

RIMA: Yes.

ME: Okay … and where did you live when you went overseas?

RIMA: For one year I lived in Pakistan, and then for eleven years I lived in Bahrain. I had no family in Bahrain, no ties to Bahrain. I had never heard of it before I found out I was moving there. We ended up spending eleven years there and actually lived through the Arab Spring.

ME: Oh my gosh! I love that you got to go to your country of origin and then explore another place for a while. I'm guessing this was because of jobs that you moved?

RIMA: My husband's father was actually a three-star general in the Pakistan army, so we lived with him. He was the senior-most general on the Pakistan-India border, so I lived in what is called the Flagstaff House for eight months, which was an experience in itself.

ME: What is that? I've never heard of it.

RIMA: So there were two boundary walls to the house. There were like approximately 150 staff members for that one house.

ME: Wow!

RIMA: We would travel with military police … it was a whole new world to this girl from Carmel!

ME: Yeah, I would say so! So were your children all born there?

RIMA: My daughter was born in Pakistan, which is another whole story in itself, and then my son was born in Bahrain, which is also quite the story. Then my [second] daughter was born in Noblesville, Indiana.

ME: Okay. What brought you back to the States?

RIMA: It's always been home; my parents live here. But eleven years ago, there's a company that came out with a bad batch of contact lens solution. So in the solution, there was a bacteria that's called *Pseudomonas*, and it ate through my left cornea. I think like, six, seven years ago, I had a full corneal transplant that failed. So I'm actually completely blind in my left eye.

ME: *Oh my gosh. I'm terribly sorry to hear that.*

RIMA: It's okay. I always tell people two eyes are overrated, and I call myself "Cyclops," lovingly.

ME: *Well, you would never know.*

RIMA: I'm very, very lucky …. It's still annoying and frustrating. The desert wasn't the best place for care. My doctor is here in Indianapolis, so just after that transplant failed, we had to make that decision of moving back home.

ME: *That's something about yourself that people might want to hear a little bit more about. What sorts of things do you have to do that others don't with full eyesight?*

RIMA: So what happens is I actually have the herpes simplex virus in my left eye—that'll flare up. This side of my face will sometimes flare up, and it's significantly swollen. You can see they look completely different, the two sides of my face. Or I'll feel a lot of pressure. My eye sometimes spasms. It's a little awkward in public because I'll start going like this ….

ME: *Readers can't see it, but it looks like she's winking.*

RIMA: There are a lot of things I can't do, so many things that a lot of people do that I found out later that I just can't do anymore.

ME: *How's driving for you?*

RIMA: It's fun because sometimes people will be like, "Are you blind?" I'm like, "Yes. Do you feel bad now?"

ME: *Right, got you!*

RIMA: When we first met, I told you I just resort to humor because I think in every situation, you can either feel bad or you can just laugh about it. There are certain times where that won't work—it doesn't always work in every situation—but in situations where it can work, I like to just laugh about it rather than cry about it.

I did feel very sorry for myself. I got sick for quite some time, and then I figured out that it's not gonna do me any good and I'm going to have to pick up the pieces. My youngest was five months old at the time, my son had just turned two, and my eldest was five. I knew that they needed me, and I [couldn't] really sit and feel sorry for myself much longer. So I had to learn how to open my eye again, and I had to learn how to drive and do all these things again.

When I had my surgery, I had thirty-two stitches in my eye, so it took a very long period for those to be removed. But it was like baby steps and now, for the most part, I'm okay. I'll get headaches if I'm looking at my screen, which I am all day. I'll have pressure; it'll swell up sometimes. It'll be like [four times] the size of the other one. I'll have some people say, "Oh my gosh, what's wrong with your face?"

ME: That was my next question, because you mentioned sometimes it swells up on that side, and I bet people think that you got injured or something.

RIMA: I've had a few times people say, "You're so brave to go out in public looking like that." Well, I gotta do what I gotta do, right?

ME: Wow. Well ... so you came back in 2014? You said your son was born in Noblesville. Did you live in Noblesville for a bit?

RIMA: My youngest, my daughter, she was born in Noblesville. My husband went in September 2008 to INSEAD—he did his MBA there, in France. So I moved back home with my parents for a year and we actually scheduled my daughter's birth around his spring break. So I was joking with the doctor and I was like, "Usually people go to Cancún for spring break; we are giving birth, right!"

ME: That must have been tough.

RIMA: It was.

ME: Here you have little ones and your husband's far away for a year.

RIMA: Yeah, it was hard. But it was a year-long MBA program and we got through it.

ME: And now you live back in Carmel?

RIMA: Yep, right back home. I'm actually ... [almost] quite literally where I grew up.

ME: Okay. So I'm looking at your last name ... your husband is also Muslim?

RIMA: Yes, he is Pakistani and he is, as of this summer, now naturalized and an American!

ME: Oh, wonderful! Very exciting. So ... you've got this wonderful family. I hope I get to see them someday.

RIMA: Yes, that would be nice.

ME: *Have you faced some struggles, as a family, from society?*

RIMA: For sure. My daughter, my eldest, the day after the 2016 election—and I'm not making this political in any way, this is just what happened to my family—the day after the election in 2016, she got pulled out of class in her first period by an adult who did not introduce themselves with their job, just by their name. They said that they needed to ask her some questions. This adult asked her a series of questions, which included: Where were you born? Do you speak English? Do you speak any other languages? What other states have you lived in? And then proceeded to send her back to first period. Kids can be mean and kids were saying, "Well, you're going to be deported." And she was texting me and saying, "Mom, I don't know what's happening … please find out what's happening." I kept calling the school, and I was told that the principal and vice principal were in closed-door meetings. The vice principal called me back about 4:30 p.m. As we know, children are usually home by then. He asked me what happened. I told him what happened and he said, "Well, have you talked to your daughter about honesty?" That was his first question. And I did, because adults can exaggerate, and children can exaggerate—okay, it's true.

ME: *Right.*

RIMA: I said, "Yes."

And he said, "Are you sure what you're telling me is the truth?"

It was the second question he asked me and I said, "Yes."

He said, "Well, if you're sure, then we will pull out the tapes from the hallway because there are cameras in the school."

ME: *Fantastic.*

RIMA: They pulled out the cameras and, lo and behold, there was an adult that pulled my daughter out of class and asked her questions. They can see that on camera for five minutes. When they figured out who this adult is—the vice principal never called me back—that adult called me back. She was an English as a second language teacher … except my daughter is a born American.

ME: *Right.*

RIMA: So that assumption was made ... assumptions ....

ME: Yep.

RIMA: And my daughter was in honors English, so [this teacher] didn't even look at the classes she was taking. I kept asking this woman, "Why did you call her out of class? Why wouldn't you look at her class schedule? Why wouldn't you call her parents?" I kept pushing and kept pushing and kept pushing.

Finally she said, "Yes, it's because your daughter's brown." Then she told me, "But Mrs. [last name omitted], I understand. We come from a biracial family! My husband is Italian American and I'm Irish American."

ME: Uh ... no!

RIMA: I then—because I remembered my time at Cathedral—I went to the vice principal and I said, "Listen, this is what I do for a living. I'm the executive director of the Muslim Alliance of Indiana." I was then serving as the executive director. "I'd love to talk to your staff or your students or anyone else about Islamophobia, about understanding your Muslim students—your Muslim classmates."

And he said, "No, no, no, we've got it covered. I'm Black, and our custodian is Black, and our Spanish teacher is Latina."

ME: Oh God.

RIMA: I said, "I'm not gonna charge you. I would do this just because it's so important."

And he said, "No, we're good. Thank you very much."

ME: That's sad.

RIMA: Yeah. I mean, I've had moments. My son's name is Arabic for Moses. He once asked me, very soon after he moved back, he's like, "Can I put 'Bill' on my club jersey?"

And I was like, "Clinton? Are you getting foundation money? Where is this coming from?"

He said, "No. There's some kids that say they can't be friends with me because I'm Muslim."

ME: Oh, that's sad.

RIMA: It just takes me back to when I was in school, and things haven't changed. If anything, I think they've gotten worse.

ME: Patricia told me that you have gotten death threats?

RIMA: I have. I made it to Breitbart [an ultra-conservative news website]—it was one of my shining moments! I received death threats. This is true. I believe it was the summer of 2017. There was a billboard on 465, on the east side. It had some very absurd and problematic things written about the Prophet Muhammad. I was then, of course, serving as executive director of the Muslim Alliance. I knew that I could either get ahead of the story or play defense. I don't like to play defense! So I got ahead of the story. I was the one that alerted the media and what I asked is that, whoever's responsible for putting this billboard up has spent a great deal of resources—money and other things—to put this up. All I want to do is sit down and have coffee with them, and understand why they would spend so many resources spreading hate. And that spiraled. I had to change my name on Facebook because I cannot tell you the number of people that were sending me death threats.

ME: Oh my gosh.

RIMA: Somehow, somebody got my cell phone number. I received a few death threats over the phone. Somebody said, "We know where you live." But again, I didn't say anything bad. I didn't say anything mean. I actually acted the way that my prophet would have. I just wanted to understand …. It received national media attention, NBC nationally, a few other publications, and, as I shared, Breitbart. People were mad. I had people from Wyoming and Texas … I had a few people that were sending me death threats. The picture that they had as their profile picture was people in uniform. Now, of course, they could have taken those. They could have been stock images; those could have been stolen images. I completely recognized that. But that didn't make me afraid. I was never afraid, because my mother and my religion always teach me that those that stand with the truth should not be afraid. But I was deeply disappointed as an American.

ME: I don't blame you one bit. You weren't nervous having little kids hearing all that and people saying, "I know where you live"?

RIMA: I was actually down at Monument Circle once, and I was speaking, and somebody started screaming. I would often take my children—my parents used to take us when we were little wherever they went, so I would often take them. I was speaking and someone from the back started screaming, "Why can't we gang rape and behead her like they would do to her in her country?" Except *this* is my country.

ME: Holy hell!

RIMA: As of recently, in the fall of 2019, I was driving ... it was 7 a.m. I was going down to the WIBC studio to do an interview, and I was sitting in my car. Someone spit on my windshield on Monument Circle ... spit on my windshield and called me the "B" word and said, "You don't belong here! Go the 'F' home!"

ME: Dear God.

RIMA: I was like, "Okay ... well I'll just get right back on 465 and go home." Like, what do you do? I am home.

ME: Your attitude is terrific. I mean, wow. You can just tell that you've got this strength and peace within you. You're not going to give up at all and you're going to keep fighting. If people dig into Women4Change, they'll see what the organization stands for. So what have you learned through all of these struggles?

RIMA: People fear what they don't understand, and people refuse to understand what they fear.

ME: That's sad.

RIMA: I went to the region—Gary, as we Hoosiers call it—and I was doing a talk there with the ACLU of Indiana. And I had four students that were yelling at me, heckling, saying really mean things. Saying, "How do you sleep with blood on your hands?"

And, as you know, I joke. I said, "I actually sleep with Bath & Body Works lotion on my hands." I was really trying to ease up the tension in the room.

As such, we had to have security come and walk us to our cars. And one of the students, finally, he asked me, "You know we've been saying all these things to you and you haven't given up."

I said, "No, because you know why? My prophet. He used to take this route every day. And every day, this woman would throw garbage on him. And then one day, she didn't throw garbage. He went to her neighbor and asked, 'Where is that woman that would throw garbage?' And they said, 'She's sick.' And he went to her and said, 'I hope you get well soon. I'm sorry that you're not feeling well.'

"[So] your yelling at me? It's noise in the back. It doesn't bother me."

ME: Good for you. All right ... so we've heard some pretty eye-opening stories to say the least. What would you want the world to do differently?

RIMA: Understand one another. Don't understand people at the people level. Understand that we are all different, but there are common threads that unite us all. Whether that's religious difference, whether that's political difference, whether that's ideology, there are always common threads. When we can understand one another, we can be happier with who we are; we can feel more confident in who we are. We also don't have to live in fear and hate.

I'd rather you yell at me to give me a chance to answer back than you go home and say, "There's that person there ... I wish I would have said that to them. I wish I would have known about this." Ask me whatever you want. There's nothing that's going to offend me—except for if you ask me about my weight. I'm just working on that piece.

Ask me anything you want but don't let that moment go. You have a question on your mind? Ask me, fact-check me, don't let that moment go. If I have a question, I'll ask you.

ME: Right! Well, I know Women4Change does a lot to open up doors and build these bridges, but are there any national organizations you might recommend that people can be a part of or support that help spread this message? Are there any organizations that help kind of dispel all these myths about Muslims?

RIMA: I would say the Islamic Society of North America. It's actually headquartered here in Plainfield. If you don't live here in Indiana, go to your local mosque. Don't rely on the national organizations, go to your local mosque. It might be five minutes away from where you live, ten minutes away from where you live. Go and participate in Iftar, when we break our fast during the month of Ramadan. People will be open, and they will be fasting, but they will make sure you have a plate—and that's good food! Even if you go for the food, go there! What brings us closer than breaking bread together? Go to your local mosque. You will be welcomed, I can assure you.

ME: *I've never done that.*

RIMA: You should do it! At my mosque, when people come there, it's like royalty! We really appreciate it. We will teach you how we pray, we will have you sit with us, we will make you a plate and tell you which foods are maybe not good this week! [Due to COVID], when we're able to and when it's safe, I'd really recommend people doing that. You'll have a deeper understanding because those will be your neighbors in your community that are there. And who knows, you may run into them at the grocery store, at the bank, and that's something you'll always carry with you.

ME: *It sounds really fun!*

RIMA: It is. I would really recommend going to a Friday prayer, go during the month of Ramadan, and experience that firsthand.

[*Rima and I had to cut our interview short, so we continued on another night.*]

ME: *I have to tell you, you inspired me. I looked up Ramadan and I thought about the sacrifices you all make. Then I was thinking about [my] own—in Christianity—season of Lent, right? And I thought,* Geez, we don't give up anything. *I mean, we do ... but it's nothing like what you all do. I think I want to do more this year, so I'm pondering. Ours starts this Wednesday. You've inspired me. I'm gonna do a little more.*

RIMA: Oh, that's so nice! You have fish on Fridays. I remember walking into the Cathedral cafeteria every Friday. I'm like, "We have fish again!" I never understood that. I think, again, it's not just about abstaining from food and drink, but let me tell you, when you're on hour eight, nine, ten, eleven, twelve ... the only thing that I think would have any person give up all of that and wait that long is God. And with every trial that God gives us, He also knows that we're able to get through it. I don't think that there would ever be a time where, you know, somebody's life would be in danger. There are different aspects to it, but I have to tell you, my productivity is actually at an all-time high in Ramadan!

ME: *Interesting.*

RIMA: When you're stripped of everything—you know, let me grab the snack, let me munch on this, it's lunchtime, let me grab a cup of coffee—when you're stripped of all of that, I find my mind actually focuses better.

ME: *That's what I hear about people who intermittent fast. I do it but it's [16/8] and that's a baby fast. So all I do is I stop eating at six and I don't eat until ten the next morning. So I don't do what a lot of people do, which is fast for twenty-four hours, but people who do that say, "Yes, I am focused. I am razor sharp. I get so much done."*

RIMA: Interesting.

ME: *Well, you have inspired me. I'm really glad you want to do this because once I went through the initial transcript, I did have more questions. I want to go back a little bit in your story. I'm curious, you said that the birth of two of your children were stories in themselves. Does that relate to the issues we cover in this book?*

RIMA: My son, as you know, he was my middle child, so I had the experience of [already] having gone through childbirth with my daughter. At the time, it was uncommon [in Bahrain] for some women to receive an epidural. So my doctor, who is not Bahraini and not Muslim, advised me that she felt that the doctors that would administer the epidural did not have a lot of practice doing so. She said, "You can't afford to do that, so you're going to have this baby naturally, without any epidural."

It was an experience, but I got through it. After he was born, of course we wanted to name our baby. So his father's name is Sayyid. Sayyid is the family whose lineage gets traced back to the Prophet Muhammad. My father-in-law, mother-in-law are both saying my husband's name is Sayyid Muhammad Muneeb .... We wanted to name our baby Muhammad, just like the tradition of their family. [Musa, or Moses, lived a life parallel to Muhammad, so Rima named her son

Musa Shahid.] So you have to go to the ministry and get the name approved. Once the name is approved by the ministry, then you go back to the hospital and you register the baby's name in the hospital. That's the process. After you do that, then you can, based on both of these board certificates, apply for his US passport. We went to the ministry and they said, "Sorry, you can't name your baby that."

ME: What?

RIMA: Yeah, and we were like, "Okay, this is interesting ... why?"

And they said, "Well, his name is too close to his father's."

ME: Oh my gosh. What did you do?

RIMA: So then we went back, and we asked when the person that oversaw that particular branch will be back so we can petition and ask for us to name our baby this. So we went back a second time and it was denied. Then we actually had to petition all the way to the minister to have his name approved. So much time had lapsed during that process. So in the hospital, my husband and I ... my blood type is negative and his is positive, so my children have to stay in the hospital because of jaundice. My son was in the hospital for nine days. And the entire nine days, we called him "Musa," but the hospital staff just referred to him as "Baby Boy" because the name was not approved.

ME: So how long did it take for him to be named?

RIMA: About a week.

ME: Yeah, that is crazy. So a lot of readers may not know what the "Arab Spring" is that you mentioned. Would you mind explaining that and your experience with it while you were living over there?

RIMA: So the Arab Spring started out of North Africa with a call for a change in power. You saw that across different North African countries. When I was living in Bahrain, or what people refer to as MENA—Middle East North Africa—so across different MENA nations, you saw the Arab Spring happening; in Tunisia, in Egypt, and in a few other places.

Bahrain is a little island. It's kind of between Saudi and Iran, two adversaries. Now what's interesting is that Bahrain, their monarchy is Sunni Muslim, the royal family is Sunni Muslim. But the majority of

Bahrainis—around 70 percent of the Bahraini population—is Shia. And here's the problematic part: Bahraini law forbids—or at that time, I'm not current with current Bahraini law—but at the time, they, Shias, were prohibited from serving in the police and armed service. So they would import people from the Sunni majority countries that made up their police and their military. What are these Sunni majority countries? Pakistan, Yemen, Jordan are the top three that they imported people from.

The Arab Spring first started in Bahrain [in] a very famous place that's no longer there. It's called Pearl Roundabout. Bahrain is known for its pearls, and people kind of set up camp there. Everything seemed to be fine, there were different things that they were asking for, but that situation quickly turned violent. I found myself in a situation where I was going to work—I was working at the Pakistan Embassy—but the embassy was now a target. So that was really problematic. There were a few incidents that happened. The government asked for a crane operator—someone, a company—to physically tear down that Pearl Roundabout. That poor man that was operating the crane, he was Pakistani, as a lot of the labor class was from Pakistan, Bangladesh, India, and the Philippines. I think he operated it wrong. So that entire thing [roundabout] fell on the crane and crushed him to death.

ME: *Oh God.*

RIMA: There's another incident of a man that was performing the call to prayer—the Adhan—and he was in his early twenties. He was the sole breadwinner for his family and would send money every month back home to his family in Pakistan. An angry mob took him out and cut off his ears and his tongue.

Our embassy was made in a Moghul style. So if you can imagine, there was a building that was kind of in almost a U shape. In the middle, there was an open courtyard. My office was on the second floor, as were many of the offices. You could hear this like very animalistic sound; it's a noise that you would never forget. I opened my office, and I looked, and there was a woman on her knees screaming and crying. What happened was her son, who was eleven years old, was playing soccer, and the children that he was playing soccer with beat him to death because he was Pakistani. Arranging for the body of an eleven-year-old to go back because of his origin ... his heritage ... it was a fear. It always brings tears to my eyes. It was a very difficult time. A very, very difficult time.

We evacuated out of Bahrain and we went to the closest country to us—to Pakistan—during the entire Arab Spring. That was Bahrain's version of the Arab Spring. I think less than eleven people died [that day].

By the time we landed in Karachi, there were more than fifty people that died [in Bahrain]. So it was still a very, very difficult time. Especially going in as an American and not understanding Bahraini law, and then working at the embassy and suddenly having Molotov cocktails being thrown at my window ... not because it was my window but it was the window that was facing the street.

My son had a very good friend—he was three or four at the time—and my son's friend, his mother was praying and she asked his older siblings to watch him. But the little boy kind of wandered off into the yard and his ball fell in his swimming pool. So those days, I remember, were very windy. They had a fence around the pool, but one of the pieces was loose. That little boy managed to get in and drowned. The mother couldn't make it to the hospital because of demonstrations and tires that were being burned in the street.

I remember so many times driving, and we would have to reroute ourselves or we would have to wait in the car because there would be eight, nine, ten, twelve tires that were being set ablaze at any time. And what do you do? You just sit there in this thick, rubbery, smoky fog. It was a very difficult time. And I talk about this time a lot because that is what happens when you do not have a government for the people, by the people.

Our democracy, as fragile as it is, we have to stay engaged. I have seen on the flip end what happens. Our democracy is not something that we can take for granted because trying to arrange funerals for children ... going to visit a man in his early twenties that's in a vegetative state ... is not something anybody should do ever. So when people say things like, "I don't like to vote because I'm not political," it's upsetting. It's upsetting. I'm not suggesting people run for office that don't want to, but your basic duty as an American is to cast that ballot. To make sure that that fragile democracy does not break because it is, it is fragile.

ME: *Yeah, it is. Oh, Rima, you're in the right place with what you do now.*

RIMA: Yeah, most definitely. It honestly always brings tears to my eyes because that mother ... and the way she was screaming ... and the way she was ripping her hair and crying ....

ME: *Yeah ... you were a mom at the time. I know ever since I've become a mom, I have just ... I'm surprised I'm not sobbing right now. But stories like that, I could not listen to. I just could not. It changes you. It's hard to hear before you're a mom, but then when you are a mom ... oh, Rima.*

[*At this point, we both had to pause.*]

How long were you there—how many months? Were you there during all that time?

RIMA: We were there [in Bahrain] for the entire time except for maybe a week, ten days, but we were there the whole time.

ME: *Wow.*

RIMA: There was actually at one time—again, I'm sharing this with you from the perspective of what I saw and what my family went through and what relates to my job as well .... There was one time when the protesters had suggested that when you go out to protest, have the children stand at the front of the line, because there's no way they're going to open fire on children. And according to the Muslim faith, when we bury our dead, we actually bury them in unstitched white cloth. So think of like, six, seven yards of unstitched white cotton. But they had told parents when you send your children at the front of that line, when you send your children to set fire to those tires, put a white cloth on them when you send them out the door. And we saw it. We were driving and on the other side of the highway. There was a massive amount of people—it brings chills to me—with four to six rows of children wearing that white cloth.

ME: *We do not know how good we have it here. We don't. Oh my gosh, Rima.*

RIMA: I will also say—this has nothing to do with the Arab Spring, or with the problematic laws, or with the conditions that the laborers find themselves in. But according to Bahraini law, every single Bahraini is eligible for a home. They are eligible for a certain number of Bahraini *dinars* [currency]. Their education, through college, is free if they go through public education. They also receive cash when they get married and all of their utilities are subsidized.

ME: *Really?*

RIMA: Yeah.

ME: *It kind of sounds similar, I think, to Denmark. Kind of.*

RIMA: Kind of, yeah, and gas is actually cheaper in Bahrain than water.

ME: *You're kidding! Well, thank you for sharing all that. I read about it online but to get your perspective, somebody who lived it … wow … On a lighter note, tell me about the Muslim Alliance of Indiana.*

RIMA: So the first mosque in Indiana was actually in the northeast part of our state and it was built around 1924 by Lebanese immigrants. It was a Shia mosque. Coincidentally, per capita, the number of Muslims—we're like, I think, in the top five states, again, per capita—Muslims represent about less than 1 percent of the US population.

There is a false narrative that we are coming in hoards and taking over and trying to implement our Sharia law. It's not true whatsoever. But a Pew research study showed that the majority of Americans had an unfavorable image of Islam and Muslims. But the majority of Americans that they had surveyed did not know a single Muslim.[7] Now if you look at me, and if you were to meet me, I could be many things. I could be Hindu, I could be Sikh, I could be agnostic, I could be many things because I don't wear a hijab or head covering. But once those same Americans actually met a Muslim, their image of Islam and Muslims changed and they had a favorable image.

People have a fear of the unknown, that's just how it is. We take what we see on television, whether that is the news or the horrid job that Hollywood has done portraying us, and take that to be how they would view their Hoosier, Muslim neighbor … there's a lot of misinformation as well. Although [the internet] is your friend, we all subscribe to the news we want to receive. So my job was to go through all ninety-two counties—to your Rotary Club and Key Club and schools and churches and worship centers—and talk about Islam and Islamophobia. To help answer questions that are on people's minds. I always told people that there was not a single question that would offend me. Ask. Because what I didn't want is for people to leave there and say, "You know what, I wish I asked this," or "I don't believe her when she said this."

I also conducted cultural taboo workshops as it relates with domestic violence. Like, how do you approach certain situations? What would be the cultural thing to do? Not just for Muslims but for other minorities. This was a workshop that we conducted across the state. Then a big part of my job was also to help with interfaith relationships and building bridges, having different government agencies understand Muslims and their needs. Because we're not a homogenous community either, by any means.

There have been many women that were the executive director of the Muslim Alliance of Indiana, but that was the most natural thing because our prophet, his wife was his boss. That's right. She was a leader, she was a thought leader, she was a community leader. She was also an entrepreneur and a very wealthy woman. So having a woman lead that, it's a very natural thing to happen. But I was asked that question, "So as a woman, how can you do this job?"

And I said, "It would actually be very unusual for a man to hold this job."

ME: *Right. Oh, I love that. I bet you enjoyed it.*

RIMA: I really did. My religion … talking about my faith always brings a spark of joy and you can see my eyes light up. I deeply, deeply love Islam. I love my faith and I love everything that it stands for. My mentor passed away in October, but I would tell her often that every time I open the door for somebody, I wish I could tell them, "I'm Muslim. Why do you hate us?"

She said, "Rima, that might be a very odd thing to do. You don't need to do that."

Right? Awkward. It might be unusual, but I'm very proud of my faith and who I am. That's all thanks to my parents.

ME: So was it hard for you to leave that job when the Women4Change opportunity came up?

RIMA: No. I spoke at the first women's march here in Indianapolis. I was the only woman Muslim speaker at the event, and I remember very well standing out and looking at the crowd and thinking, *I'm only here advocating for this small group of people.* Not because Muslims didn't come; because there are just not that many of us. With my current position, I get to advocate for Muslim women and men and families, but I also get to advocate for so many others while continuing our—my—faith tradition of women leading. I get to talk about my faith all the time, so this is kind of the best of both worlds for me.

ME: Was that the mission of the Muslim Alliance of Indiana, to grow understanding throughout the whole state?

RIMA: Grow understanding, grow civic engagement, build bridges and understanding. We hosted every year, on Iftar, the governor in Ramadan. And that's a tradition that we continue. We had Muslim Day at the Statehouse so there was that understanding, the civic engagement. There were the workshops around cultural taboos, as it relates with domestic violence, and then interfaith work.

ME: Did you work with our governor [Eric Holcomb]?

RIMA: We did. He spoke at Muslim Day at the Statehouse a few times. He hosted Iftar at the Governor's Residence, and we broke bread with him there. He actually quoted Hadith at the prayer breakfast that we would have. During the 2016 campaign, he had a very short window of time, of course. I sent two texts asking for a roundtable with the Muslim community. And he said yes.

We met with him—a number of us—and we took photos, and they posted those photos on social media. You should have seen the comments. "I'm no longer voting for you." "I just took your yard sign off." "Why would you be with those people?" So I called his campaign and I said, "Listen, we appreciate his time, we appreciate all that he's given us, our intention was not to hurt his chances. Take the post down."

We appreciated it, but I didn't want it to be the reason why people were doing that to him and he was coming under attack. I received a call later and they said, "Those people don't want to vote for us because we took pictures with you and we stood with you. We didn't want their vote anyway. The pictures stay."

ME: Oh, I love that!

RIMA: So I have to give credit where it's due.

ME: Yeah, absolutely …. Well, I wanted to make certain to give you some time to talk about anything we might have forgotten the other day or didn't have time for. Anything else you'd like to share?

RIMA: I think within the Muslim community—within the community of folks that are of Pakistani heritage—what I shared with you is my experience and my story. Certainly I would say that no person can be a spokesperson for so many people. I think that's really important. I think that we look at people and we say, "Well, that person is this"—especially as it relates with minorities—"I have this one friend that's this and they're all like that." We're not. You will find good people and bad people. You'll find friendly people and introverts and everything in between. We're no different than anybody else. I would just remind people that when it relates to anybody, these broad strokes and things that we have … it's very troublesome language.

ME: Yes, I want to emphasize—that these are sixteen glimpses. Sixteen stories. It's not the end-all, be-all. This is not, "All right, this is it on the Muslims, you know. I've covered it all." Not at all. But it's more like just a glimpse, and I hope a spark, for people to be like, "Well, I want to learn more."

RIMA: Exactly. And I'll stress that I would also say the question, "Where are you from?" is one that many of us have heard so many times. I think a better way to phrase that is, "What brings you to Indianapolis or Denver or San Francisco?" It can be something like, "I was born here," or it could be, "I moved here because of a job," "I immigrated" … there's so many different ways. But the question, "Where are you from?" When I tell people I'm from Indianapolis, nine times out of ten the follow-up is, "No, really, where are you from?" So I'll say, "Okay, well, Eighty-Sixth and Ditch ... from Saint Vincent ... like, I don't know the room number I was born." But that question is very troublesome. I would encourage people to maybe think about, if you want to understand somebody's past and their history and more about them, there are different ways to ask that.

ME: *You raise beautiful points. This has been great.*

RIMA: Thank you for this opportunity!

Organizations mentioned during this interview:
- The Muslim Alliance of Indiana: www.indianamuslims.org
- The Islamic Society of North America: www.isna.net

Imperfect = I'm perfect. You're human. You're gonna screw up. Other humans are gonna screw up. Let it go.

–JEN SINCERO

JEFF

o you have some individuals you knew when you were a teen who, when you look back on those days, just make you smile with warm memories? Jeff is one of those people in my life. His kindness, intelligence, humor, and love for humanity have always inspired me. I was thrilled to reconnect with him on social media years ago and even more so to get to speak with him for this book.

> **NAME:** Jeff
> **AGE:** 51
> **IDENTIFIES AS:** Male
> **ETHNICITY:** Italian American (with a little Belgian)
> **OCCUPATION:** ICU Nurse

ME: Well, I first want to hear about you and your family growing up. I have no idea if you were in Mishawaka the whole time before you went to college or what. So give us the scoop!

JEFF: I was born and raised in Mishawaka. We moved into the house that I grew up in when I was three. It's interesting—it helps me date my memories. I have one memory, a random one from our first house, and that's it. I grew up probably a very typical kid in Mishawaka, as you know, public schools the whole way.

ME: Remind me, how many siblings do you have?

JEFF: I am the youngest of four, so my oldest is my sister and then two brothers and then me. So I was in Mishawaka, as you know, all through high school, then went [to college] with Dave [a mutual friend], who was interested in Northwestern's journalism school. I always assumed I would go to Purdue, which is where my brothers went. My sister went to Saint Mary's. I really loved Northwestern and my parents were sort of like, "Well, that's great, but don't get your heart set on it. It's an expensive school." I applied and was pleasantly surprised that I got in. Luckily, between grants and the fact that I was the last kid, my parents had a little more financial flexibility. I was able to go to Northwestern, where I met my closest friend for the last, gosh, thirty-five years or so. I like Northwestern. I think if I had to do it all over again [but still] know her [my closest friend], I think I would have liked a smaller school that was more focused on their undergraduates. The chemistry program at Northwestern was a little harsh. I was a little bit of an easily intimidated kid from the Midwest ....

ME: Did you and your family have some good traditions growing up?

JEFF: We did. The Italian American traditions probably dominated. [My family and I] were talking about this when I was home: food's a big part of our family life. Even my Belgian grandmother, who was a very good cook of some traditional Belgian foods, learned to cook Italian foods and cook great food. The region that my grandparents come from in Italy is called Emilia-Romagna. There's a lot of traditional soups, a lot of sort of meaty sauces, still a lot of tomato based. I think, as you get further north in Italy, it's a little more cream-based sauces. But at any rate, a lot of traditional soups. Food was a big tradition for us in a very Catholic family. Maybe more in kind of just a mechanistic way. When I was young, we went to Mass every Sunday. I went to catechism and everything. As my parents got older, they, my mom especially, became a lot more religious. Definitely Catholicism was kind of hand in hand with our traditions.

I don't identify as Catholic anymore. I haven't been back for a long time. I went to St. Bavo's [Church] for all of my youth pretty much. I'm trying to think, Amy, if we had any other traditions. We didn't have an annual vacation spot or anything. As I got older and left the house, my family has rented a cabin or cottage. It's funny, if you say "cottage" out here in Seattle, people think it sounds quaint. People don't call them cottages. But a cottage on a lake either in Indiana or Michigan, as we've moved around over the years. So that's been kind of an annual tradition for us as adults and for this next generation of kids.

ME: *Oh, that sounds fun.*

JEFF: Yeah, it is! My boys have a blast.

ME: *So now I have to ask the question that I wanted to ask you before I ever started this book. I want to know when it first hit you that you were like, "Hey, I'm gay."*

JEFF: As you can imagine, it's a little bit of a complicated question because, at a young age, especially when we were growing up, there wasn't a real conception of what it was to be gay. So I remember traveling with my family on a trip cross-country when I was eight or nine, and we would stay in these motels. It's so funny because, to save money, my parents would go in alone or maybe with one kid because they would charge more if you had more kids.

We would stay in the car and then we would go up to the room and sleep on the floor. I remember one night we had been out by a pool and there was like a hot tub or just a separate little pool next to the pool. My family made their way back to the hotel room. This was in the days where you didn't really worry so much about your kids. I hung out with another kid who was my age there.

I just remember having that first glimmer of feeling—I'm gonna put an adult word on it—*attracted* to him. There was plenty of time later where I struggled with the rightness or wrongness of it. But at that point just knowing that maybe—I think, some dawning awareness—that maybe this wasn't what most boys felt or were supposed to feel. Or what I was *told* I was supposed to feel. But I just knew that I didn't want to leave and I wanted to hang out with him. It felt different than wanting just another friend. So I would say that's my first memory of sort of, maybe, something being not what I was told it should be in terms of attraction.

Then of course as I got older, by the time I was in middle school and playing football and stuff … you're in a locker room. It was obvious that I was attracted to guys and at that age, of course, every other joke is a gay joke. So you're really nervous about dropping any hints that someone might pick up on. I certainly never acted on it for many years.

It's probably a familiar story for many men of our generation … of this kind of bargaining where you're like, *Okay, so I'm attracted to men … but maybe I'm also attracted to women.* Then as I got older and I was like, *I'm attracted to women in the most aesthetic way.* I can appreciate beautiful women, but not in a kind of visceral way. Then you're like, *Okay, that's okay. I'll marry a woman because that's what I'm supposed to do.* And I was pretty religious.

Interestingly, because of my friend Brian who was Methodist—and me growing up a Catholic, especially at St. Bavo's, which, at least when I grew up, was a little bit stuffy, I started going to a Methodist church. That type of worship and kind of open friendliness … I loved it. In fact, it caused a lot of grief with my parents because I would go to Methodist church *and* go to Catholic church. When my mom found out I took Communion at the Methodist church, she freaked out.

ME: *My family would have been the same.*

JEFF: As a kid, you're a bit naive. I'm like, *Okay, I'm not doing drugs. I'm going to church. Isn't it all the same God?* But now I understand some of the way people can cling to their set of beliefs and get a little fearful. It's difficult to paint with a broad brush. I think my family has a lot of good qualities, but among their probably not so good qualities is they're not a very, like, "Live and let live" family. It's very much kind of like, if you don't believe what they believe, they struggle with that.

I think what I used to envision was that by the time we were all adults, there would be this sense of, "Okay, well, maybe we don't have the same beliefs, but maybe we can be curious about that." It's more distressing to them because they very much feel like their way is *the* way. So if you're not believing that, then there's something wrong. Families are like that.

ME: *Very true.*

JEFF: So that has presented some struggles ... what was I gonna say ...?

ME: *Church ... did that [switching churches] kind of help you think, "Wait a minute ... maybe it's okay that I feel this way"?*

JEFF: It was a strange time. Whether it's religion, or new love, or some other profound experience at that age. For many people, when you don't have all the burdens of adulthood on you yet, but you have some of the more mature capacity to start appreciating these deeper things ... that summer hit me like a bulldozer.

ME: *How old were you?*

JEFF: I was sixteen. I didn't know it, but looking back, I fell deeply in love with Brian, who is now a good friend of mine. We talked about this years later and he's been just a doll. When I came out to Brian and his wife when I was in my twenties, he started crying. I was in love with Brian. I was very much kind of on fire with Christianity because I hadn't experienced this flavor before. This ... just very open, personal kind of religion that Catholicism—at least the type of Catholicism I grew up with—wasn't well versed in. It was just, in all directions, this very intense experience.

I can remember sitting with a group of the guys, young men from the Methodist church ... I'm forgetting names. But one of them lived on the Saint Joe River. We had a bonfire in the backyard, and between this kind of newly expansive feeling of God and religion and the closeness I felt with them, it was just, in some ways, a more intense feeling than I've experienced.

As you get older, of course, it doesn't compare to that [initial experience] maybe. It's hard to compare it to, like, the depth of love you have for your kids or your partner or whatever. But just in terms of pure, unadulterated intensity, you know what I mean? At that age you don't have a lot of other baggage to worry about. It was pretty amazing, and when it ended ... I think Brian probably picked up on something being different. I don't know if he identified that I was gay, but I think maybe he did.

At one point Brian sat me down and said, "You know, Jeff, I don't think I can give you what you want." He kind of distanced himself and

I think I fell into something like clinical depression. I remember my dad, who is a good guy but who isn't well versed in emotional language, he came downstairs and in the basement where I was practicing piano for hours and hours. He was like, "What is going on?" I could never explain it. It was an intense time. By high school, I remember Dan, who was in our class—he would probably laugh his ass off to hear this—but I just secretly envied Dan. Because, on one hand, I didn't identify with Dan because I had the whole, "Well, I like guys, but I'm not a feminine kind" hang-up, which is ridiculous to me now. But part of me really admired Dan because he wrote some love letters to guys and would suffer for it. But, I'm like, "Hell, that's a lot braver than I ever was!" It's one of those things where, if you can pass, it's great. Except [you're] not forced to cope with who you are. So there was that whole dynamic too.

ME: *So did you go to college and start to say, "Okay, I'm gonna come out"? Or was that later?*

JEFF: I wish I had, but no. It's funny, Northwestern would have been a very good place to come out. It's not a huge school, but I was north campus where it's mostly science engineering and the Greek system dominates up there. South campus—it used to be, who knows now—was journalists and artists and musicians and so much more progressive. My buddies in the north campus weren't homophobic, but I didn't have any gay friends there. I had one friend who was a lesbian.

I remember I would toy with the idea of two things. One was walking into the student union and going into the gay/lesbian student alliance office. I would look at the doorway and walk away with this kind of irrational fear that if I walked in, someone would see me and it would be all over. Two, I used to look at the L—because the elevated train goes up into Evanston where Northwestern is and we go to Chicago for different things—and be like, "I think if you got on that train and got off in Wrigleyville, they'd probably let you in a gay bar." Like I could actually meet gay people. And never working up the courage to do it. It's a little hard to re-create now because it's been so many years. My mindset has shifted so much. What was I so afraid of? But there were some powerful feelings of not wanting to be gay.

So it wasn't until I was twenty-four and I was at a little lab in West Lafayette. They did contract assay development for a pharmaceutical company. I loved that job, it was a great little company, and so I came out when I was twenty-four and living and working in West Lafayette.

ME: *Okay, and how was that? Were you just terrified?*

JEFF: I was, and it happened very strangely. Mike and I were roommates. Mike was working at Purdue at the time. I think sometimes these ideas percolate in your subconscious, because I went from thinking, *I'm not gonna be gay,* or *I'm not gonna acknowledge it,* to one day I was like, *This is ridiculous. You're gay. You can't marry a woman and put her through that.*

I had never, at this point, kissed a man. I'd never done anything— never been to a gay bar. It was a weeknight, and I hopped in my car, and I drove the two and a half hours back to Mishawaka. My parents were surprised to see me with no plans to be back. I told them I had something to tell them. We sat down … and it's one of those things that was so intense that my memories of it seem hazy … but there were a lot of tears on both our parts.

There was obviously a lot of disappointment on my parents' part, but initially, some of what felt like some support. I think my parents were so worried about me. They saw how distraught I was. They kind of came across as, "Well, we'll work with this." I left that night feeling better, and I got a call from my parents within the week saying, "We found the name of a therapist in West Lafayette. Would you consent to see him? We really just want to make sure you're okay and you're happy."

Here's the interesting wrinkle of the story—that was my response, right? I'm like, "Oh, this is great." Then I found out he was a Catholic priest as well as a psychologist.

ME: *Hmm ….*

JEFF: Exactly. I told my parents and I told myself, "If I work with him and he tries to sort of push me to be straight, I won't see him anymore."

My parents said, "That's fine, we just want you to feel better and see him."

So I went to see him and he was the perfect guy .... After our intake session, he said, "Well, I can't know for sure, but I think you're probably dealing with clinical depression. I don't know that you're gay, but you may be gay. You need to understand that all my training as a psychologist has led me to believe that people don't choose their sexual orientation. All my training as a priest has led me to believe that God doesn't punish people for things they can't choose. If you want any kind of traditional church counseling, I can't provide that for you."

And I was like, "No, you're like, the perfect guy." Because religion played a role for me. I saw him for a while and the interesting thing was, maybe three months into it, my parents asked me how I was doing with counseling. I said, "It's great. I feel better than I've felt in years." And, almost as an afterthought, I said, "Oh yeah, and just to let you know, I *am* gay."

Then the bottom fell out. My parents were like, "What? Isn't he going over Bible verses with you?" That's another part of the deal. There were kind of like dueling expectations. I thought that they had one goal and they had another. It was hard.

I think this is hard for anybody, but being an Italian Catholic family, it's kind of drilled into you from the time you're young that family is everything. My mom would phrase it basically like, "You can't trust anyone but your family." It's just this kind of almost mantra of your life. To suddenly go through a phase where your family becomes kind of like a proposition is a hard thing to kind of stomach and understand.

Unfortunately, it was a lot of years of struggle. Really no one was very supportive. I didn't have any sibling that was like, "You're gay ... no issue." My sister was the most, like, in the middle. My brothers were pretty antagonistic and my parents were just terrified that people would find out. My parents begged me not to tell my siblings. I told my siblings, but everyone begged me not to let the grandparents know, which I never did. That was awful in its own way because I was close to all four of my grandparents. I'm like, "It's not really your place to decide what my relationship is." My mom was afraid my dad's friends were gonna find out.

It was probably one of the harder times in my life. You feel like here is this group of people where, if the situation were reversed ... I can't imagine what it would be ... but if there's something about my parents or my siblings that I was worried my friends might not like, honestly, I'd be like, "Well, then you don't have to be my friend anymore." To realize that that wasn't reciprocated ... it was hard.

My parents would say things that were, to my mind, were pretty intentionally almost destabilizing. Like hoping that they could get me to reconsider. My mom sent me this horrible literature from the Catholic Church—not just the Catholic Church, but the most, like, reactionary branch of the church. Basically, you know, saying that "Gays are all addicts of different kinds," and I don't even want to repeat some of the medical stuff in there. It was so wrong and so offensive.

When I confronted my parents on that years later, my mom was like, "Well, I was so upset, I was crying." It's hard to criticize my mom because I love my mom. We just went through a very intense year. For years we just struggled, and then that continued. Me bringing my first partner home was a huge fight there, where we were at a stalemate for a while, where I just wasn't gonna come home. Then I was told how selfish I was for insisting on this and it just went on and on.

Even in 2014, when my husband and I were getting married, my parents initially weren't coming. They made an excuse—a ridiculous one. It was Easter weekend. They said they had plans to have Easter dinner with my aunt whom they saw every week. I just said, "Enough. You don't need to dissemble for me. I know what's up. I have my own chosen family here who support me, and if you don't want to be there, I'm okay."

Eventually they came around and they came. My dad, who's usually not great at kind of serious talk, pulled me aside before the end of the weekend and said, "Your mom and I just can't imagine if we had missed this." It was a very sweet moment and then, for better or for worse, I think getting the boys sort of cinched the deal.

For my family, having kids is a big, important part of family life, right? So when Josh and I had fostered and adopted the boys, I feel like, for the first time, they kind of fully accepted everything.

Things don't always happen for the reasons they should happen. I don't feel like I would have been any more accepted as a father than I would be as a single guy or a guy with a husband with no kids. But in my case, it definitely kind of pushed things forward with the family, to the point where we don't talk about me. My siblings are mostly careful about not talking about too many contentious things, or political things, because we don't see eye to eye on many of them.

But I think there's mostly full acceptance in my family now after quite a few decades of struggle to get there.

ME: That's great, because I was going to ask about your siblings. I was kind of nervous that maybe there were still problems.

JEFF: There were still problems there, but I think that's finally softened. If we had a more abstract discussion about gay marriage or things like that, I don't know what their opinions are, to be honest. And I probably am happy not to, at this stage.

Just in terms of accepting Josh and I, and not this anxiety that was there for years about who's going to find out and, "Oh my God, you can't let this person know you're gay!" I think that ship has sailed. They're great with everyone. My boys are part of the family; there's no difference there. It's been really good and I'm grateful, because had my mom passed during one of these more contentious periods, I just think it would have been super hard.

But at this point, my parents were coming to Seattle every year. We were having a great time together. I was going back with my family to the cottage every year. My boys really got to know my parents quite well for being at a distance. I'm grateful for all of that.

ME: Oh, that's tremendous! Let's talk about some of that fun stuff. How did you meet Josh, and then how did you foster and adopt the boys?

JEFF: I had that period where I lost my job, and my partner and I split up. After that period, I had actually had the one and only long-distance relationship I've ever had, which was a guy in Sydney, Australia, of all places. He was French Algerian, so there was a little bit of that, "Oh, I have an exotic boyfriend." And he was a great guy.

We chatted online for a long time and then I flew to Sydney and spent time with him and had a great time. He flew here ... but that ended. He's a super great guy, but a super possessive guy. He used to say things that were borderline frightening. Like, if he ever caught me with someone, like, he might kill me and throw me in a river. Like, half joking, but I had this realization. If I move across the world and this goes south ... I was old enough to be practical about it. I'm gonna be in Australia, waiting to get work rights, totally dependent on this person whom I really cared for but who had a degree of possessiveness that frightened me. I just decided, as romantic and as exciting as that life sounded, it probably wasn't the prudent thing to do. So I ended that, and in the aftermath, maybe six months later, I met Josh at a dinner party at a friend's house. He asked me out afterward and I was in that phase—a lot of us go through these phases—where I'm like, "Well, I'd love to go on a date with you, but I'm not really looking for a relationship right now." I was just kind of recovering from that whole thing.

Then we went out and had such a good time together that you sort of break your own rules sometimes. You're like, *Okay, I'm not letting this slip away.* Like a lot of couples, we had a really great start. We had some struggles for a while, before the boys, and then kind of got through those and felt a lot stronger. Then Josh brought up kids and, at that point, I was in nursing school and forty and thought the stage of kids for me had passed. It was never, "I must have kids." But I thought, *If I'm with a husband or a partner that's really working, I would certainly entertain [the idea.]* I have some friends who are like, "Even if I don't meet someone, I want to have a kid." It's just really a focus for them and it wasn't for me.

Instead I had traveled. I'd done that trip to Sydney that same year. I went with my best friend from Northwestern to Peru. I had been in the Peace Corps in Africa. I really loved travel and I had this fantasy of owning this new career—it's got a lot of flexibility. Josh and I can start traveling. So when he brought up kids, it was a real kind of seismic shift for me. All I could see was shackles and restrictions and loss of freedom.

But I said, "I love Josh." When you care for someone, you don't want to shut down their dreams. We went to some adoption agencies, and the first ones were all newborn adoption agencies. It was fine; a lot of them meet with expectant moms who identify as not wanting or not able to take care of the new baby. They match them and you do a video and it's expensive, which is okay. But it's like $35–$40K. You realize pretty quickly: This is definitely a want thing, which is fine; it's no different than if people have bio kids. They want kids, but it's not like these kids needed homes. There were lots of families lined up for them.

Then we went to this agency called Amara. What Amara does is work with the state foster system and they sort of smooth the way a bit for you. They do some services in lieu of the foster system that they're certified to do. They help with communication with the foster system, which can be tricky. They help you navigate through the system. I was really charmed by their presentation.

They brought in a family that had fostered and adopted two young boys. As you can imagine—and you may know people in your own life who've been through this—there's no guarantee that a kid or kids that you foster are going to end up being kids you can adopt. There are some heartbreaking stories of having [to] not just give up kids who you've grown close to, but maybe sometimes [send them] back to situations where you think they shouldn't go back to their parents.

I'm a pretty strong believer that kids belong with their bio parents; if the state can help make that work, I do think that's important. But we went in a little naively because we've been steered this way a little bit. They kind of maybe aren't fully upfront with you. They present it as you can sort of predispose yourself toward kids who are likely to need a permanent home. There are kids who are technically free and I forget what the term is—it's not free and legal—but it's basically that they're [emancipated] by the state. [The state has] already decided they can't go back to their parents, but you realize once [potential foster parents] get in the system, that's very rare. And most of the time, kids are in kind of a gray state where you don't really know the chances that they're going to reunite with their parents. You just kind of have to roll those dice. So we did.

We were actually just looking to adopt one kid, but the social workers are pretty good because you know multiple siblings are harder to place. I remember reading a story about some family a few years ago who fostered and then adopted seven siblings, which is amazing. So we had put in our application ... It's so funny to think how different life could be with one of those early ones. There are different stages, but they try to match on various criteria and the kids didn't match with us. Then the boys came up and we were both just charmed by their application. They were in that gray area. Their parents were, as we know now, struggling with meth. They had come up here with their dad and a girlfriend ... I think it was more of a neglect issue than abuse; pretty badly neglected. There was very little to know at that point about what the chances are that they would be reunited with their bio parents. But they were in Washington state and their first set of foster parents ... unfortunately, it was not a good situation. There was some abuse toward my older son.

So it was a very accelerated process because the plan was once we matched with them, they would come spend some time with us periodically, like on weekends. Then if we felt like it was going well, we would move forward and foster them. But as soon as that plan was formulated, the state called us and said, "We've decided they need to get out of their foster home this week." Within a few days ... I remember because I was able to get out of my nursing shift ... Josh still had to work, he's a PA, so he has clinical shifts as well. And the social worker shows up at your door and drops the two kids off with a cardboard box with some other clothes—and you're a parent!

ME: *Welcome to parenthood!*

JEFF: Luckily, the boys have really sunny dispositions. They're really fun-loving kids. They're very social. So it wasn't like you'd worry that maybe they dropped them off and they would be sullen or scared or both. We started playing right away and, suddenly, we were foster parents.

There were some struggles, like there often are the first eighteen months. My older son, Aiden—the one who's going to be thirteen in June—at six, when he came to us, would have these terrible tantrums where he would be screaming and kicking doors for hours. It was scary and it just put that kind of knot in your stomach as a parent about, "Okay, what am I going to do with this?" We worked with a family therapist for many months who kind of guided us. But it's funny talking to Aiden now because he's such a happy kid. He'll sometimes be like, "I used to, like, freak out, right?" And we were like, "Yeah, many years ago." Even in his mind, it's hard to map himself onto that person, I think, just because it's not his reality anymore. He's a very normal tween now, a sweet kid who occasionally has moments of attitude. It's been really gratifying to see that growth in him.

Eighteen months into this process, the dad was sort of half engaging. I didn't know much about the foster system, but basically it requires the parents to engage with services before they can entertain getting the kids back. Dad was sort of half engaging, half not. Mom never would engage. So after eighteen months, the state allowed us to adopt the boys.

The part I'm really grateful for is that the dad came to trust us a lot. The first conversation we had with him, we were told he wasn't really interested, that he wasn't doing phone visits with the boys at the previous foster home. He corrected us on that. He said, "Their foster mom would let me talk for maybe two minutes and the boys were often quite sullen and sad. They're so happy here." So there's a lot of trust in some ways between us and their bio dad. He keeps in touch. We do [video call] visits. They come and go. We'll do a few weeks in a row and then he will disappear for a few months. But we have an open adoption. He came up and submitted a statement in support of our adoption.

That's been really lucky because—I don't know what the numbers are—but there are quite a few kids in the foster system where they just don't have contact with their bio parents. I think that's kind of this gaping hole for kids. Even if their bio parents have serious flaws, they do better knowing them, and knowing about them, and periodically having contact than they do if you just sort of shut that off. So we're now just a normal family struggling with remote schooling and COVID and trying to keep the boys active and all the things everyone's struggling with these days.

ME: Yeah! Now I'm guessing Seattle is a pretty open-minded place, from what I've seen. I've never been there. How are you accepted? How are you received overall as a family?

JEFF: It's pretty easy here. I would say if you would have asked me this in Indiana when I was in my twenties, I never would have envisioned a time where I could say "my husband" without some self-consciousness about it. It's pretty rare here that I have any self-consciousness about it. People … it doesn't seem strange to them at all. It probably seems less strange in a lot of Indiana now than it did in the early nineties when I came out. It was a different time.

I can remember coming out in West Lafayette, there was a group called Dignity, which is a gay Catholic group—it was like the only gay group in town. Not officially embraced by the church because [the church's] position was you can't be gay, and act on those desires, and be with a same-sex partner, and still be Catholic. But still, [it was for] gay men and lesbians who were interested in their Catholicism and being gay ….

Dignity did a trash pickup like a lot of organizations do. So West Lafayette put a sign by the road by this park that said, "Trash cleared by Dignity West Lafayette." I remember one of the city council women, who was a super-religious conservative, wrote an editorial in the paper and she was shocked to find out what Dignity was. She said, "I worry that they'll be picking up our children instead of picking up trash." It was the worst … the worst stereotype, prejudice.

It was an interesting time to come out because at the same time, [the local government was] considering a very contentious antidiscrimination ordinance. They were expanding their ordinance to include sexual orientation. It was the most surreal experience because I was pretty new to being out. I was nervous to go to these meetings—but even to sort of sit with those people who were in support of adding into the bill and let it be known that I was gay ….

I can remember holding the door for this older gentleman, then later seeing him get up and speak and say in the council meeting the most horrible thing about gays. It was just such a surreal experience. Turns out my picture was on the front page of the *Lafayette Journal & Courier* the next day, just randomly. I was speaking as being part of the group in favor of it. It was interesting.

When I came out at work, I didn't have many negatives there. Maybe just one funnier side is there's a coworker, a woman who used to always make homophobic comments. I had come out to my other coworkers, and we were in our twenties. I wasn't there, but they were out drinking one night with her in West Lafayette. They had had a lot to drink and she said something homophobic, and one of the guys who I knew from work said, "You know, you shouldn't say that stuff because Jeff is gay."

And she said, "That's a really mean thing to say about Jeff, you shouldn't say that."

He goes, "No, no, Jeff is actually gay."

But she broke down crying and said, "Oh my God; he must hate me." She couldn't look me in the eye for weeks.

I was like, "It's okay!" We were fine after a while, but it was just a funny story from that coming out.

I was very touched, actually. The little company I worked for, without me ever thinking to ask for this—and I have no idea if this was because of me, but it happened in the same year I came out—added sexual orientation to their own nondiscrimination policy.

It was cute … I had some coworkers, like one guy came up to me and said, "If you don't mind me asking, is it true that you lead an alternate lifestyle?"

And I was like, "I think you mean alternative … I wouldn't call it a lifestyle, but, yes, I know what you're getting at." So there were some funny experiences those first few years.

I knew very few gay people, like I said. I hadn't been with a guy or anything. So I was going to Chicago, starting to meet people, going to Indianapolis because a lot of my friends just moved down to the city after college. It was an exciting time. Things were very new. I was still working through a lot of my own internalized homophobia, looking back at it. It was like a lot of people's twenties, I think, a lot of searching, a lot of trying to figure out who you are.

ME: *I am curious, how were the boys? Were they like, "We were picturing a mom and a dad," or were they just like, "Oh cool, this is great."*

JEFF: No, it's a good question. In the beginning, I don't think they thought about it much, which is surprising. But then again, you'll appreciate this as a parent … I didn't until I was a parent … even though I had lots of nephews and nieces, it's not the same. Kids have such a different way of seeing the world than you think. You forget how much of your "adult way" was shaped at some point.

They weren't freaked out by having two dads, but they also, I don't think, understood what that meant. So eventually when we explained that, "No, we're married," there was some confusion. It took them a while to understand.

I remember a few years later when we kind of gave them the birds and the bees talk. My older son didn't have the reaction to the birds and the bees talk that I thought he would. Being a parent of kids these days, there's not nearly—at least among my boys—the embarrassment about sex and bodies and stuff that there was when I was growing or we were growing up. He said, "So you and Josh are together but gay people don't have sex." And I was like, "No, we do." It's been like a stepwise process of them to understand what it means. It's been, in some ways, very sweet. My older son at some point had kids at his school saying that they thought being gay was weird and some homophobic stuff. He kind of, unprompted, said, "It's not weird." Just on his own he would see like gay pride flags and be like, "That's a gay thing, right? Like you and Josh?" So he was just very sweet and supportive and always has been.

My younger son just came around to the point where it just seems normal to him. He talks about his two dads. In the beginning, they called us "Dad" really quick. We never asked them to call us that when we fostered—that wasn't ever going to be a requirement of ours—but very quickly they called us "Dad." Then over the years they've reverted back to calling us Josh and Jeff.

We've had our own kind of struggles with this—"Do we ask them to say that?" We said, "You guys can call us Josh and Jeff at home because it's easier." I don't know, because we both grew up calling our dads "Dad," it always felt artificial to say "Call me Papa" or something. I don't know why, it just never felt right. "When we're out in public, maybe it'd be nice if you call us Dad." I think over time we've just let it be what it is. They're so expressive of their emotions; they say "I love you" all the time. My family was not a big "I love you" family growing up. There's no doubt about the closeness there. But they mostly call us Josh and Jeff. Some people have a visceral reaction to that. There's a mom at the school—when they say Josh or Jeff in front of her, she's like, "You know it's a respect thing. You mean your dad." I'm just like, "It's okay. They don't mean it with disrespect at all."

ME: *I never thought about this, though. If they say "Dad," which one of you is that?*

JEFF: I know! So I think just for practicality they have switched to names. When they are talking to other people, it kind of just depends. Sometimes they'll say, "My dad said I couldn't come over because I have to do my homework or something." Probably in situations where it really doesn't make a difference which dad said that. A lot of other times they'll say our names. I think Josh and I have completely made our peace with it.

It does help that in Seattle—for a couple years—I think we were the only, at least the only one I know of, same-sex couple with kids at the school. Then there was a couple in the younger grades after us. Now among our friends are my son's best friend—he's also still a foster kid, actually, but he probably will be adopted. He has two moms. So at least there's some visibility there and they don't feel alone in that respect.

ME: *Well that's good! I don't think I've met anybody around here with two moms or two dads. Maybe that'll change as time goes on.*

JEFF: I have never seen the statistics, but my sense is that it's probably more common for lesbians to have kids, whether they're bio kids or adopted. My boys have a lot of uncles who dote on them and so they brag about how many uncles they have. In some ways it's nice to have this community of uncles who don't have kids of their own to shower attention and gifts on them and are excited. We have people who are so close to the boys that they, for example, in our will if we pass, the boys would go to them .... It's just been nice to see the boys—because we don't have a lot of family close by—kind of develop their own uncles and family and a community of people that care about them here.

ME: *That is fantastic! You're the only family in this book with two dads or two moms, so having that experience, I think, is really good to share and give everybody a little perspective. I stress to everybody as I'm talking to them that this book is not meant to be like, "This is the gay experience," or "This is the Jewish experience." It's just a sample of different lives to increase understanding. I'm excited to let people kind of glimpse into a world that maybe they don't see very much.*

You've gone through the questions beautifully. I would say that "What have you learned through all this?" would be a perfect final question. Unless you belong to any organizations that support couples like yourself that you want to plug at the end here.

JEFF: No, I don't. I saw that question; it made me reflect. There are some same-sex parent organizations. We've never—and some of this may just be us, someone that may be living in Seattle—we've never felt that that is specific support we need. I don't know; if we were in Mobile, Alabama, I might feel differently. But in Seattle—this won't surprise you—when we meet other same-sex parents, there's about the same chance that we will identify with them and find commonality as heterosexual parents. It's not really a defining factor for us either way. So I don't belong to any organizations.

You were asking what I feel like I've learned from all this. As someone who I think has had my struggles in life with things like self-confidence and feeling good about myself ... looking back and seeing the periods that felt really shaky where I took steps forward were actually a lot braver than I thought. It has served me ... I've learned that I will never be that person who is like, "You know what? I'm good enough. And I'm going to feel good about this," unfortunately. It's not that I don't like myself. But this is the part that I struggle with. I'll always be that person that's like, "I don't know if I'm good enough. Should I do this?" but I've learned to just do it! I've learned to persist anyway. I'm grateful for that.

ME: *That's beautifully said; thank you! Is there anything else you wanted to say that I might have forgotten to ask you?*

JEFF: I will just say that I've really enjoyed this, but it has also felt—and I know this is the point of the interview—but it's felt a little selfish because I feel like I've talked with Amy whom I haven't seen in decades and I've been talking about myself for a while.

ME: *Nope, that was the point! It feels really good just to hear your voice and reconnect after all these years. It was great talking to you.*

It's okay. Keep trying.
Keep practicing. You'll get there.

-P.J.

P.J.

I instantly liked P.J. when I met him eight years ago in my hoop-dancing world. Back then, he still identified as a woman. Our conversations have always been deep and made me think about things in different ways. P.J. has expanded my world even before this book, and I'm incredibly grateful! He is a wise, loving soul, and I'm glad to know him.

NAME: P.J.
AGE: 57
IDENTIFIES AS: Male, masculine, he/him pronouns
ETHNICITY: Caucasian "mutt"
OCCUPATION: Office Manager

P.J.: I am probably one of the only people you will know that was born, raised, and grew up [here] and has never been many places. I was born in Indianapolis, just about Seventy-Fifth and Keystone, and we lived there until I was three. I was the number six child in the family. So there are six of us and I am the youngest. At that point they're like, "We need a bigger house."

They started building a house right at the edge of Carmel in Indianapolis, at the most northern part, so about four miles from where I was born .... By the time I was four, we were living in [that] house. I grew up there and have never moved, other than short-term moves to apartments here and there within the Indianapolis or Carmel area. I live in that house now. My dad passed away when I was twenty-three and he asked that I stay and take care of my mom, and so I did. I stayed in that house—both my children have been raised in that house their whole entire lives. I have two kids, they both identify as girls right now. They were born/assigned female at birth. They are adults— thirty-one and thirty-three.

My mother is ninety. She is still alive and I am her primary contact to the world, her caregiver. She is in a senior living facility in the Fishers area, and so not far from my home, right between my home and office. I take care of her on the regular. If I don't see her every day, I get twelve phone calls. I know you can relate.

ME: I do, definitely. Did you and your family have any traditions or do any fun things growing up?

P.J.: I was the youngest of six, so we had kind of a very diverse family when it comes to what we did. Nobody was really ever pigeonholed. I grew up in a very religious family. My dad actually studied theology and philosophy, which is an odd combination, I think. Psychology, philosophy, and theology. He actually studied to be a priest in the Orthodox Church, which is similar to Catholic except it's stricter and has no pope. Being the youngest of six, it went two girls, boy, two girls, and me. So I was kind of always my father's little buddy and always the biggest tomboy in the house. "I'd [rather] decapitate a Barbie than play with it" kind of thing.

ME: [Laughing] That's awesome!

P.J.: It was a very strict, religious household. We did not cuss. My dad had a really creative way of letting off steam, so he taught me how to use lots of substitute words. I was working on a motorcycle with him once, and he smacked his hand so hard and his thumb busted open. He said, "Gosh, golly, darn, drat." Never a cuss word. That was the kind of household we grew up in.

I was a latchkey kid. My mom returned to the workforce about the time I was six. I remember being carpooled back and forth by her in kindergarten, or sometimes somebody else. But by the time I was in first grade, she was back in the workforce, so pretty much a latchkey kid all my life. Between my dad, my mom, I was never bored. There was always something to do and that something was usually outside.

ME: Excellent, as it should be! I'm gonna dive in. I've got burning questions. I would have had this conversation with you even without a book, girl, because— sir—see, I told you I'd screw up.

P.J.: It's okay, Amy. Before you go any further, here's my standard phrase: "It's okay. Keep trying. Keep practicing. You'll get there."

ME: Thank you. I will. I know you got married. You mentioned it in the very beginning today. So we'll start with that and then I'll ask you later on, When did you start to have inklings like, "Hmm, this isn't right"? Anyway, how did you meet your husband and when?

P.J.: I was in high school. I was emancipated when I was in high school. So my junior and senior year, I lived on my own.

ME: Wow.

P.J.: My choice. I asked my parents. I said, "Look, I'm the only one out of six that hasn't run away. I'm asking permission. Can you emancipate me? I would like to go, move into an apartment, and spread my wings a little bit and see what it's like." And they granted that. Basically, end of junior year/senior year, I lived on my own for a majority of it. Until I had a car wreck and lost my mode of transportation and had to move back to finish my senior year at home.

During that time is when I met my ex-husband. My family situation was very strict, like I said. So to have a man be dominant and controlling was not a question. He was that, but it was not a good situation for me. Because I am very stubborn, I kept trying for thirty-five years.

There [were] four different points in our marriage that I said, "I can't do this." One was before we even had children. When I got to the courthouse [to sign for a divorce], the judge informed us that we were in the wrong court, that we belonged in Hamilton County, not Marion County, and sent us away. The ex was like, "Oh see, it wasn't meant to be. You were supposed to be with me forever." We did get back together and had kids, and then I focused on raising the kids and staying out of his way—for the most part in appeasing that situation. But he was not a good man.

ME: *Oh gosh, P.J., I'm sorry. Did he abuse you in any way? It sounds like it.*

P.J.: Yes. So there are five types of abuse. There is sexual abuse, there is mental abuse, there is physical abuse, there is emotional abuse, and there is financial abuse. I went to an amazing group in Noblesville and they helped me basically identify what was going on. I came to them with the understanding that if I left, I was risking my life. They said, as we went down through the list of things, "Well, you meet all five of the criteria for the abuses."

ME: *Oh, my.*

P.J.: So, yes, there was an abusive situation there and I needed to get out. And I did, with their help. I got out—and I don't mind if this goes in the book either, I am fine with this because it might help somebody else someday. When I got out, I had a restraining order on him and I removed all his guns from the house because I didn't want to be at risk. I didn't hate him, I just needed to be free of him. So I removed all the guns. Then when we went to divorce court, the judge said the physical violence had not been recent enough so he dropped the protective order.

ME: *Oh my God.*

P.J.: My ex bought the house directly behind me. He still lives there and this is four years later. My house is the one I grew up in.

ME: *That's right, so you don't want to go.*

P.J.: I desperately want to move. However, I am taking care of my ninety-year-old mother and I work at a job right now where I'm working seventy–eighty hours a week. I am salaried so there is no way for me to move right now. Although I would love to.

Since that divorce went through, I refiled for a protective order again. It was declined. We've had the police out a few times and then my ex stalked me constantly. He would just stand out in his backyard every time I went out, or out in his yard, and watch me every time I cut the grass. So basically, the abuse never stopped. I am a survivor, so I'm gonna keep going. Last August, he drove down the road and threatened my partner's life. So we got to put the protective order back up for my girlfriend, for my fiancé, but mine was denied again because it went before the same judge.

ME: *That is crazy!*

P.J.: It is, but it is more about the judge than it is about me. Some judges do not want to change their opinion when they've done something because it's a matter of their standing, not a matter of the situation. So anyhow, fast forward ... the divorce happened four years ago and I got out of the abusive relationship as far as I could.

ME: *Very good. So from what I could see on social media—and maybe I'm wrong—you kind of started to do some self-exploration, or you had an inkling years ago ....*

P.J.: As far as my gender ... Okay, so when I was in elementary school, my nickname in fifth grade was "flat-chested maniac" because I was always getting into fights with boys. I was always my dad's little buddy. I was happy to be a tomboy. I did not fit into the mold of the girls. I always had a very difficult time bonding with girls and usually hung out with the guys. Even when I got married, the thing that was attractive to my then spouse was that I had no problem working on cars and busting my knuckles with them. I had no problem climbing a roof and hammering in nails. I was every bit of the guy that he needed to have as a helper. So that was always there. That part was always there.

Sexuality and gender are two separate things. So you can be attracted to women if you're a man. You can be attracted to women if you're a woman. You can be attracted to women if you're nonbinary. Somebody asked me the other day, "So if you're a guy now, what does that make you?" And I said, "Well, it makes me straight, I guess." So in my world, the opportunity arose prior to—probably my first trip to PlayThink—to start doing some self-exploration, as you said.

ME: *What year was that, P.J., do you remember?*

P.J.: It's probably been ten years. Maybe eight. When I was out there, it was amazing because I went by myself. I did not camp with somebody else. I was just, *I'm going to this thing. It's a learning festival and I'm very excited about it and I'm going.* I was allowed to go because I was going by myself and I knew how to camp. That was something I knew how to do. Although my spouse was not an outdoorsy person; he was more interested in sitting down and watching a race than being a part of life. So I went to PlayThink and I learned about movement and dance. But even more than that, I learned about myself and I learned about people. And I learned that there were more people out there in the world than what I was seeing in Carmel, Indiana. And you don't know about this until you step out of your comfort zone and you see that, right?

I went that year and I came back so excited, so happy and euphoric, just absolutely happy; and I found my place that's the happiest place on the earth. I saved up my money and went again the following year and came back with that same feeling of, "I found a place. I belong." I have never fit in with all the girls, I've always been one of the guys, but here it didn't matter if I was a girl or a guy. I was just a person, and I could be appreciated as a person, and that was beautiful.

That's about when I started exploring that part of who I am and I noticed that I was attracted to multiple people all my life. What I did notice, the attraction was more about their intelligence than it was about their physicality. They had to be intelligent for me to have interest. And if they were intelligent—and that doesn't mean they have to be part of Mensa or anything like that—it just means that they have to want to experience, to grow, to understand, to listen.

ME: *Yes! So ... much ... this! That is what intelligence is to me.*

P.J.: Yes, the ability to do that. I had been married to a person that was the opposite of that all of that time, right? So thirty years in, I'm just still going, "Why don't you want to see what life is? Why do you have all these prejudices against Blacks, Hispanics? What have they done to you? What has this group, culture done to you personally?" Well, nothing.

It is not a cookie-cutter world. It is a big messy plate of spaghetti where we're all intertwined with each other, in each other's lives. And it just might be a surprise when you turn around and find out who you're intertwined with.

So going to PlayThink opened up that door. Opened up my mind and brought me to the realization that I wasn't happy when I was at home. It made me step away and take another look. And I grew a little bit more into the flow arts community because that's where the people came from. I discovered there, in that community, that it's okay to be you, no matter who that is, as long as you are being kind. That's what mattered. And it didn't matter how you dressed, if that's how you felt comfortable, and being you was more important than putting on a mask every day. I kept coming back to that and back to that and kind of discovered that not only was I unhappy in my marriage, I was unhappy with how I was walking through life. Then I met some people that were transgender and I watched a few go through transition before I really started questioning myself.

Then that goes to, "Oh no." It's that panic [others have] of, "Oh, it's contagious!" No, no, that's not what it is. Being transgender is not contagious, but seeing someone that is and then questioning your own identity, you might come back with, "Well, I know I'm a woman. I was born as a woman. I know I was meant to be a woman. I am happy being a woman." Or you might come back with, "I never fit that place and I don't really feel like I'm a guy. I don't feel like I'm a woman. My body says this, but I feel like some place in between ... or neither ... or all of it."

You might say, "I was born a woman. My body says this; my brain doesn't line up with that. My thoughts don't align with how this looks. I look in the mirror and no matter what outfit I put on ... no matter what I do ... what hair or makeup or expression I have on my face ... I don't feel happy with who I see in that mirror. It's not because I'm overweight or underweight. It is because the person in the mirror is not reflecting who I am." That person in the mirror did not reflect me.

Growing up in a very strict, religious household, there were things that you did not cross. And one of them is, "Oh, girls are soft and pink and supposed to be kind and submissive." Submissive was a big part of that. And they are supposed to help and do nothing but help, and cater to, and take care of ... and going from that to a marital status situation of someone that was also in that mindset ... if I made any waves, there was a price to pay and I would be back into that position.

Going to PlayThink and going to explore my internal self and expanding on my yoga took me to that place where my body doesn't feel like my body. I don't belong here in this way. I don't hate myself; I love myself. But I am not happy with me when I see myself. Like I said, I had met some people that were transgender and I went to a night that changed my life. I went to a thing called Transgender Day of Remembrance. They call it TDOR as an acronym. And what that does in November is it brings the community together to mourn all those that we have lost in our community. A lot of it has to do with suicide because they are trying to live their true self, and their family or their others or whoever is stifling them so much that if they cannot live being themselves, they would rather not live.

Some of it has to do with addiction because they are numbing that person [who they are not]. Some of it has to do with, unfortunately, transgender women … are more likely to have been sexually assaulted than any other women, period. The highest numbers of women are Black Americans. They are more likely to be killed because they are transgender.

ME: *I've been seeing that all the time lately.*

P.J.: It is absolutely terrifying to be a transgender woman that is Black. That night changed my whole life. I met people, just from the surface, that maybe they didn't look cisgender. (Cisgender means that you were born that gender and you identify as that gender. It is not a slang term that's saying that you're less than or more than. It just means that you're born a gender and identify as that gender, and that's who you are.) You could see, you knew right away, "Well obviously, this is transgender." That is okay, because transcending themselves beyond what they were born as, to me, is just the fact that they have changed their gender to what they truly should have been.

That night I walked away in such awe and disbelief of all of those who have fought through so many fights … struggled and survived. I'm in disbelief in what our nation … what the world has done to this marginalized group of people. Not knowing why it affected me so deeply that night, I came home … and my husband was absolutely livid because I went to this event and I was absolutely forbidden to go. I went and when I came home, he said, "You chose them over me." And my answer was, "No, no, I didn't choose them; I chose me."

I did the right thing ... one of the first times that I ever stood up for myself and did not regret it, because no matter what he did after that point, I did something that made me know who I was.

ME: *My heart just kind of went crazy hearing that. Oh my gosh, so wonderful.*

P.J.: Yeah, so that was my night of change. I still did not know I was identifying as transgender at that point. I just knew something was different in me. As we were going through the divorce, he would threaten to kidnap me a few times and have me deprogrammed or unbrainwashed. That's one of the reasons why I wanted a protective order. Meanwhile, through all of this, my daughter had gotten pregnant. They were having a baby. Or actually, even prior to that, he was still saying those things, and that was actually right after the divorce that she got pregnant. But before that, she was in the hospital because she is an alcoholic. She had basically almost drank herself to death.

ME: *I remember that.*

P.J.: Yes, and I would have to sneak my way to the hospital at ten o'clock at night so I could go see her because there were threats that I was going to get kidnapped because I was transgender. So we go through our own stories. Not everybody goes through this. Some have amazingly supportive parents and siblings. Some people go through their own form of torture. I am less likely to be raped as a man—doesn't mean it's unlikely but less likely—than someone that is a transgender woman. And I have to say that when people say, "You're brave," that is kind of a disservice in one way. Because all you're trying to do is live and survive. If somebody [walks] up to you and you say, "Oh my God, you're so brave. You're living and surviving," when you're living yourself, that's kind of like, "Well, but no. I'm just trying to live."

So sometimes people saying that is also hurtful and disrespectful. Sometimes somebody needs to hear ... you know, "Hey, you're doing it; you're doing it." But a lot of times when people go, "Oh my gosh, that's so great, congratulations," I don't know how to take that. They mean well, I'm sure they mean very well, but it always leaves me a little bit like, "Well, okay, I'm just trying to live."

ME: *When was your divorce?*

P.J.: We are four years past now.

ME: *Then you were friends with a lady, and you've been for a long time. And you and she got closer, right? I'll let you explain it more.*

P.J.: Yeah. So as we progress through this divorce, [my girlfriend] is kind of my back support here. I have a couple good friends—[her] and Misty—and my hoop people are support. But I am not big on drama. If you read through my Facebook, it's usually not drama. It's usually, "Hey, I'm thinking of you, listening, I'm sending you support."

ME: *Your posts are always beautiful.*

P.J.: I just want people to know life is worth living. So do what you can to live. But I don't like drama, so I tried to keep it to a small group of people that knew what was going on. When I would run into someone and they would say something like, "Sorry you're going through a divorce," I'd say, "I'm living with my sister right now." But [my girlfriend] was always there and she was my confidante.

She, at the same time, was going through a separation with a partner that she had and we kind of, like, leaned into each other. We kind of discovered each other. We went to an event once, and I did not know that I was attracted to her until she did something, and all of a sudden I went, "Wow, she's sexy." And I was smitten at that point.

Then I realized, "Hey, wait, that makes me a lesbian." Because I wasn't into that path of my journey yet. I was like, "Okay, I'm good with that." So I had to come out as a lesbian at that point in time and I was good with that. Actually, I just say bisexual because I'm attracted ... it's not about, again, the gender, it's about the brain for me—sapiosexual.

ME: *I'll never forget the post where you just put, "Bi!" I thought,* Oh, she's bisexual.

P.J.: Yep, that's all I said.

ME: *It was brilliant.*

P.J.: That was it. That was me coming out. That was the coming-out day. That was my announcement to the world—"Bi!" Some people got it, some didn't. But, yeah, our relationship grew, and then the following year it rolled around to TDOR [Transgender Day of Remembrance] and we went together again. It meant something new and different to me because it wasn't me watching other souls. It was me connecting to it and understanding it and feeling. Right around that time was the first time I said, "Hey, be my girlfriend forever." So I gave [her] a promise ring that year. Then a year later, I gave her an engagement ring. So we are officially engaged and we have not set a date because the world decided to have COVID.

Yeah, the world kind of paused for a moment. We are officially engaged, but we don't have a date. We're just kind of waiting for the world to open back up. And for my ex not to live behind us or for us not to live there.

ME: *Right. So, outside of your ex, what were people's reactions?*

P.J.: To me coming out as gay?

ME: *[Yes] what has their reaction been to you saying, "I'm going to go ahead and transition/process to transition."*

P.J.: Coming out as gay was like, "I already knew that." For most people they were just like, "Yeah, all right." Some people were like, "Ew." I didn't really lose a whole lot of friends over that.

ME: *Really? How was your family—your siblings?*

P.J.: Well, I come from a pretty diverse family. When you have six kids, and when they have kids, then all of a sudden you're up to—my mom has, I think, fifteen grandkids, something around forty great-grandkids, and also has like seven great-great-grandkids at this point. So being in a family that large, we have some gay people in our family. It was not that big a deal. It was kind of like, "By the way, I'm gay … okay, moving on."

ME: *All right. What was the reaction to you transitioning? You told me earlier you lost some friends?*

P.J.: During this divorce stuff with my ex, one of the things that I had said to the judge was that I want to protect some people because they might be transgender. He has a lot of prejudice against people that are transgender or gay. He has a prejudice against everything that is not him. It's just a basic narcissist.

I had some friends that were supportive of what was going on. I said, "You know what? I'm going to let him tell his side of the story. I'm going to tell mine. I am not going to slam him. I'm just going to say he was abusive. I needed out. I should have done it thirty years ago. He's not the person you think he is, because he's really good at that [lying]."

My safety is I have not come out to my brother. … [W]hich is sad, because it would be great to have a brother … but right now I do not. All my other siblings are fine with it. I am fifty-seven years old and my oldest sibling said to me, "You know if you do this, you can't go back."

I said, "Yes, I know. I am not doing this as a flighty thing." I have never been a person that jumps into an idea and just does it. I do a lot of research. I dig and I will continue to dig. I know it doesn't go back once you do things, but I am really good with this.

The things coming out of my office were different too. The person that I lost was [a friend], someone I spoke with every Wednesday via text. It was a guy and I came out to him with a phone call on a Saturday, so there wasn't the pressure of a workday or anything like that going on. He had told me that his daughter came out as being a lesbian. And I asked him that day when I came out to him, I said, "Todd, how's your daughter doing in the relationship?" and he said, "Oh, they broke up. She's a hot mess. But I'd rather have her being gay than not have her at all."

So I felt like that was an open door. And I said, "Do you remember when I told you to ask her about people that are transgender?"

He said, "Yeah, I never got around to that."

I said, "Oh, well, that's unfortunate because I want to tell you that I am transgender and I wanted to tell you over the phone. I didn't want to message you this."

And he paused for a moment. He said, "Well, P.J., I've always thought of you as the classiest woman I know."

I said, "Can't I just be the classiest person you know?" We had a little bit more discussion, and since then, I have not spoken with him.

ME: *Oh, P.J. ….*

P.J.: I've messaged him on our normal Wednesday twice. The first time he didn't answer at all. The second time he just said, "Busy, can't talk." He hasn't messaged since. So I lost that friendship. And that was somebody I communicated with on the regular. The other person … things have been said like, "Well, you'll always be a girl to me." It has been said by other people and that's hard. Because that is absolutely denying who I am. That tells me right there … well, they are not supportive and they are not my friend because they don't know me. So I've lost a couple friendships that way.

ME: *Can I confess something to you? And I know we're not like super-duper close friends.*

P.J.: Yeah.

ME: *When you cut your hair, I have to admit, I was like, "She cut off all her beautiful hair! Why did she do that?" I can't believe I'm telling you this. But when I reached out to you for this book and you explained [that you were transgender], I went, "Oh my God, that makes perfect sense." I kind of learned something, like, "Don't just assume things, Amy." The light bulb went on and ever since then, when you've shown off your haircuts and stuff, I'm like, "All right, that is who this person is now." I was a little ashamed of my initial reaction. Now I'm like, "I get it. He's becoming who P.J. needs to be."*

P.J.: Well, you know, razor burn and all that other stuff is going on! I definitely don't have that long hair anymore.

ME: *So have you been taking medication, I assume?*

P.J.: Hormone therapy. Depending on which way you're transitioning, you will do different kinds of therapy … how old you are when you're transitioning. Because for younger people, it might be a blocker if somebody's a young kid and they're like, "I've always been a boy; why don't you let me be a boy?" And they'll kind of delay puberty. I know it is a very big point of contention for a lot of people. But it doesn't say that they're not going to continue to be a girl or a boy. It just says they're not ready to make that choice yet. Give them a little time so they can figure that out, which is kind of cool.

But when you're F to M, which is female to male—that's me—you do testosterone. It is the most common thing and there are different methods of taking that. Some people wear a patch, some people use a cream and that is applied to their genitalia. Some people do full injections ... which, again, that's me. Some people do subcutaneous injections. So there are multiple ways to get this hormone in your body and it all aligns with how your body responds the best. Some people take smaller doses, some take bigger. It all depends. It does not mean that you *have* to take hormone therapy to transition. That is not a given. There are people out there that are F to M that have never taken testosterone. There are people out there that are M to F, which is male to female, who have never taken any estrogen or any of their medications that they do to transition the other direction. So you don't have to chemically, medically transition that way.

To be transgender is not a pill or an injection. What it is ... is where you identify yourself, your internal, who you really are. It is not—I know that that's kind of a rough phrase to say, "I identify as female. I identify as male." Then the people start throwing up the thing of, "I identify as an airplane," or whatever. No, that's not it. It is who you are. There are many studies on brain scans and stuff like this. Unfortunately, you can't do that until somebody's dead—to do all this research in the brain. But that shows how their brain works if they were, you know, male or female or whatever. And it's actually wired differently. So I've always been me. I've always been basically kind of stuck in the wrong body. I'm just trying to get my body caught up with who I am.

I started my chemical part—or my medical part—of my transition July 23, 2020. Prior to that I really didn't think I was going to be able to ever do anything about it. But the graces of COVID allowed me to have to work from home, and allowed me to make the decision that I didn't have to go through all the levels of transition in front of everybody, and practice and whatever in front of people. So I was graced with that. Some people have to do this right in front of the world. I was very fortunate with that. And then I had to come out at my work here because obviously my voice doesn't sound the same. Right now I'm kind of straining it, so it's kind of skyrocketing right now.

Chemically, I've been transitioning a lot less longer than I have already been outwardly transitioning to the world and saying I identify as male. [These are] things that I have to do to survive in my body because I've not had any surgeries—they call that pre-op. Not everybody who transitions will ever have a surgery. That doesn't make you less transgender than anybody else. Chemically taking the injections does not make you less or more transgender than anyone else. Who you are, it isn't a status of what you look like all the time, which is a tough one to explain to somebody. If you're walking around in jeans and a T-shirt and they don't know what to call you, the easiest thing to do is, "I go by P.J.."

ME: But are you going to do surgery?

P.J.: I will tell you this because of the interview situation .... First off, if you were ever talking to a transgender person, you are not allowed to ask that. That's one of those "no-nos."

ME: Thank you. I am so glad you said that. That's something I didn't know and others need to know. Okay, right.

P.J.: Here's the thing ... if you've gone through life, and every day in the morning you woke up and you had to go put on a clown outfit and put on the white makeup and the sad face and the tear and the hat and the hair ... and you had to go out into the world like that every day, knowing that you look like you and this is what you're supposed to look like ... is this right? When you finally get to go out in the world and look like you and not look like a clown ... because that's what everybody told you that you were all your life ... it is very, very freeing. So cutting off my hair was kind of like my first step of, "Hey, by the way, I really look like this."

ME: You were excited, I could tell.

252 AMY THORNTON SHANKLAND

P.J.: Thank you, COVID, for that. The first haircuts I did were all myself.

ME: *I remember that.*

P.J.: So I was like, "Look what I did! I did a thing!" So that was me coming out. My family and my siblings and stuff, that was later. I had already looked like this. I was talking to them and then was like, "Okay, time to tell them," because my voice sometimes sounds like this, and when it's like this, you can't hide that.

ME: *Yeah, it's deeper, readers!*

P.J.: This is actually generally where I hold my voice ... down in here. But I know I'm doing a lot of talking, so I have to change it from being in my lungs [lower-pitched] up higher to push there. So I bring it back up here into my head voice [high-pitched] and this is where I talk to my mom, which is the other person who does not know in my family.

She does not know because she is ninety years old and she has dementia. I would have to come out to her every day for the rest of my life. She does get confused when she doesn't see me because my voice is down here. She doesn't know who she's talking to. She'll say, "I want to talk to P.J.; I want to talk to your wife. Put P.J. on the phone." I'm like, "Mom, this is P.J.." That one's tough.

For the most part, with the other people that have reacted to me, most of it is ... okay, if you are over the age of thirty, you will question it more. Just because this is the world you live in. If you're over the age of forty, you will question it even more and be a little confused. If you're over the age of fifty, you're like, "What?" But yet you'll still, if you're a good person and you're accepting of people, you'll say okay and you'll work your way and maneuver your way through it. If you're over the age of sixty, you'll get there, but after that, you'll either say yes or you'll say no. And that's where you'll stay. Unfortunately, this is what I'm noticing. It doesn't mean it's that way for everybody. Hopefully, if somebody loves you, they will just accept you. That's the hope.

Hopefully, if you tell someone, "I have male pronouns," if they respect you, they will use them. If they forget, that is on them. It is not on the transgender person to educate them. It's on them. Do not make a big to-do about it. You simply say, "Oh, sorry," use the right pronoun, and move on. Don't sit there and apologize ten thousand times. It makes the matter worse. It's kind of like, yeah, the wound's open now, you just keep pouring salt in it.

I will be happy to educate people and generally my common statement is, "It's okay. Keep trying, keep practicing, you'll get there." If I don't be gracious, because I am the person that is representing—possibly the only person that you know who is transgender—I'd better do a darn good job of representing. If I come off as an asshole, you're gonna think all transgender people are. So how about if I come off as a good guy and be gracious?

To normalize it—this was something that was said to me—when we start writing down numbers for a date in January of 2021, we would slip back and write 2020 on things all the time. By February, you're pretty much out of that habit. *I've gone thirty days writing 2021. I'm good.* So that kind of normalizes it.

I expect people to make mistakes. When somebody does it on *purpose*, that's malicious. That is just wrong. That is them just being disrespectful. If somebody tells you, "I'm not gonna go by that," [and] says, "Hey, you are still a girl to me," that is disrespectful and hateful and not what you want from people.

I answer the phones all day. Right now with my voice, it goes up and down. My voice will crack and break and then I'll drop back down and I'll go back up again. I am a thirteen-year-old boy with my voice right now, because my vocal cords are getting thicker. All of these things change. Your body fat distributes differently, your vocal "cords" change, my face is changing shape. And I shave. When I'm talking on the phone, I'm finding that I'm getting about fifty-fifty on phone calls saying "sir" or "ma'am." I know in the next four months, it'll probably be sixty-forty. I'll keep going that direction to where everybody will be saying "sir." If they say "ma'am," it'll be weird, or they weren't paying attention.

But my look is changing as well. Right now, when I'm walking through a store, people frequently "ma'am" me, because first off, I'm five foot five. A lot of guys are not five foot five, but there are a lot of guys that are. My body fat has not distributed enough to where my hips are narrowed down enough ... or, I still have a chest because I've not had top surgery.

You did ask about the surgeries. Yes, I intend to have top surgery. It does cause me a lot of what they call "dysphoria," meaning I get dressed and I look in the mirror and I go, "Shoot, you're still there. I'm gonna get 'ma'amed' all day."

ME: *That's exactly what [our mutual friend] Jack said. They said when it was done, they looked down and went, "Finally, yes!"*

P.J.: Yeah, so it is hard for me to go out in the world, knowing that when somebody talks to me, if they cannot see my face—which we are behind masks [due to COVID]—they don't see my five-o'clock shadow or hear my voice.

ME: *I didn't even think about that!*

P.J.: It's more likely they're going to "ma'am" me. I've stopped turning around when they say "ma'am," and if they keep "ma'aming" me, I'm going to keep walking. If they "ma'am" me as they're facing me, I'll look at them and say, "sir." If they want to be rude about it, I'll just walk on. I won't continue the conversation. I'm not going to engage in an argument for their satisfaction to have them tell me something that is wrong. I have to—again—I have to represent a community by my actions. If I'm going to get argumentative with them, it's not going to help educate that person.

ME: *That's been a theme throughout this book with a lot of people.*

P.J.: Yeah, I would rather educate somebody and represent my community the best I can.

ME: *So that leads me to one last question I wanted to ask. Do you belong to any organizations that help in that respect?*

P.J.: Yeah. Some of the organizations ... I've been going through therapy. I started therapy a couple years before I even filed for divorce, or even decided, *I am being abused, and this is not okay, and I want out of this.*

By the way, to back up on that a little bit, one of the other key things that struck me was that my mom married a man—because she has already outlived two husbands and two boyfriends—she married a man [after my father died] because she did not want to be alone. He was the most abusive man I have ever seen in my life next to my husband ... because she did not want to be alone. That was her biggest fear, was to be alone. So she married an abusive man. And as I was driving her back to the airport, I was like, "Mom, you don't have to go. Just stay here, you're fine, we'll get your things brought back, there's no reason for you to go back to him." And she was just bent on going back to him. What finally happened on that car ride ... that was my day that I said, "Mom, I'm going to get a divorce. I don't want to live the rest of my life in a situation where I have an abusive person involved in it. I found a group called Prevail. It has helped me escape."

ME: *They're the best!*

P.J.: They are. They helped me get out of my situation. Meanwhile, I was going to a group called GenderNexus on Tuesdays during my journey through all of this. Before I even said the words, "I identify as male," or "I have he/him pronouns," or "I am a man; I am a transgender man," I was going to these meetings. I would sit there quietly, listening to everybody's stories, and not communicate very often, but listen and realize that I'm not alone.

What helped more than anything was I have gone to now four Transgender Nights of Remembrance. We did not get to have one last year because of COVID. But at the first one, it was my awakening. And at my next one I will be grieving, because I do know people that have lost their lives at this point.

ME: *I'm sorry.*

P.J.: I don't know them personally, physically, presently. I knew them through the avenues or the groups that I belong to.

Queering Indy is another group that I belong in. I belong in some Facebook groups, but there are a lot of Facebook groups out there ... please be careful. There is a lot of information out there in the world via YouTube or via Reddit or whatever that people will act like they are transgender, or they will be saying this is real clinical information about transgender people ... and they are misleading and misguiding people into believing something that is not true. Please be careful when doing research to look deeply at their credentials and who these people are, and see if they're legitimate. People are really good at deceiving people when they want to make a point. They are—not to get political—but you see this every day through politics. And it is politics when it comes to this because we're fighting to just be able to use the restroom. I don't know if my friend Jack touched point on that at all. But right now, because of how I look, I can't just walk into a restroom. I will hold it for seven hours if I have to, until I can get home. Or I go to Starbucks because they have single bathrooms.

ME: *Right. Jack did touch on it. I guess a friend called them from San Diego and said, "Jack, you won't believe this. They've got all the restrooms in the airport! It's great!"*

P.J.: It's something that people don't understand. You have to kind of think of it like this. When I was in "girl mode"—you can use that phrase all you want—when I was in girl mode, I had no problem walking into a men's restroom if there was no restroom to be used. But right now, it risks my life. I risk getting beat up, because they're gonna go, "Oh, you're transgender. That gives me the right to beat you up."

A transgender woman walks into a restroom, somebody starts screaming, "There's a man in the bathroom!" A little kid [can crawl] under the stall ... but you know, [people think] it is terrifying [if a transgender woman is in the bathroom]. The likelihood of transgender women getting a UTI because they've had to hold their going to the restroom for hours and hours ... it's just normal. That is a normal thing. You get UTIs because you can't go to this room. So these are the little things that get in the way.

ME: *Is there anything else you wanted to say before we conclude today?*

P.J.: I hope that I'm presenting or representing my community in a better light. But I do not speak for the entire community. It's always better to seek knowledge than it is to throw trash. Remember that. Like how Black people, Latinos are treated ... transgender people are a minority. You might be surprised that you already know someone that is transgender and you have no idea. That happened to me. You might be surprised by who people are when they take off their mask. So be cautious and be careful with how you speak to someone. Always offer respect. Respect is something you can offer and it's free! It's not really going to hurt you to be just polite.

ME: Yeah, this has been beautiful. I have been enthralled, and I've learned so much.

P.J.: Please do watch this one person that does podcasts—and you might have to dig into his archives a little bit—but his name is Jammidodger [Jamie Raines]. If you look it up on YouTube, he's hysterically funny. He is actually a doctor. He has his doctorate in gender studies basically. So he is not missing knowledge and he is very wholesome. So you'll enjoy that.

ME: I'll watch it, and I will share that link!

Organizations and individuals mentioned during this interview:
- Jammidodger's YouTube: https://www.youtube.com/watch?v=iqKWp1clXzU
- Prevail of Central Indiana: www.prevailinc.com
- Transgender Night of Remembrance: www.glaad.org/tdor
- Queering Indy: https://www.facebook.com/groups/QueeringIndy

The people who put limits on your
abilities, goals, or dreams may not be the
people you want to associate yourself with.

−ROBERT CHEEKE

SUSAN

Yumi, now known as Susan, will always have a special place in my heart. She taught me to be more confident as a nerdy girl/teenager. Susan was there for me for my high school graduation and first wedding, even though we hadn't seen each other often. I was thrilled to find her on Facebook and reconnect a few years ago. She's one of the inspirations for this book. I think you'll see why!

> **CURRENT NAME:** Susan
> **GIVEN NAME:** Yumi
> **AGE:** 51
> **IDENTIFIES AS:** Female
> **ETHNICITY:** Korean American
> **OCCUPATION:** Surgical Territory Manager

SUSAN: My birth name—because I wasn't born in the United States, I was born in Seoul, South Korea—is Yumi Choi. "Che" is how you pronounce it. The Koreans actually put the surname first, so last name first, first name last. That's how I would always introduce myself in Korea. But you come to the United States and I become Yumi Choi. *ME: I've never asked you this—why did you change your name in your teens, to Susan?*

SUSAN: I feel like it was sixth grade, maybe fifth grade. My parents became American citizens. And as dependents, [my sister and I] became American citizens because they had to go through the whole naturalization process. We studied, meaning me as a fourth/fifth grader had to learn US history at a high school level. That's what was required to pass the test to be a naturalized American citizen.

When you pass that and you're able to become a US citizen, you're given an opportunity to assimilate. Back then it was assimilation, you know. So you can choose an American name. For me, my mom picks Susan, because in Korea there is a Sujin, and she said that was one of the names that she was kind of thinking about naming me [when I was born]. But she went with Yumi, so it's very close to Susan. She liked the sound of that name. Even my mom changed her name to Gina, though, because that was the process back then to become White America.

ME: Did all five of you—your father, mother and all three of the daughters—go by your American names?

SUSAN: Lycia, my youngest sister, was the only one born in the United States. So she already had an American name when she was born in South Bend Memorial Hospital. My dad, he's that traditional Korean male, he didn't want to change his name. His name was pretty simple. He just took part of his first name, "Moon," so everyone called him Moon. It was just my mom, myself, and Jennifer. [Jennifer] picked her name.

ME: Okay, interesting! … Ethnicity?

SUSAN: In a lot of the documents, I would identify myself as Asian or Pacific Islander. That's usually the box I check. I identify myself as American, Korean American.

ME: All right! Well, here's the fun part. Tell me about where you were born and how you grew up.

SUSAN: I don't remember a lot of Korea because I came here when I was about five and a half. I remember a little bit about the neighborhood and maybe some faces. But I was born in South Korea. My mom, my dad, and my sister who was two years younger, Jennifer—back then she was Yu Chung—and [I] came to the United States in 1977.

I remember more about Mishawaka [Indiana] .... Why did we land in Mishawaka? Because my dad's side of the family had already moved to the United States and had settled in New York and Mishawaka. We were kind of sponsored to come to the United States, so we landed in Mishawaka.

ME: *And why did they come over to the States?*

SUSAN: Back in the late seventies there was a lot of opportunity for—I'm sure there were other countries but in particular, Korea—there were a lot of opportunities to come to the United States. Opportunities for your children, education for your children. It was just a matter of being able to come to America, the land of opportunity, and being able to work hard and succeed. That was the story. My parents bought that story.

They had two girls, so they wanted to give us the opportunity to pursue education, things like that. It took, I think, five years to get here ... the visa process. Americans are very interested in [how] you come to the United States ... under what circumstances and if you're legal. I don't think people really understand the process that it takes to come here legally.

ME: *So did you live in that yellow house on Jefferson Street right away?*

SUSAN: No, we were close to Elkhart. I went through first grade there and I think we were at maybe low-income housing there—more apartments. They were really nice because they had just built them. And the reason I mentioned that is because when my mom was pregnant with Lycia, we had to leave because it wasn't gonna accommodate five people in that apartment. And that's what brought us to the yellow house on Jefferson. We were only there [the apartment] maybe less than two years and then we had to move. I think by the time you and I met, I was probably going into second grade.

ME: *Yep, I remember second grade! What were some of the struggles that you and your family had at that time?*

SUSAN: At that time the language barrier was huge. I didn't speak English very well because I had only been in the States for maybe a year, year and a half. My parents were worse off because they're adults, so they weren't at school. Kids pick it up quickly. Mishawaka was very blue collar, very White. There wasn't a whole lot of diversity going on when I landed at Mary Phillips School. In fact, I couldn't even tell you if there were any people of color besides my sister and myself.

ME: *I don't [think I could] either.*

SUSAN: The struggle, I think, for our family was language and probably finances. My dad worked at the factory because it's an RV, blue-collar manufacturing area, so he was a welder. Back in those days, they didn't pay very much. At Mary Phillips School what were my challenges? I think because I was different or I looked different. I used to have my hair braided really tight into pigtails. Some of the teachers thought I was Native American, which is very interesting because I had no idea what a Native American was because I was seven! I remember thinking, *What is that?* I didn't know what that was.

ME: *I remember those pigtails!*

SUSAN: Yeah, my mom … we would bathe at night and she would—in the morning it was so rushed—so she would braid all of our hair, all three of us, because we had long hair and we would be ready to go in the morning.

ME: Oh, I love it. You are taking me back, girl. So language and income. You told me some stories I think … I think your sister got picked on one time?

SUSAN: So I'm the oldest, right? I have a more dominant personality whereas my sisters are not as—I don't want to say aggressive. But as the oldest, I remember we'd have to walk home and we would get picked on, and it's not a big deal for me. I just kind of let it go, but I remember in one instance where a boy had thrown a rock across the street, and it hit my sister on the head and she started bleeding. It wasn't a huge rock, but enough to make her bleed. She was crying and it was unexpected, of course. I remember running across the street and pretty much attacking that boy who was probably a lot bigger than me, because I wasn't very big in grade school. I was like fifty-five pounds.

The funny story is, later that evening, that little boy and his father showed up at our house. The dad was very upset that I attacked his son. My mom—and you know she doesn't understand much English, and my dad doesn't understand much English, so she gets the gist. She looks at me and she goes, "Why did you do that?" I told her the story and she was very apologetic to that father and the son. "So sorry, it won't happen again."

That dad got a look at me because he didn't come in, this is all at the front door ... he took a look at me ... I think he had a different impression after that. He was more mad at his son that he got beaten up by this little Asian girl. So they walked away, never to bother us again. That boy just, like, avoided me like I was the plague. I think that was a good lesson for me and probably set a little bit of a precedence that I wasn't going to be this meek little person. I was going to be able to just kind of address it at the moment and kind of handle it.

I think if I didn't have some of these experiences that I might have a little different personality. But I always say this—I share this with my husband all the time—I'm the product of the US. I was able to take these experiences, kind of master them, if you will, and then use those experiences to go through my life.

ME: *Have you and your family faced a lot of outright discrimination?*
SUSAN: Oh, of course, yeah. I don't think it was ever, like, physical danger like maybe some of the other ethnic groups may face. I never felt like I was going to be attacked physically or harmed. But there are always subtle—which could be pervasive—prejudices, racism, whatever. Maybe not the same opportunities ... We all do it, it's just human nature.

You look at someone, you've already kind of assessed them based on what they look like. How they're dressed, how they speak. I get it. I'm guilty of it myself. I try not to do it, but I would say that's the kind of racism that I have faced in my years. I still face those stereotypes. Some are good stereotypes that I don't mind. A lot of Asians get the stereotype that we're smarter, we're driven, hard working. A lot of times we might not be seen as maybe poor or taking advantage of society and the systems. That's, I guess, a good stereotype, if you will.

If I were [typecast] in some way, some of the negative stereotypes is that by looking at me, a middle-aged Asian woman, that maybe I'm supposed to be more subdued, maybe a little more submissive, kind of quiet, shy. So in the business world, that's not helpful. Those stereotypes are damaging economically, career-wise. There's a female component to it too. I know that the book is not about being a woman, but in my line of work where it involves a lot of technology and electronics and imaging, women still aren't seen or perceived to be knowledgeable in that field. We're judged by a lot of, like, doctors, surgeons, bioengineers, biomedical engineers, even staff. You still have that perception in my field that you're gonna be pretty much a six-foot, White, Caucasian male. I have kind of a double whammy sometimes that I have to kind of navigate depending on which scenario I'm in. I have to be able to kind of adjust and adapt. I've been very good at that. I think part of that is because I've had that on a daily basis. No matter how small, those little racial prejudices are kind of what I have to deal with on a daily basis.

ME: *Is there one example you can think of specifically?*

SUSAN: I'll tell you the story. I think I was in southern Indiana. I literally stopped at a Walmart to pick up some soda or something like that. I was in line to check out and there was an older gentleman. He looked, like, farmer-ish. Anyway, he was looking at me. He seemed like he was having some kind of thought issue. He was making certain noises.

I said, "Would you like to go ahead of me?" because I thought *maybe he's in a hurry.*

He goes, "No, that's okay. I'm just kind of waiting anyway."

He keeps staring at me. It's an uncomfortable stare. And I don't know this gentleman—not that I was afraid. Then he goes, "So where do I get me one of you?"

ME: *Oh my God!*

SUSAN: This was probably, I want to say eleven years ago, so it's not like a long time ago. I looked at him—and I am very tolerant of older folks, not peers or younger folks because they should know better. It's a different generation. But with the older folks, because I'm very good at collecting data—I feel like a computer a lot of times—I scan the room … like I said, older gentleman in a rural area. So I'm more accepting of some of the flaws maybe or things that I may not agree with, it's not as shocking to me as opposed to if I were in a different forum with college graduates and educated people. People who are professionals, I would expect more, so it's different for me. I don't know how to explain that, but every situation is different.

Anyway, in that situation, humor came out and I said, "Oh, probably the internet." He just looked at me. I don't know if he knew what I was talking about. Then I paid and was on my way. But that's what I mean. Some people may take great offense to that. I do not. Like I said, I scan the room and act accordingly.

I do have another story that's kind of interesting—and this is maybe shocking to others, but at the time it was not shocking to me …. This is a colleague who is probably fifteen years younger than me and she's a female. Same position as me. We were going to a training session and we had arrived early. We were shopping at the Mall of America—I'll give you that reference point. We stopped at Sephora, the makeup store. I'm not into the makeup store, but she wanted to go buy some things. There was a clerk or associate and she was Asian. She wasn't Korean, but she was Asian. But [my friend] looks at her … and she was pretty because she works in the makeup store, so she had makeup that was perfect. So my friend, she says to her, "So what colors are good on Orientals?"

ME: *Oh my gosh.*

SUSAN: This was probably five years ago. So here's where there's a disconnect. You could see it on her face; it totally threw her, because she was younger … I would say midtwenties. I'm late forties at that time, so I'm not taken aback, but [the sales woman] clearly was uncomfortable. So I started laughing and I looked at Lindsay—a White female. Lindsay looks at me and she is clueless. I mean, this was not in malice. This is just what it was, so you can't be angry about that. But I kind of laughed and I said, "What are you asking her?"

And she goes, "Well, you know, there's certain colors that look better on certain skin tones. So what looks good on Orientals?"

And I said, "We're not rugs. We're not faces." She had no idea ... no idea.

Later that evening when we met our other colleagues for dinner, the story came up. I asked her if it was okay. I didn't want to put her on the spot and make her feel bad. She was fine with it. The whole group of White men and one White female were very offended, *very* offended by it. And I said, "Why are you guys offended? I wasn't." It's so minor compared to the experiences I've had. I don't want to say I'm numb to it, but those kinds of things don't trigger me, you see what I mean?

ME: *Yeah. That's an interesting perspective because everyone gets super offended even though it's not about them at all. So, wow, that is interesting.*

SUSAN: Yeah. I tell you that story because I think we need to be less ... we, everyone, not just the people of color. This is just my opinion, we need to just maybe relax a little. Not be super hypersensitive or triggered and go off. But maybe take the moment to kind of share. Maybe share it in a way that's not uncomfortable, not accusatory, or you know, hanging someone out to dry. But sharing the story where everyone can chime in.

It worked out beautifully. It wasn't my intention to do that, but just for her, the shock of our peers—male White peers—that she had said that in public ... it made her kind of understand. She did not know. I was surprised that she didn't know because that was five years ago—so, you know, 2017 or '16. [And] because she's educated; she's very professional. It was a teaching moment. She didn't mean anything in malice, and everyone needs to kind of assess the situation. There are certain times ... you're never gonna educate certain people. You're never going to change their mind. I don't know if giving up on them is the right word ... maybe a little.

ME: *I'm curious, were you and your family able to continue your Korean traditions? I know you did with food. I remember I had some.*

SUSAN: We did do some of the Korean traditions. Like you said, food is a big part in any culture. That's how you celebrate all the good moments, the milestones in your life. I think we spoke a mix of English/Korean at home because my parents still were more Korean dominant in their language. English was their secondary language, but they never were formally educated in English. They just picked it up through the process of being in the United States. So they relied on me quite heavily because, again, I was the oldest. I picked up on things very quickly. I was managing our checkbook at like eight years old!

ME: *Oh my word!*

SUSAN: Yeah, I was writing out the checks. I wasn't when they were working. But I had to learn—physically write the checks out—because they couldn't write in English. And then balance the checkbook and read all the mail that came to the house. Whether it was utility bills or school, anything that came through the house I had to read and interpret. Circling back to the time where all of us—the whole family—had to study for my parents to go for their US citizenship. I had to read all this US history. It was like a workbook and I had to record and my parents would listen to it all night.

I would have to say, "Who was the first president of the United States?" Then I would answer, "George Washington." It was probably a good 200 questions, maybe 250. I would read all these questions, and they would listen to it, and that's how they learned. It's interesting, you never would have gotten that perspective. "How many branches of government are there in the United States?" What eight-year-old knows this information? So that's how they learned. Actually, it wasn't really learning; it was memorizing the government facts.

ME: *Yeah. Were there any Asian grocery stores around us up there?*

SUSAN: No, not at that time. I think the only Asian restaurant was that Hi Ho Chop Suey place. I want to say it was on Lincolnway but I can't remember. The grocery store didn't come till toward the end of my junior high. We know the people who own that store. I think there was one Asian store, but that was maybe eighth or ninth grade.

ME: *I didn't even think about that because living in central Indiana for so long, we've got the ones in Castleton and I know there's so many others.*

SUSAN: Obviously food is a connector of people. Look at how many Thai restaurants and Vietnamese restaurants ... it's not just Chinese as an offering. You have Japanese. There's so much Asian food. All kinds of food.

ME: Did your parents ... did you tell me they opened up a restaurant?

SUSAN: Yes. So I went to middle school ... oh, I have to tell you about middle school because I did get bullied at middle school. That's a funny story.

ME: Oh yeah, we'll have to hear about that.

SUSAN: We left Mishawaka because this one Korean lady had a little Chinese restaurant; it was more carryout. There was only, I want to say, seven booths. Very small place. She was gonna retire and she went to church with us. She knew my mom and my mom was like, "This is an opportunity that we probably should take." So that's what made us move to Elkhart and that was after my freshman year. My parents worked at that little Chinese restaurant. It's called Egg Roll Heaven. We sold, like, so many egg rolls—like probably seven hundred to eight hundred a day.

ME: Wow! Okay. So what happened at the middle school?

SUSAN: Oh yeah. I was tagged as one of the smart kids. But John Young was kind of rough, if you remember. It was kind of different going from little Mary Phillips School. It was kind of a scary little walk from my house because you had to ... go through this, like, alley and through this fencing. You kind of had to squeeze through. It was weird.

There was a group of kids—I think they were a lot more experienced than me. I think they were doing a lot of, like, drinking and drugs and sex and stuff. There was one girl in particular—I don't know if you knew [her]—Stacy. She was a smart girl, red hair. We had a lot of classes together and she would sit behind me and she would just kind of pick at me. Going back to my standing-my-ground personality that I acquired as I was living in Mishawaka, I said, "Stop messing with my hair." I turned around and told her that. Well, she didn't like that. She made a point to kind of pick on me with her group and we had some words in the bathroom. There was some shoving and then I think one day, there was talk that she was gonna fight me after school. The principal came out and she got expelled.

ME: *Wow!*

SUSAN: Yes. You want to hear the funny part of the story? When we moved to Elkhart, I started to go to Jimtown—very small school. She worked at … back then it was the Revco, which was the Osco Drugstore. So I hadn't seen her for a year because she got kicked out for multiple reasons, and one of them was trying to fight. But she was working at the Revco where I was applying, so we both worked [there]. That was like, "Well, this is a small world. This is just kind of weird." Here's the funny part—she apologized. I don't know, her life story might have been rough as well. I'm not quite sure all that had happened, but she did apologize to me. I forgave her; I didn't forget. So we would be coworkers and we were nice to each other. I thought it was interesting that it circled back.

ME: *Yeah, it's super wild! So you graduated from Jimtown and then—I know where you went to school. You went to Notre Dame, right?*

SUSAN: Yes.

ME: *So when did you meet your wonderful husband?*

SUSAN: Thank you for bringing that up. We just had our twenty-fourth anniversary.

ME: *Happy anniversary!*

SUSAN: Thank you. We've known each other thirty-one years. We met at Kroger. It was our summer job …. We dated seven and a half years before we got married. We had a long engagement. I think quite a bit about commitment, any commitment. I don't want to commit to something unless I know I'm going to be able to deliver. Marriage was a huge commitment decision. So it took me a minute.

ME: *His name's Joe, right?*

SUSAN: Yeah, he's a very good man. Our dynamic is number one because we've been together so long—more than half our lives. But when we first were dating, we were complete opposites. I'm the oldest child; he's the youngest child. He kind of grew up in a Beaver Cleaver type of upbringing and had an older sister. His mom was a stay-at-home mom, do you know what I mean?

ME: *Oh yeah, I lived it!*

SUSAN: Exactly. Your lives are completely opposite of my life. We struggled as a family; my parents worked and we all had to do our part, some more than others. We all had to excel. It was just this mindset, this work ethic. It wasn't optional. So anyway, a totally different way. He had this kind of mindset of, "Well, it'll work out." Whereas I had to plan things. There was next step, next step, what's next. Where his was like, "Oh!" It was just totally different. So my point is, [we were] complete opposites. Now we're very similar. It's kind of interesting.

ME: *Well, I have to point out the obvious. He's White, I believe. Did you guys ever get any flack about that?*

SUSAN: Of course we got it. So my parents—they dropped us in Mishawaka, Indiana. My parents were very opposed to me or any of us dating White.

ME: *Wow!*

SUSAN: Yes, it's still very much … even in 2021, it's still a little taboo. It's a little bit more accepting. But you gotta understand that Korea is very homogeneous in its own right. There's not a whole lot of diversity in Korea. They're all Korean! It's getting a little better. You've got to think of it in that mindset. But if you want to be realistic about it, there were no Koreans in my school. Like, where am I supposed to meet the other Koreans? So my parents were … especially my father … part of that is probably because he's, you know, Dad. I don't think any dad wants any daughters to date. But part of that was they just had this vision that it was going to be, you know, us marrying Koreans. Where they thought we were going to find these Koreans, I have no idea, because we had never gone back to Korea since we came here in '77. We didn't have the funds. Then later in life we did better, when I was about in high school. But work—the restaurant was open six days a week, 7 [a.m.] to 10 [p.m.] every day except Sunday. Sunday was for church. So we never went back to Korea.

When we were dating, this was probably '89, '88, I don't know if we got a lot of stares. I feel that sometimes we would get certain … I would sense it. But not that we were being shunned. We could go out to dinner. We would be served; there wasn't gonna be an issue.

But I remember one time we were in Valparaiso meeting my sister Jennifer and her husband, who is also White. We walked in to the restaurant and the restaurant got really quiet because there were two Asians and two Whites coming in together for dinner. You know how you come into a restaurant—it's busy—you hear that dinner noise throughout the whole restaurant? Then when we walked in and we were being seated, it was quiet. I remember that so vividly today because Joe felt it—my husband—my sister felt it, I felt it. But my brother-in-law did not feel it. He didn't even notice. I thought it was interesting—the perspective. You're in the same place, you're at the same table, but everyone has their own perception. He was with us and he did not notice.

ME: *That is interesting! So you have two beautiful sons.*

SUSAN: Thank you. They are outstanding. I think I was meant to always be a boy's mom because I'm not so warm and fuzzy. I am, but not all the time.

ME: *Yeah. How's their world? Have they faced any issues?*

SUSAN: Well, they probably have. We don't talk about it as much. I think we've had the opportunity to live here in Carmel, Indiana. Both my husband and I are well-educated professionals. They've had a lot of opportunities. They've had a charmed life. That doesn't mean that they haven't faced certain prejudices from other kids as they went through school.

My conversation with them has always been, "Do your best. Work hard. Don't judge people just by what they look like or how they're dressed. Try to get to know people for who they are. You don't have to like everyone and not everyone's gonna like you. The only solution to equalize the playing field is success." So that has always been my message to them.

I think early on, maybe in grade school where they wouldn't be accepted into certain cliques because they were different … I'm not sure if that's it or if it's personality. I don't know because I wasn't there.

I would say to them, "The only way that you're going to be accepted is if you're successful." What does that mean? At school, you're smart, you're great, you're successful in that, so you're going to be included in those groups where you know those kids are smart kids. If you're doing sports, go out there, do your best. If possible, in sports, you're going to be accepted; you're going to be included. It's an equalizer. So if you're not going to be successful, if you're not going to work hard, try hard … it's not gonna be given to you like how it is with some kids. Because maybe their parents are coaches or their parents are teachers. You know what I'm talking about.

There are a lot of politics involved and it's always gonna be like that in any arena. So nothing is going to be given to you; nothing has been given to me. So if you want it, you've got to work hard and be successful at it. I think that message has been told a few times, so my kids have always really strived for excellence. It's not really an option here.

ME: *You are a big-time football mom.*

SUSAN: I am a big-time football mom! My kids, like I said, they've had a charmed life. They've been able to participate in anything that they wanted to. They both played football and loved it … different positions. Nico's my bigger, my oldest. He's a big guy. I don't know where he got it from. So he's my strong, big guy. My younger one has always been just really dominant as far as speed and ability.

ME: *Nice! So this is the toughest question of the night, and that's, What's currently happening in our world? I cannot believe I'm talking to you—what is it—two, three weeks after Atlanta? [I am referencing the spa shootings that occurred in March of 2021, when several Asian Americans were targeted and killed.]*

SUSAN: Yeah, I know, because you probably didn't even think about this.

ME: *No.*

SUSAN: I'm a little mixed about it. What I mean by that is ... not that I've ever felt physically threatened. I think I feel more physically vulnerable as a woman. Like, I would never walk down a dark city street by myself or on campus. I don't think it's an Asian thing, an ethnic thing. It's more that it was a woman thing. That's been my experience.

But I have felt some of those racist prejudices. It's hard to say. I'll share it with you. So everyone is going to judge people based on this outward appearance. You have Black folks, you have Asian folks ... this is how we're born. We can't change our appearance. I just feel like in America for some reason, there seems to be a need to blame or have a scapegoat. I'm basing this on really nothing but my own observations.

So you're going to have periods or times where you're going to target more, maybe, Black Americans. And [there's all the] suffering and discrimination that they have to face. Then there's some protesting and there's more visibility. There's more light shed on that. It gets a little too hot—and I'm not saying by the collective. There's no, like, grand scheme. Then it moves to a different ethnicity or different folks. I just feel like it's a spinning wheel. Like a roulette wheel. It's just constantly taking turns. I share this with people and they look at me like I'm kind of crazy, but that's how I feel.

So right now, Black Lives Matter—that was at the forefront. And rightfully so. But it's too hot right now. The people who are wanting to create that chaos, wanting to create harm ... [they] can't target Black folks or it's too hot for them, so they're gonna move on. So you've got the Asians. Schools are not being targeted as much because [of their] awareness, all that preparation. So now you're going to get small stores, small restaurants, small businesses because they're not prepared for these kind of attacks.

So what's my point? ... Before [Black] Lives Matter, it was the Mexicans or the Latinos ... the whole border thing and the whole particular jobs thing ... that whole mantra, then it was "Black Lives Matter." Now it's "Don't hate the Asians." Who's next? I don't know. Jewish, Muslims? Someone's always got to take it on the chin. I don't know how to explain that, but that's what I see in my fifty-one years.

Does that mean that there's no hope? I don't think so because I feel like in my time in Indiana, there's been progress. Just like going back to what you were saying about Asian stores and Asian restaurants and the influx of different cuisines, Asian cuisines. It's changing, but you're still going to have a huge population of people that lack a couple things to be more accepting and enlightened. One is education. I'm not just talking about going to college. I'm talking about learning different cultures and different people. The knowledge and empathy … there's very little empathy going on. Because it's all about "me," and how *I* feel, and what *I* want to say. Without those two things, you're still going to have racism; you're just going to have it. That's my opinion.

To go back to your question about my thoughts on this targeting of Asians … I think it's disgusting. It seems to me from the news that they're targeting women and old people. I mean, that is cowardly. That is so cowardly. It's sad to see that in 2021, we're still having all this violence. But I watched a really good program on PBS. I feel like it was last year. It was a really great four- or five-day docuseries. It was about eight Asian Americans. It wasn't just on Koreans. It was the Chinese, how they came and built the railroads. And the fact that people don't really know; it's just a little blurb in our history.

Because it's not White American history. How all those folks came here for whatever reason, whether they were brought here, kind of indentured-servant slaves—not to the degree of Black Americans, but they came here not willingly, some of them. Some of them came here willingly to send money back because they're so poor and opportunities, what have you. They literally took a leap of faith like my parents did. But they were lynched all the time. There was no reason. There was no trial. There was constant lynching of the Chinese. *ME: Really? I don't think I've ever heard that.*
SUSAN: Yes, they were strung up all the time for any of [them] looking at you as you were walking by. It's horrible. There was that and that was a long, long time ago. There is that history. They had the worst jobs. They were looked upon as like dogs or animals. Worse than that. They struggled through that and that was blatant racism.

When Japan bombed Hawaii ... how they took all these Japanese—a lot of them born in America—these *Americans* and took them to different camps and held them there for years. Not for a week. Not for a month. But for years. Children, old people, and some of those folks were not Japanese! Because you can't tell. So how does that happen in America? That's a stain on American history. It was a really interesting documentary. It's called *Asian Americans*.

They were talking about some of the stereotypes that we have of Asians being smart or not poor. What do you call it? Being good contributors to society. Not troublemakers. That was all tagged. I found this to be super interesting. The American immigration policy back in the seventies and so forth, when they wanted that influx [of Asians]—they would only give visas to professionals. Doctors, scientists, mathematicians, physicists. So unless you had family here or a company that would sponsor you, you couldn't come here. You've got this "brain trust" that came to the United States. That's why there's this perception and that's why there's a negative perception on maybe, like, Mexican citizens.

If you came here sponsored by a company, you could be a surgeon, you can be a physicist ... it's super interesting how these stereotypes come about, and that documentary was just really enlightening.

ME: *I'll have to watch that.*

SUSAN: It's so good ... so much information. Like you didn't know about the lynching that went on all the time. They were hating Chinese people—men—left and right for no reason. They were in the way. It's not like Asians haven't faced these dangers. Then with the Vietnam War, there was kind of that anti-Asian, antigovernment sentiment you kept hearing.

ME: *I cringed when I heard people say "China virus" last year. That just made me sick. I'm like, "Don't call it that!"*

SUSAN: It just, again, goes back to what I'm talking about—education and knowledge. Not to change the subject, but Corona beer ... their sales went way down because their name was Corona. It's not even made in China or in Asia, so it's kind of interesting. Crazy. The logic, or the lack of it, just amazes me.

It's hard to know how I feel with all the news and the video clips that I'm seeing on social media where there's these unprovoked attacks. It makes me feel a little unsettled. I feel fine where I live, but we're planning a trip to New York to check out a college. They just started to do on-campus visits in New York. I'm a little nervous about being in the city. As we walk through the city, are we going to be targeted? I don't think so, but it's a different feeling. An unsettled feeling because I'm not a New Yorker. If I walk down the street, are we gonna be targeted because I'm an Asian woman? My husband's not gonna be a target—he's White. But you see what I'm saying? There are certain neighborhoods that we should probably avoid. I don't know … just kind of unsettling.

ME: *I'm sorry that you feel that way.*

SUSAN: Do I feel like that here or even when I go to Indy? No, because this is what I know. My world. But if I were to go to, like I said, New York City … or certainly I wouldn't go visiting down South. I have no desire to go to Atlanta or something. I just feel like it's probably not good. It puts myself in danger. I don't want to do that. They're targeting people without being provoked.

ME: *You've pretty much gone through everything I was going to ask today, and you kind of answered the one that is next to the end where I ask, What would you tell the world to do differently for people like you? I think I'm summing it up pretty well when you said … to just have some conversations and share. There's no need to be belligerent; just try to take those opportunities and educate [each other].*

SUSAN: Like I said, it's about education and it's about empathy. I think you know in certain scenarios, people get triggered even if that prejudice or racism is not on them. They feel the need to just jump in and, you know, save the day and set these people right. I don't know if that's a good strategy, because no one wants to be attacked. No one wants to be told "wrong." No one wants to be singled out.

You know, it escalates. I think that's a key word: "de-escalate." Everyone needs to de-escalate. That's probably what needs to happen, because without those two things [education and empathy], you're going to have racism. Because people are afraid of what they don't know. There's still a lot of people that I know through my kids' school … they don't have any friends of color. They might have coworkers, or they know someone who has a friend. But everyone's safe in their little pods still.

The other part is, like I said, people of color or people who want to kind of help and support people of color. They have to understand that you can't just come in and just yell and try to educate people. It's not really maybe the right time or the right venue. I think people need to de-escalate. If you shove things in people's face, it just makes things worse. What I see is you have all these people just kind of jumping in because they are so passionate about it. They want to make things right, but I don't think that helps a lot of time. You've got to do something, but there's a way to do it right.

ME: *Do you know any organizations that are doing things like this?*

SUSAN: No …. So me and a lot of people like me that were either born here or came here as young children, we walk a different path than some of the other folks because we're not … I mean, obviously, genetically DNA-wise, I'm all Korean. But [I] haven't grown up in Korea. So I miss some of those innuendos and those little inflections.

I'm not completely Korean. I'm not completely accepted by the Korean community. As Koreans, when they see me, they see me as a White girl. But in the White circle, I'm not really White; I'm Korean. I'm not a mixed child like my kids are, but I still have to play that part because I'm not completely accepted by White[s] as White. And I'm not completely accepted by Korean[s] as Korean. So I have a different perspective, I think.

Some people—and I would say that is true for other folks that you know—have kind of grown up here and became Americans. But we still have our food. We still have our cultures. We still have our superstitions. But we have become American. We're Americans too. So we have all the American traditions.

ME: *Well, before we finish up, is there anything I have forgotten that you might want to say?*

SUSAN: I don't think so. I was just kind of open to the conversation. I hoped to give you some of my thoughts on it. It doesn't reflect, probably, the mass thought on racism and targeting Asians or whatever. I'm just sharing my experiences. My experience with racism has been subtle, but always present. Everyone's got different experiences, and I really think it depends on what city, what state, even your home life. It just depends. Someone who lives in the inner city is going to have a different experience than someone who lives in the suburbs. It's just human nature. It's just life. We all try to get through it, but we're all human beings. I personally don't know why this still exists today.

ME: *I know. Honestly, it's sad, isn't it?*

SUSAN: It's super sad because we all just want to live. We just want to be happy; we want to raise our kids. This is a common goal, belief system, of all human beings, and I don't understand why it has to get political and why it has to be economical. It's sad. I feel like there's a solution. We're intelligent. We're supposed to be intelligent. I don't understand why it's still to this degree. It seems to have ebbs and flows, which is also sad. You see all these news clips of the fifties, the seventies, but flash forward to just last year, this year, and it's like it seems more violent.

ME: *Well, thank you! Thank you so much for your time, my friend.*

Resources mentioned during this interview:

- *Asian Americans* documentary: https://www.pbs.org/weta/asian-americans/watch/

Although we're not responsible for history, we are responsible for what happens today, and for what happens in the future. Racism impacts all of us. And we all have a role to play in ending it.

–DERRIK ANDERSON, EXECUTIVE DIRECTOR OF RACE MATTERS FOR JUVENILE JUSTICE

ROB AND DENISE

*R*ob and Denise are two more of my hoop-dancing friends. Their remarkable faith, amazing marriage, and kindness have inspired me from the start. They are both gentle yet strong people. I'd never talked to them about Rob's disability until now. I learned a great deal from them.

> **NAME:** Rob and Denise
> **AGE:** 64 and 50
> **IDENTIFY AS:** Male and Female
> **ETHNICITY:** White
> **OCCUPATION:** Retired

ME: How did you two meet and when?
ROB: In a singles bar!
DENISE: He says a singles bar, but I say a salad bar …. Okay, but it really was church.
ROB: Yes … I was thinking, *Here I am handicapped—severely handicapped,* and I'd say, "No girl would want me … I'm single …" So I have been, from the very beginning, saying I should meet someone that knows me and likes my Christianity. I thought that the best place would be church. In that way, they have all the same values, tendencies, and characteristics that I like.

DENISE: Now if you have trouble understanding anything, just ask. Did you catch that? [*Rob has some communication challenges and some people may struggle to understand him upon first meeting him.*]

ME: *I did ... that he was thinking, "No girl would want me because I'm handicapped." I'm embarrassed ... I've known you now two or three years and I don't think I've ever asked: Rob, what happened? Have you been like this all of your life or were you in an accident? What brought you to having this disability?*

DENISE: He wrote a book about it.

ROB: Yeah.

ME: *Wow!*

DENISE: We probably should go back further.

ME: *Sure.*

DENISE: I grew up with a mom who's a nurse, and my parents took care of foster children. One foster child had spina bifida and was in a wheelchair. And the family that lived in the house behind us, both the husband and wife had cerebral palsy. They had a daughter who had no disabilities, and she was a good friend of mine. So I was with disabled people, with my foster sister that lived with us for four years and the neighbors, a lot.

Then when I was thirteen years old, Rob was in the car accident, but I didn't know him. I heard about it because a friend of ours who went to his church asked us to pray for him.

ROB: On Halloween night, 1983, Marshall—my brother—and I went down to Broad Ripple [Indianapolis] to look at a Chevrolet Z28. A big guy—not fat, just big—named Douglas wanted to take us on a test drive to show us how well the car held the road. We went a quarter mile from the dealership. Everything was going fine. We speeded up to pass a car and then, for some reason, I have no idea why, Douglas stomped it. First of all, I've been told this by Marsh. I don't remember. When we impacted ... we killed two girls in the other car.

One of the girls was so badly injured that her boyfriend, who was working with a fire department, he didn't know who she was. She kind of fell out of the car into his arms and he had no idea. He didn't recognize her until someone read her ID.

ME: Oh my gosh ....

DENISE: [Rob] took a good long nap after that for four months. He was in a coma.

ME: Oh my word! And what age were you at this time?

ROB: Twenty-seven. Four months in a coma. Some people come to me and ask, "What happened when you woke up?" Marsh had to tell me what happened.

DENISE: His brother—he calls him Marsh, but his name's Marshall.

ROB: I couldn't believe it. I couldn't believe there was a car wreck. My memory is completely intact up to the time of the wreck. You know in my logbook from flying—

DENISE: He was a pilot, he had his own plane.

ROB: Yeah .... I wrote, like, a diary two days before. I remember the events in the logbook, but the day of the wreck and the following four months, I remember nothing.

ME: Oh my gosh ... So what did this leave you with? What injuries?

ROB: I sustained a closed-head injury similar to a small stroke.

ME: Wow.

ROB: Douglas lost his eye and had plastic surgery. He had some complications. Marshall had problems walking just for a short time. He's fine today. The problem was, I was the innocent "bysitter."

DENISE: He was sitting ... "bysitter" versus bystander.

ME: Got it!

ROB: It was Douglas, me, and Marshall. We impacted right there on Westfield Boulevard. There were a hundred officials at the center of the accident ... police ... firemen ... paramedics ... in 1983.

ME: Oh my word. So physically, I'm guessing, things were broken that night.

ROB: Dad came to Methodist Hospital and talked to the doctor. [The doctor] said, "Rob's behind this curtain ... his right hip is completely out of the socket. I'm going to go in and try to set it. If I don't, he'll require a pretty serious operation ... with an artificial hip."

DENISE: But he really wasn't that worried about the possibility of doing a surgery later, because they all thought he was going to die anyway. But he thought he'd do his duty and put it back in place. He said that Rob would not have been able to withstand the anesthetic, or the painkiller.

ROB: Yeah. Then talk about God working in mysterious ways. Here he's about to go behind the curtain ... but the thing was, I was unconscious so he just went to it. And I never felt a thing in four months.

ME: That's good! So you woke up slowly ... Did you have to have therapy for quite a while? Physical therapy and things like that?

DENISE: Oh yeah. He went to Hook's Rehab, which was at Community Hospital at the time. He still has physical therapy. We do our therapy at home. Ten to fifteen minutes of home therapy every night.

ME: So, for readers, just as an observation ... you are able to walk with a cane.

DENISE: For years he was able to walk without one, but he's gotten worse over the years.

ME: Gotcha.

DENISE: And now he has this walker that's called a hemiwalker. It's for people with one hand because he can't use both hands very well.

ME: Oh, I see. Okay.

DENISE: He has a motorized scooter—

ROB: To use at one of those places like shopping centers, grocery stores, or the fairgrounds.

ME: Right.

DENISE: And when we bought it years ago, we asked if it would be covered with the Medicare insurance that Rob had. The salesman said if you can walk, they won't cover it.

ME: Oh ... wow ....

DENISE: So we bought that and the scooter lift out of our own pocket. We also bought a minivan, which the scooter lift is in. Which was fine for us, but for a lot of families, it would be impossible to pay for all that. But it's made a huge difference in our ability to go places.

ME: Right, exactly! So, Rob, were you able to continue to work after this?

ROB: Yes and no.

DENISE: His dad owned the company Best Lock where Rob worked.

ROB: Because the company was owned by family, I kept going to work.

ME: Cognitively, you're sharp from what I've always seen. I mean, some of your jokes fall flat, but overall ... [I give him a wink and a smile, and we chuckle, as Rob is always telling jokes.]

ROB: I worked for about ten years afterward.

DENISE: Then when his brother took over the family business, he retired.

ROB: I thank God now I'm not in the rat race of the business world again. I feel like I've been there, done that.

ME: Me too, guys, me too. I like having my own business. I'm much happier. Oh my ... what a story. I'd like to read your book sometime, Rob. How do I get it?

DENISE: We could just bring you a copy. I'll just put one on your porch someday.

ME: Yes, please do. I'd like to read it, Rob.

ROB: It's called *Be Still*.

ME: Okay, that sounds wonderful. So how old were you when you both met?

DENISE: I think when we first met I may have been twenty ... I know I was twenty-one when we started dating. When we got married, I was twenty-two and he was thirty-five.

ME: Okay, and what drew you to him, Denise?

DENISE: Well, he wasn't gonna give up! No matter what, he was persistent. My brother worked at the company that his dad owned and he found my brother, got my phone number, and ... my brother couldn't say no to the boss's son!

ME: I love it!

DENISE: He just assured me that he just needed a nice lady to go with him to this event—it was this business dinner. But he just treated me so sweetly, so kindly.

ROB: She fell for it.

DENISE: He would just stare at me and act like he was just enthralled with my every word.

ME: Of course he was!

DENISE: And no other man did that ... a lot of them ... it was kind of like they were sort of afraid to invest too much. I didn't date that many different guys of course, I was only twenty-one when we got engaged.

ROB: And around that time, Dad was giving some advice. He was saying what you need to do is find someone that is really your friend.

DENISE: But he decided to settle for me. *[We all chuckle.]*

ME: I love it! So let's see ... you were married at twenty-two ... wow, twenty-eight years now, right?

ROB: Yes. I tell people, when they ask me about my marriage, I say on the scale of one to ten, our marriage is at eleven.

ME: That is outstanding!

DENISE: As you can imagine—I know you would not feel this way or think this because you are a more enlightened person—however, some people do seem to be surprised that disabled people are married.

ME: I bet.

DENISE: I have had people just kind of assume ... I mean servers in a restaurant asking if we want separate checks. A lot of times when you're with your spouse, they assume it's one check.

ME: Right.

DENISE: People referring to him ... like maybe we're at a shop and they'll say, "Well, does your buddy want this?" or "your friend" a few times over the years ... or "your brother."

ME: Wow ... that is odd.

DENISE: Sometimes people tell you things that somebody said about you that they should have never told you.

ROB: But if you tell someone what I'm going to tell you, we'll have to kill you. *[We burst into laughter once again.]* Nothing personal at all ... but somehow I found out that one of my relatives, through the grapevine, said, "Rob will never get married." The lady he told that to told us.

DENISE: Really she shouldn't have probably ....

ME: Right, oh my gosh. That's terrible.

ROB: I can pat myself on the back and say the thing that I stuck with from the very beginning ... I was determined to find a girl that had the same beliefs that I did. Because [your spouse's] beliefs are really important to you. If your faith is really important to you, it helps if it's important to your spouse.

ME: Oh yes, it does definitely. You are one determined person, Rob. I admire that about you.

DENISE: He's patting himself on the back.

ME: This man … I kid with him, but he really does have a great sense of humor and one of the best attitudes I've ever seen. So what are some of the good times you guys have had? All these years of marriage … what are some of the great experiences that pop up in your mind that you've shared together?

ROB: Well, believe it or not, one thing that impresses me is the daily … time when we go downstairs and do therapy. I learned myself, I have to … bend this and that way and then the stretches ….

ME: So you do that for him, Denise?

DENISE: We've got a mandatory "date"! We've been together all the time lately.

ME: Wow, so every morning you do physical therapy with Denise?

ROB: Every night.

ME: Every night. Okay, wonderful. I know you've shared that traveling can be a struggle, but what places have you been?

DENISE: Before the disability became more severe, it was hard, but we went to Germany, Austria, Switzerland, Mexico, the Bahamas, Alaska. We've been to several countries, back then you know, but we're sticking to the US and Canada now. The US is even better than Canada, for the most part, for disabled travelers. That's our experience anyway.

ME: Oh, well that's good to hear. There are sometimes I wonder about our country in that respect, but I'm glad we're leading in that area from what you've seen.

DENISE: Yeah, everything around here is so new. It's all handicapped accessible. We've been told, "Don't go to Italy. Don't go to these other places … there will not be any easy way to get around." Places like Nantucket. It's a fabulous place but there are cobblestone streets and you just have to be prepared to know whether or not you're going to be able to get around somewhere.

ME: Yes. So can you do research pretty easily nowadays thanks to the internet?

DENISE: Yes, but I think it's best to call directly to the actual place you want to stay. We don't stay at bed-and-breakfasts anymore because a lot of them don't have handrails on both sides of the stairs, and they're just really old houses, typically, that aren't accessible for Rob ....

ME: Well, I'm so thrilled you guys have had all those travels and all those experiences.

DENISE: We've gone to Beef and Boards [dinner theater venue] and different places. We like going to shows, to museums, to zoos, aquariums. We like watching movies together, going out to eat like everybody else ... festivals.

ME: Not much slows you guys down. You mentioned some weird things ... the servers that thought you weren't together .... Overall, how do people treat you?

DENISE: Most of the time, really great. Most people, in fact. Once in a while, I've noticed little things ... like somebody looking at me saying, "What do you think he wants?" instead of asking him, like in a restaurant. I know they're not trying to be impolite, they just don't realize it.

ME: I wonder ... we're in such a world of "rush, rush, rush." It just takes you [Rob] a little while to get your thoughts together to say something, from what I've seen with our friendship. I bet people just don't give you that time ... am I right?

DENISE: I think some people don't and some people also ... they're not that familiar with all the different types of disabilities. Like what might be a physical disability is not necessarily indicative of the inability to tell someone what you want to eat.

ME: Right .... So you find people are very kind. Do they help you open doors and things like that?

DENISE: Oh, yes. And sometimes people will ask, "Do you need help?" And that's always nice because sometimes you don't know. They don't know what you might or might not need, especially when it comes to our scooter. Sometimes people offer to help us with the scooter and it's very kind, but that is one thing that is pretty easy for us to do with a scooter lift.

ROB: I make a once-a-week trip to a grocery store and I always use their motorized scooters when I get there. When I get to the door, the guy invariably asks if I need help at Kroger.

DENISE: Yeah, they offer to help.

ME: Good! Is it tough to get a motorized scooter sometimes? Are they all taken?

ROB: Never.

ME: Oh, that's good.

DENISE: That way he doesn't have to take ours.

ME: Yeah, that makes it easier, I imagine.

DENISE: I'm not having to get it out of the van, and he doesn't have to take the van if he wants to take his car.

ROB: Yeah, I just drive and walk in and get a motorized scooter.

DENISE: They're surprised he drives a car. Neighbors have said, "I didn't realize Rob drove." Then other neighbors have been very scared that he's going to fall on the ice. They want us to go to Florida in the winter, but Rob doesn't care for hot weather. People just don't know.

ME: Yep, they don't know. I know one side is a little weaker than the other? Your left side?

ROB: The right side. I'm gonna say the right side of the brain controls the left side of the body and vice versa. So I'm paralyzed on my right side … which means the left side of the brain was injured.

DENISE: I actually think some physical therapists … occupational therapists … doctors and nurses sometimes actually like talking to Rob because they learn things about how treatments have changed so much over the years. He has scars from surgeries they don't do anymore from when he was in the accident in 1983.

ME: Interesting … So you're teaching people some things.

ROB: I have mementos. *[We laugh at that one.]*

ME: Awesome … I'm so glad, overall, you've been treated kindly. That is fantastic. One thing I like to ask everybody in the book is, What have you learned through all this? I know you've asked God, "What do you want me to learn?"

ROB: Yeah … we're not sure.

ME: From an outsider, I'm thinking your life isn't all easy peasy. Just a little guess here.

DENISE: Not everything's easy, yeah, we have to hire a handyman. Some things I just never learned how to do because in the "traditional" home, it was my father's job ... it was the guy's job. I have had to learn to do some things that we would have traditionally considered the man's job. But I know millions of women have to do these things because they aren't married or maybe their husband's in prison or in the military. A lot of people have to do things that they didn't grow up knowing how to do or plan to do.

ME: *Well, it seems to me like your faith has been tremendous through all this. How has that helped you through everything? Through your struggles?*

DENISE: Well, we can pray and ask God to guide us and read scriptures that are encouraging. That helps. The people at the church are very kind people, just very accepting. People prayed for him back when he had the accident and were a real encouragement to his parents. His mom was really taken back ... [His dad] was strongly, solidly believing that God was saying Rob's going to get better. The doctor said his parents were not being realistic. They were holding on to hope and being unrealistic.

ROB: One time they [the doctors] asked if I wanted to be an organ donor.

ME: *I know this is part of your story ... Denise, you recently were diagnosed with breast cancer. Do you mind sharing how [that has] affected you, because [you] are Rob's primary caregiver. How did you all work through that?*

DENISE: Yes, I was diagnosed in December of 2019 and it was one year to the date of my niece's death. I was still kind of shocked about that. When I found out I was going to have to have surgery and have a mastectomy, I didn't know how much care I might need myself. I knew Rob would probably not be able to do that much. I thought, *We'll just have people come clean the house and Rob will go out to restaurants and get carryout.* Then the pandemic hit, and we were concerned about being around anybody. We didn't want to have anybody come in. But it turned out that after just a few days, I was really doing quite well. My mom came and stayed with us maybe five nights, but I made her breakfast like two days after my surgery!

ME: *Wow!*

DENISE: My sister-in-law came one time and folded laundry ... and she maybe made the bed and a little bit of stuff. But I was able to keep up with the housework. I drove myself to some of my chemo myself. I drove myself to every radiation appointment. I even drove myself to surgery, but then Rob drove me home.

I actually did very well. The medicines they give you now to prevent nausea work well. A lot of ladies from church brought food and both the husbands and wives came. It just all was okay. The house wasn't maybe quite as pristine—I didn't have everything dusted—but it was okay. We already have somebody that mows our lawn. I was kind of concerned with Rob having physical therapy, because I didn't think I could do it after the surgery. And the physical therapy office closed due to the pandemic. But they sent someone to our house about three times. Then I started to heal enough to do his therapy again. It just took a little while to get the strength back in my arm and all after surgery, but the pain medicines they have today were very effective for me.

ME: *What a blessing.*

DENISE: I have exercised for years and I try to take good care of myself. I don't know if it makes any difference, but I've taken vitamins; I drink a lot of water. I had a lot of people praying for me, a lot of people sending cards and encouraging us, and we did well. The day of the surgery was before the actual lockdowns. My brother, and my mom, and a friend of my mom's came—and a pastor from our church. But then after that, everything else I pretty much had to do alone. But I don't mind. I'm not afraid of going to the doctors or hospitals by myself.

ME: *Good for you. I was amazed when I brought food over and you were just like, "Hi!" I'm thinking, My gosh, she's awfully perky! It wasn't that long after your surgery and there you were .... That leads me to my final questions: What would you like to tell the world to do for people like you? What would you like to see the world do a little differently for people with physical disabilities?*

DENISE: What do you think, honey?

ROB: Contribute to the [Robert] Retirement Fund.

DENISE: That's terrible ... he's being silly. I think it would be kind of interesting if there were a way in our culture that we did some things to help raise awareness overall for a lot of different kinds of disabilities. I wouldn't necessarily know how to help people ... I would not know all the best ways to communicate with a deaf person, because I haven't done it very much. Or the things to do to help a blind person, because I'm not that familiar with it. I think it would just be interesting if we just had some type of broad, educational ... I don't even know the correct word. The younger generations have grown up where people with disabilities have been included in the classroom.

ME: Right.

DENISE: My generation and older did not.

ME: Yes, they were separate ... in their own world practically.

DENISE: Yes. They had separate schools ....

ME: You and I are the same age, so I know what you're saying.

DENISE: It's really much better in the United States than a lot of other places. I met a lady who told me that she lived in Crete, which I think is somewhere around Italy, and she said they still hide the disabled.

ME: Really?

DENISE: I was astounded at a country like that. Maybe twenty-five years ago, a lady from the island of Barbados said they just kind of kept disabled people home and hidden away. So we really are a lot better than a lot of other countries. I do think that it would be nice, though, if we all had maybe more opportunities to learn about disabilities ... to know more about helping people with disabilities ... helping kids with autism.

Several years ago, I went to a talk at church about having children with autism in the Sunday school classrooms with the other children. They talked about how sometimes less activity and quieter things can be a lot better for children with autism. But I wouldn't know that if no one had taught me. I wouldn't necessarily know what to do, and people just don't know.

ME: Right …. Have any organizations helped you, that could maybe provide information like what you're saying?

DENISE: Fishers has a Disability Awareness Month in March about increasing accessibility. They are trying to help raise awareness about different disabilities. Last year they did something, and we didn't go to any of it, but I would like to see more of what they do if it's COVID-safe for us to go. I'm still being kind of careful because of the pandemic.

ME: Right.

DENISE: But we have never participated in anything that I can think of that is for the disabled other than just going to medical things like physical therapy.

One of the things I think it said they were doing [in Fishers] was having some kind of an art display of artists with disabilities. I do remember reading about them having it last year. Isn't there a lady who's trying to get Indianapolis to be known as a kinder city for kids with autism … or a gentler city for kids with autism?

ME: I'll look that up.

DENISE: I'm sure I saw something on the news about it. It seems like you always hear something on the news about somebody trying to do something good. Then you don't always find out the results. Oh … Rob likes this. We might have shown you when you were here ….

[They show me a plaque.]

ROB: Enjoy life. This is not a rehearsal!

ME: Oh, I love it!

DENISE: So we do enjoy life.

ME: I am thrilled for you guys. You're showing me—and readers—that anything is possible. Truly, you two are a very happy couple, that's for sure, and you're an example of what a married couple should be. Like you said in the beginning, you're friends and you work together and you have faith together, and that's tremendous.

DENISE: People do make a lot of assumptions though, which I know I do too … I make assumptions about people. But people also assume that … that we couldn't have children, but we chose not to have children. As far as we know, we could have. We never tried, though.

ME: *When it comes to that, I just never ask, and I try to never assume.*

ROB: I absolutely love not having kids.

DENISE: We have a lot of freedom.

ME: *It's not for everyone, and it is sad in our society how some people kind of make you feel bad when you choose to not have kids. And that's crazy to me.*

DENISE: Yeah, we really haven't had that with us, but I know some people do. Probably because people think we can't have them. It can be a really sensitive subject to some people.

ME: *Well, I thank you so much for your time. I was so pleased when you said yes because not everybody has said yes. And I understand … not everybody's outgoing, and for some people, sharing these things, it's really hard. So thank you for sharing!*

Rob and some of his homemade bread

Rob meeting a new friend

Rob out and about with his scooter.

And, finally, Rob and Denise on their wedding day!

Organizations mentioned during this interview:
- Indy Autism Project: www.indyautismproject.com

ACKNOWLEDGMENTS

I realized when I was interviewing these remarkable people that this was no longer *my* book—it quickly became *our* book. Each and every one of these individuals had the courage to be vulnerable and share their stories. As they spoke, I knew the interviews often brought up a myriad of emotions ranging from grief, anger, fear, and sadness to hope, happiness, relief, and awe. I lost sleep playing and replaying our conversations in my mind and worrying about how these interviews affected everyone. But each person knew that just by giving the world a glimpse into their lives, they could help make it a better place. While these stories don't represent everything about someone who is queer, non-White, or disabled, etc., they do offer glimpses to help build understanding.

I encourage my readers to find your own group of people—or more!—who are different from yourself to talk to over the next few months or years. "Just talk to me" was a common theme throughout this book. Instead of resisting what we don't know, let's *learn* about it and stop fearing it. Visit a synagogue or temple. Ask your friend in a wheelchair to have a chat over coffee or tea—at an accessible location, of course! Instead of making small talk at a party with a Black or Brown person, ask them what they like to do, where they grew up, and where they've lived throughout their lives. Maybe you, too, can "get a clue" and learn more about their experiences. Don't worry about saying or doing the wrong thing. Recognize you'll stumble and make mistakes; come clean right at the start. Most everyone will appreciate your honesty.

Thank you to Amy, Andrew, Anne, Bryan, Chip, David, Denise, Gloria, Jeff, Jordan, Laurie, Maria, Mookie, Patricia, Patrick, P.J., Rima, Rob, Sonya, and Susan. You all took time out of your busy schedules to do something that was uncomfortable at times. I will never forget that.

Thank you to my family and friends who supported this idea in the summer of 2020, especially my husband John, my sons Jonathon and Jacob, Stacey, the Gang, Yumi, Patricia, and, of course, Bryan Fonseca. Bryan, I hope you've been watching all the steps of this special project and smiling from above.

Thank you, Liz, for helping me find an easier way to create transcripts!

Thank you to Mindy Kuhn for taking a chance on me and helping me get out of the self-publishing world. Not that there's anything wrong with that, but I was ready for the next step and you took me there—big time!

Thank you, Parker Palmer, for your support of this little-known author and responding to that card in the mail months ago. I've enjoyed getting to know you. You're one of my heroes!

Thank you to my editors, Amy Ashby, Melissa Long and Erika Nein, for making the suggestions to help make this book even better. My deepest gratitude goes to Lacey Cope for her skilled guidance on marketing. That's an area that I, along with many authors, have always struggled with. She helps me breathe easier. And to the Warren Publishing team, all I can say is wow! Thank you for helping my book to reach audiences all over the United States and beyond. I truly believe the world needs this book now more than ever. You made that possible.

ENDNOTES

1 Parker Palmer, "Naropa University Presents Parker Palmer & 'Living from the Inside Out,'" Naropa University, streamed live May 15, 2015, YouTube video, Parker Palmer. https://www.youtube.com/watch?v=OWRDKNXPq3Y.

2 "Fatal Violence Against the Transgender and Gender Non-Conforming Community in 2021," Human Rights Campaign, Resources, https://www.hrc.org/resources/fatal-violence-against-the-transgender-and-gender-non-conforming-community-in-2021.

3 "An Epidemic of Violence: Fatal Violence Against Transgender and Gender Non-Conforming People in the United States in 2020," (PDF), Human Rights Campaign Foundation, 56, https://hrc-prod-requests.s3-us-west-2.amazonaws.com/FatalViolence-2020Report-Final.pdf?mtime=20201119101455&focal=none.

4 Sharita Gruberg, Lindsay Mahowald, and John Halpin, "The State of the LGBTQ Community in 2020: A National Public Opinion Study," Center for American Progress, posted October 6, 2020, https://www.americanprogress.org/article/state-lgbtq-community-2020/.

5 Anjel Vahratian et al., "Symptoms of Anxiety or Depressive Disorder and Use of Mental Health Care Among Adults During the COVID-19 Pandemic – United States, August 2020 – February 2021," *Morbidity and Mortality Weekly Report* 70, no. 13 (April 2021): 490–4, http://dx.doi.org/10.15585/mmwr.mm7013e2.

6 Naropa University, "Naropa University Presents Parker Palmer and 'Living Life from the Inside Out,'" June 4, 2015, YouTube video, 18:57, https://www.youtube.com/watch?v=OWRDKNXPq3Y.

7 Besheer Mohamed, "Muslims Are a Growing Prescence in US, But Still Face Negative Views from the Public," Muslims Americans, Pew Research Center, posted September 1, 2021, https://www.pewresearch.org/fact-tank/2021/09/01/muslims-are-a-growing-presence-in-u-s-but-still-face-negative-views-from-the-public/.

BIBLIOGRAPHY

"An Epidemic of Violence: Fatal Violence Against Transgender and Gender Non-Con forming People in the United States in 2020." (PDF). Human Rights Campaign Foundation. 56. https://hrc-prod-requests.s3-us-west-2.amazonaws.com/FatalVio-lence-2020Report-Final.pdf?mtime=20201119101455&focal=none.

"Fatal Violence Against the Transgender and Gender Non-Conforming Community in 2021." Human Rights Campaign. Resources. https://www.hrc.org/resources/fatal-vio-lence-against-the-transgender-and-gender-non-conforming-community-in-2021.

Gruberg, Sharita, Lindsay Mahowald, and John Halpin. "The State of the LGBTQ Community in 2020: A National Public Opinion Study." Center for American Progress. Posted October 6, 2020. https://www.americanprogress.org/article/state-lg-btq-community-2020/.

Mohamed, Besheer. "Muslims Are a Growing Prescence in US, But Still Face Negative Views from the Public." Muslims Americans. Pew Research Center. Posted September 1, 2021. https://www.pewresearch.org/fact-tank/2021/09/01/muslims-are-a-growing-presence-in-u-s-but-still-face-negative-views-from-the-public/.

Naropa University. "Naropa University Presents Parker Palmer and 'Living Life from the Inside Out.'" June 4, 2015. YouTube video. 18:57. https://www.youtube.com/watch?v=OWRDKNXPq3Y.

Vahratian, Anjel, Stephen J. Blumberg, Emily P. Terlizzi, and Jeannine S. Schiller. "Symptoms of Anxiety or Depressive Disorder and Use of Mental Health Care Among Adults During the COVID-19 Pandemic – United States, August 2020 – February 2021." *Morbidity and Mortality Weekly Report* 70, no. 13 (April 2021): 490–4. http://dx.doi.org/10.15585/mmwr.mm7013e2.